Flying the Old Planes

Flying the Old Planes

By Frank Tallman

PREFACE BY ERNEST K. GANN

INTRODUCTION BY JOE BROWN

DOUBLEDAY & COMPANY, INC.
GARDEN CITY, NEW YORK

1973

Library of Congress Catalog Card Number 73–79719
ISBN: *0–385–09157–5*

Contents

List of Color Illustrations

Preface

For reasons best known to the gods, aviation has always attracted men and women who seem to be the ultimate individualists. In a world where the antihero is welcomed and even given a high seat in the pantheon of celebrities, the astronaut still commands a certain awe in his beholder, and the airline captain remains a wholesome hero for little boys—and many adults. The astronauts and the airline pilots occupy the summit of the flying profession; separated but of equal status in the caste system are those very special men, the experimental test pilots.

There are those who fly away their entire lives in less exalted atmospheres. There are the marvelously resourceful bush pilots, whose exploits continue to make legends. There are the corporation pilots whose skill and diplomacy are usu-ally underrated, although the net worth of their cargo often far exceeds that of the largest airliner. Next below the salt is the "fixed-base operator," an individual who can and does do anything about his domain, from overhauling airplanes to teaching aerobatics. He is now vanishing from the whole flying scene quite as surely as the buffalo once disappeared from the plains. In his heyday it should be forever recorded that the fixed-base operator was invariably one of a kind: a tough, cantankerous, courageous, lazy, conniving son-of-a-bitch who would often distribute largess from his aerial wisdom according to the fierceness of his hangover. If it was mild, his natural greatness of heart would shine through his wind-tormented eyes, and he might give you ten minutes' flying for free. If his mood was otherwise, he could snarl the most determined student into despair and charge double for everything. As these stalwarts disappear, their places are taken over by sleek salesmen operating from chrome and carpeted bases. No one spits tobacco on the stove any longer. No one wears a leather jacket. And much of the color is forever gone from aviation.

Military pilots are not really a part of the flying social order, since they fly under conditions unique to their times and are usually warriors first and pilots afterward. Military discipline and protocol demand that their individualism be held to an absolute minimum except in actual combat, and even then it is actively discouraged. Wars continue, but the swaggering aces of World War I were the last military pilots whose very names remain history. Relatively few people remember the high-scoring victors of World War II, and only the official records recognize the flying victories of anyone since.

Seated in respectful hush at the far end of the social scale are the legions of private pilots, who range from most expert to catastrophe waiting to happen. Regardless of their proficiency, they are also most certainly accredited individualists, or they would not be in such company. They would be driving their Chevrolets to the laundromat.

And then there is Frank Tallman.

If the man is not a reincarnation of some early aeronaut, he does his best to behave like one. And since he is a mixture of raconteur, author, actor, *bon vivant*, scholar, and gentleman swashbuckler, the performance is always worth watching.

Tallman's fetish for elderly flying machines has set him apart from all of us who know what it is like to leave the sweet earth in something other than a modern, inherently stable, aircraft. Basically the current crop of aircraft are *all* well behaved and easy to fly. The gigantic Boeing 747 is quite as docile as the little Cessna trainers. You can literally "drive" modern aircraft, and many people in the air would not be there if they were obliged to depend on their own skill. To witness their graceless, bumbling performances is to know the taste of ashes, for what manner of person is this who so flagrantly insults the art?

Fortunately, most airmen still take great pride in the business of flying, and he who walks proudest when he returns to earth is the man who is constantly honing his skill aloft.

Tallman walks with the air of one artificial leg, a handicap that prevents him from flying with the greatest of ease yet somehow seems to have enhanced his expertise. This quality, which is really an attitude coupled with rhythmic physical coordination, is very necessary for those who would fly old airplanes. Those who lack it, the ham-fisted characters who boast, "I can fly anything including a barn door if you give me enough power," often commit suicide before the eyes of whatever crowd may have assembled. Long ago there was a song dedicated to such heroes, and sometimes its mournful notes would be rendered by surviving comrades soon after the bold one's funeral.

"Take the carburetor out of my stomach,
Take the pistons out of my head,
Send my arms back home to Mo-o-o-o-the—rrr . . .
Tell her I . . . am finally dead."

The trouble with old airplanes is not so much that they are old as it is their basic design. Airplanes built before the First World War were little more than powered gliders, and their aerodynamics were mainly some enthusiast's imitation of his favorite bird. There was actually little other choice for an ambitious designer. The available sources of power were so weak, unreliable, and penalizing in weight-per-horsepower that the utmost effort was devoted to designing lightness into the aircraft itself. The necessity for lightness led to bamboo-and-linen construction, and almost invariably the necessary size of movable control surfaces was underestimated.

Perhaps if the early designers had spent even more time at bird watching they would have become more aware of their feathered friends' ability to *change* the over-all surface of their wings and flight control surfaces according to their speed. We now know this as "variable geometry," and it is much used in modern sophisticated aircraft.

The movable control areas of many slow-flying pioneer flying machines would have better suited a modern 300 mph racer. The consequence was an extremely unstable craft requiring proportionately large control movements to keep it tame, and many brave men died at less than fifty miles an hour. The wise aviators flew only at dawn or dusk, when the air was still. Even so, only a handful of those pioneers survived their era, and it is significant that even fewer men still know how to fly their infernal machines without killing themselves.

By the time World War I was drawing to a close, the urgencies of aerial combat had mothered some comparatively decent aircraft. The secret was in the frantic development of power with an energy source light enough to permit hanging in front or behind a still aerodynamically crude pair of wings.

By 1918 a pilot could find infinitely better flying aircraft than the prewar Bleriots, Eindeckers, and Farmans. The Germans had their wonderful Fokker 7's, their reasonably efficient Albatros, and their new Siemens—all biplanes. The Allies had more variety of choice if not much more efficiency. There were the French Spads and Nieuports, the English Camels and S5's, and assorted lesser aircraft for almost every belligerent purpose.

Pilots who have never flown a World War I airplane would be very surprised if they had the opportunity —probably shocked, and possibly disappointed. For with few exceptions those planes were dogs compared to present aircraft of similar size. It takes a very skillful man to get much out of First World War types, which is probably why those pilots who survived their first hundred flight hours found such easy picking when opposed by newcomers to the aerial front.

One saving grace of First World War types is their slow landing speed. If you can find an open space of even three hundred feet you might roll the poor thing up in a ball, but you stand a good chance of walking away from the debris. Aficionados teethed on World War I flying movies should not be forever deceived by the camera into believing flight speeds and maneuvers were as fast as they appear on the screen. It was true that in some types their rate of climb was remarkable, but all else transpired at a pace resembling a dreamy ballet.

Frank Tallman probably has more flying time on World War I types, both German and Allied, than any other active flying man in the world. This record is not only proof of his individualism; it speaks most eloquently of his no-nonsense approach to the business of flying old airplanes. Tallman is a brave man, yes; but he is a damned careful brave man, with a ruthless dedication to his own survival. To label Tallman as a "stunt flyer" is to miss the man entirely. Some of his movie exploits may appear to be hell-for-leather "stunts" on the screen, but you may be sure every minute detail has been most carefully planned. Tallman plays for keeps—that is, keep Tallman alive. Accomplishing same in the very old types has not always been easy.

The decade after the First World War was a time of aeronautical bastardy. Many pilots were trying to make do with war surplus aircraft, of which the "Jenny" and the "DH4," powered with a Liberty engine, were typical examples. You either learned to fly a "Jenny" in a hurry or you went broke repairing the damage you did to it, or it did to you. The "DH-4," also a graduate of wartimes, was a very much better airplane and performed admirably when recruited into the airmail service. New types with ever more sophisticated wing and control designs were constantly appearing. There were Ryans, Stinsons, Boeings, Fokkers, Fords, Sikorskys, and Lockheeds for commercial use, and Martins and Douglases and Boeing fighters for the military. Biplanes were still very much in evidence, but new aerodynamic formulae applied to monoplanes assured their eventual dominance of the latter.

The period sparkled with aeronautical color and glamor. Civil aviation had been recognized for its adventure and promise. Individualists became famous overnight, among them one Charles Lindbergh. German dirigibles were flying with admirable regularity, and people were so sold on the "air age" that a dirigible mast was erected on New York's Empire State Building. It is still there, but most of the men and women who flew through the age of bastardy are no longer with us. While many died with their boots off, too many were either victims of their own aerial ignorance or were betrayed by their aircraft, which were still relatively primitive. The much-vaunted trimotor Ford gained a magnificent reputation only because some magnificent men were flying the things. Its agonizingly slow cruising speed was hardly balanced by its slow landing and takeoff speeds. It took considerable muscle to make a Ford do what you wanted it to do, and its performance on two engines was thrilling in the wrong way. By modern standards it was as an unwieldy sailing ship to a fast destroyer. The comparison was true of most of the "tin goose'" contemporaries. All of them demanded the type of pilot who knew how to fly by the seat of his pants, which in these avionic-jet days is a much underrated art.

Although Tallman was riding his tricycle and chewing licorice sticks when many of the aircraft in this book were in their prime, he subsequently managed to fly most of them without damage to either himself or machine. Luck favors the knowledgeable. Tallman's unique record might never have been achieved if he had not learned in the beginning to interpret certain vital messages as transmitted by his butt.

By the early 1940s, when the skies were once more employed as a battleground, a quite different species of aircraft was available, although the ultimate purpose remained the same. Only a few trainers were still constructed of wood and fabric, monoplanes were overwhelmingly in the majority, and power plants were very reliable. Cruising and top speeds were high in relation to landing and takeoff speeds, and the general behavior of the aircraft was very forgiving. The

10

airborne vehicle had come of age in both a commercial and military sense, and rumors of jet aircraft were just beginning to be whispered.

These were the times of the Douglas DC-3's, 4's, Constellations, Boeing Clippers, B-17's, Consolidated B-24's, North American B-25's, Mustangs, Corsairs, Curtis P-40's, and whole tribes of lesser known aircraft, many of which are still flying. They are "old" airplanes to those who have never flown anything but a jet. Many still active pilots who flew them during the Second World War may wonder how aircraft they had been flying only yesterday could so suddenly become antiques. Their answer may be easily found in any mirror.

Tallman himself blossomed as a pilot during this era and can thank the U.S. Navy for his training. With that typical dogmatism known only to the military, his service grandly declared that a graduate Navy pilot was qualified to fly *anything* capable of leaving the ground. Tallman apparently took this dictum seriously, and even if he were the only sailor-pilot ever to wear the golden wings, no one could deny the Navy was right.

Flying old airplanes is nostalgic fun and often considerable challenge. It is also a very serious business, with severe penalties for the overly-bold. If your grandmother discovers the dusty remains of a vintage aircraft in her barn that just "needs a little putting together," be sure the job is done by one of the several experts in the land. And once the resurrection is complete, reject any temptation to first-fly it yourself, unless you were brought up on such machines. Find one of the very few genuine professionals for the first ascent, and you may be reasonably sure both pilot and machine will return unscathed. Otherwise, after all your work and expense, minutes or even seconds after takeoff, your precious antique may look much worse than when it came out of grandmother's barn.

Flying old aircraft is strictly a job for expert professionals. Of this very exclusive group Tallman stands alone —an appointment that this book should certainly confirm.

Ernest K. Gann
San Juan Island
1973

Introduction by Joe Brown

MOVIE STUNT-PILOT Frank Tallman opened the throttle of the trim Seabee pusher-type amphibian and sucked in his breath as the wooden shack loomed larger and larger over the instrument panel. In the script—Universal's *The Adversaries*, being shot for television—the pilot would be killed when the plane crashed into the shack and exploded. Tallman had well over fourteen thousand hours of flying time behind him, a lot of it flying risky, death-defying, but intricately planned stunts like this one, and he tried not to think about an upcoming crash.

To make the sequence look authentic, the shack was to be blown up just as the Seabee came out the far side. On cue, Tallman nosed into the building, but then the unexpected happened. The force of the impact neatly

sheared off both wings. Minus the wings, the Seabee quickly picked up speed, roared across a field, and plunged into a gully, just as the shack erupted in a sheet of smoke and flame.

Inside the smashed-up Seabee, a shaken but unhurt Frank Tallman calmly brushed off the splinters, gave thanks for the thick padding of shock-resistant neprene that had been placed around him in the cockpit, climbed out, and strode briskly to where his mechanic was waiting.

"Before I do *that* again," he roared, "I want an ignition cut-off switch I can *reach!*"

If you say this is a damn fool way of making a living, you deserve a medal for the understatement of the year.

But Frank Gifford Tallman III does

12

make a buck, and a damn good one, crashing more airplanes—intentionally—than many men ever fly.

For the film *It's a Mad, Mad, Mad, Mad World* he flew a twin-engined Beechcraft through a steel girder-rimmed billboard, and then through an open hangar—at 160 miles an hour. Once, he crash-landed a temperamental P-51 Mustang fighter *eight times on one wheel*. During three decades of flying, he's piloted crop dusters and tested airplanes for the government. He's flown under bridges. He flew a hot-air balloon across California's Santa Catalina Channel and had to swim the last part of the trip. He's been a wing-walker and a military pilot. All told, he has piloted more than five hundred kinds of powered, fixed-wing aircraft, helicopters, gliders, and balloons. He's flown every single category of aircraft—he likes to remind himself—invented by man, except spacecraft.

Now past fifty, Frank Tallman claims to have slowed down a bit. "Nowadays," he says with a grin, "I don't crash as many planes as I used to." At his breathtaking pace, Frank Tallman's "slowing down" is like Jim Ryun running the mile in a lazy four minutes.

As this is written, in fact, Tallman has completed a number of other film contracts, which he describes as involving some of the riskiest flying in his entire life.

In one of them, the popular *Catch-22*, Tallman scratched together twenty—count 'em—twenty twin-engined World War II-vintage B-25 bombers from remote corners of the country, put together a squadron of pilots and crewmen, and transferred the whole lot to a remote area of Mexico, where an authentic World War II air base had to be assembled as a "set" for the film.

Tallman is such a stickler for authenticity that the *Catch-22* fliers almost came to believe that they *were* World War II types during the many months of filming. Even the flak they flew through was real, and the hours they worked were arduous. "We worked so hard," Tallman recalls, "that a learned for the first time what combat fatigue really is."

For a more recent film, *Murphy's War*, Tallman piloted a single-engined Grumman "Duck" amphibian biplane, a type that served the U. S. Navy in a variety of duties from 1933 until the mid-1950s, in the jungled river area of northern Venezuela. Practicing a landing on the Orinocco River one day, Tallman hit an unseen object in the water and felt his aircraft shudder violently as a lower wing buckled and an aileron froze. He horsed the damaged craft back in the air and fought it sixty miles to home base.

More than once after a day's shooting in *Murphy's War*, Tallman had to spend twenty minutes or more pulling leaves, twigs, and jungle vines out of crevices in the Duck's fuselage—he had flown that precariously close to the jungle for the authentic flying sequences.

Tallman, in other words, is a rather fantastic guy. In his own profession, which numbers about eighty-seven stunt pilots, he's king of the hill, a man with an uncanny and inborn flair for flying, and an unlimited appreciation for both vintage aircraft and today's supersonic jets and spacecraft.

There aren't many men around skilled enough or possessing enough guts to do what Tallman does for a living. Stunt flying, obviously, requires men not only with exceptional courage, but only those with superior mental alertness and physical coordination.

So it is even more incredible to learn that Frank Tallman is "physically handicapped." Since 1965 he has been an amputee, a condition that has knocked many men out of careers far less demanding than stunt flying.

Tallman lost his left leg in a tragically ironic way—in an accident completely unconnected with flying. Previously, his only serious injury was a broken ankle, which occurred in a sky-diving accident.

Near his home in Palos Verdes, California, one day in May 1965, Tallman was helping his son, Frank IV, who was then twelve, operate a new motorized Go-Kart. The senior Tallman pushed the Go-Kart, climbed aboard, standing behind his son, and went roaring away. When the Go-Kart was hitting about 20 mph, however, it struck a bump in the road and threw Tallman through the air.

Tallman hit the ground in a standing position, but apparently at such a critical angle and speed that "my hip drove into my left knee, shattering the knee socket and splitting the tibia bone from top to bottom."

Normally, such an injury would have healed. In Tallman's case, that might have meant only a temporary grounding and more time to putter around the world's largest private plane collection, which he maintains at Tallmantz Aviation in Orange County, California. But infection set in, and the knee didn't heal. Despite all that doctors could do, the limb continued to worsen.

At almost the same time, Tallman's private world suddenly grew even blacker. In a freak accident, blamed on a malfunctioning part, his long-time friend and business partner at Tallmantz, veteran stunt flier and air racer Paul Mantz, was killed on the California desert. The tragic crash made headlines around the world.

Mantz was piloting an airplane for the film *The Flight of the Phoenix* in which, according to the script, a surplus cargo plane that has crashed in the Sahara Desert is rebuilt and flown back to civilization by a mechanic. Mantz, who was perhaps Hollywood's greatest flying stuntman for three decades, had just lifted the *Phoenix* off the desert sand when the craft split in two and plunged to the ground. Mantz died instantly.

News of his partner's death staggered Frank Tallman.

"It was the worst year in my life," he recalls. "Business at Tallmantz was down, Paul was now dead, and my left leg was growing steadily worse. I was just about at the bottom."

The seriousness of Tallman's situation was magnified when his doctor told him, "Frank, the leg infection has gone too far. We've got to amputate."

Three days after Mantz was buried, Tallman underwent surgery, and the infected leg was removed just above the knee.

Such an amputation quite understandably might bring on a wave of self-pity and defeatism. But not for Frank Tallman.

Instead, it was the beginning of a long road back.

First, of course, there was the tremendous task of getting used to the artificial limb. Doctors call it an "adjustment period."

"I was determined not only to walk again, but to fly." Tallman says. "That was the only 'adjustment' I was going to make."

Slowly, with incredible pain at first, he endured the endless hours of "adjusting" to the man-made limb. Despite modern improvements in the field of prosthetics—artificial limbs— it sometimes takes weeks, even months, before the skin of the stump that fits onto the new limb becomes calloused enough to prevent painful blisters.

Tallman stuck it out, and within a year he was able to perform most normal tasks, such as walking and running.

But the biggest job was still ahead. He still wanted to fly.

Tallman received a lot of encouragement from other amputees, including pilots, such as Navy Lt. Comdr. Frank Ellis, who had lost both legs below the knee in an accident at Point Mugu. California, a few years earlier. Ellis's story and Tallman's are similar because each fought a hard personal battle to fly again.

Tallman's chief problem was learning to use his artificial leg to operate the rudder pedal and the brakes.

"The toughest thing in flying again," Tallman says, "was getting the feel of the controls. In some of the aircraft I fly, this is an almost instinctive thing, and doing it partly with an artificial limb was difficult."

But only a year after the amputation, Frank Tallman had literally made aviation history. Not only had he remastered flying itself, but thanks partly to an understanding Federal Aviation Agency, he requalified for every single type of license he had before the accident.

Today, he's licensed to fly as an airline pilot; he has commercial licenses for both single and multi-engine aircraft, seaplanes, and private and commercial helicopters and hot-air balloons. He also holds an instructor's ticket and is FAA-qualified to make instrument flights and fly jets. Tallman believes he is one of less than twenty men in the world to hold all ratings, and the only amputee so rated.

"None of us ever doubted Frank would make it again," says an associate at Tallmantz, "because he's the kind of guy who can do almost anything he sets out to do."

Son of a naval aviator, Tallman was born in Orange, New Jersey, just after the end of World War I; he regrets having missed the war, "I was simply born too late," he says sadly. In later years, however, Tallman recaptured that golden era of flight by rebuilding and piloting many of the aircraft of the period.

He scoffs at published reports that he learned to fly at the age of three, perched on his father's knee in a World War I Jenny.

"Flying at three? That's stupid even to think about," he laughs. "Hell, I didn't fly until I was *ten!*"

Although he did sit at the controls of his father's Jenny at ten, he didn't solo until he was sixteen, the minimum age under federal regulations. (Tallman's son, Frank IV, also soloed on his sixteenth birthday.)

His love of vintage aircraft dates back to a day in 1949 when he spotted the skeleton of an 1918 model British Sopwith Camel in an old barn near Moorestown, New Jersey. The Camel was ready for the junk pile, but Tallman was determined to buy it anyway. He located the owner, who agreed to sell, but was curious as to why anyone would want it. He blinked in amazement when Tallman coolly said:

"I'm going to rebuild it and *fly* it."

He got the Camel cheap and spent thirty-five hundred dollars putting it into flying shape. Until last year, when it brought $40,000 at an auction in Santa Ana, the old Camel was perhaps the most sentimental part of the fleet of vintage aircraft that comprised the Tallman-Mantz "Movieland of the Air" museum at Orange County Airport. It was a Camel, Tallman likes to remind visitors, in which Capt. Roy Brown, a Canadian flier in the World War I British RFC, brought down Germany's famous "Red Baron," von Richthofen, who had shot down eighty Allied planes in twenty months of air combat.

At a reunion of combat aces in San Diego, Tallman startled everyone by showing up flashily dressed like von Richthofen and flying a Fokker triplane. "The worst plane I've ever flown," Tallman grumbled. "I don't know how von Richthofen did it."

Typical of Tallman was the way he became a naval aviator. Normally, two years of college is required before the Navy will even consider an aviator applicant. Tallman had attended prep school and only a year of high school. He had no college math, a requirement for Navy pilots, who must master tricky navigation problems for long overwater flights.

"The fact that he didn't really qualify didn't stop Frank," a friend says. "He simply fought to convince the Navy he was a good prospect, and the Navy took him up on it."

In Navy flight school, Tallman recalls, better-educated fellow students cribbed him on navigation problems involving math, and in return, he helped them in aircraft identification problems.

"That was a snap for me," he says, "because I'd flown many of the planes we were identifying." He spent fourteen years in the Navy, a portion as an instructor, and today holds the rank of lieutenant commander in the Naval Reserve.

During his Navy days, Hollywood was grinding out aviation movies by the dozen, and the opportunity for stunt pilots was fine. Tallman decided that was for him.

"I'd flown a lot of aerobatics as a naval aviator," he explains, "and there's no better training than that for movie stunt flying."

But in those days stunt flying was mostly seat-of-the-pants barnstorming in the face of fierce competition among the elite group who did it for a living. Pilots were getting hurt and killed all the time. Tallman decided he would not be among them. Today, he seldom uses the word "stunt" in describing what he does for a living.

"It's really precision flying," he says. "The techniques are trade secrets mostly, and pretty technical. But what counts is preparation. We rehearse and rehearse for a flying sequence just as actors do for the other parts."

Typical were the flying sequences in the comedy It's a Mad, Mad, Mad, Mad World, which Tallman handled and which he considers the toughest, roughest job he's ever had in movies.

In one scene, he was to fly a twin-engined Beechcraft through a billboard. A practice sign, using cloth tapes, was set up in an Orange County, California, pasture, and Tallman flew through it several times a day for three weeks. Then he switched to a real billboard, in which the usual wood or metal base was replaced with styrofoam and balsa wood strips, but on which, Tallman remembers now with a shudder, "the frame was plain old cold steel girders." Adding to the risk was the fact that the Beechcraft's wingspan left less than three feet of clearance on each side.

Tallman correctly predicted the loss of one of the plane's two engines in the impact. Smashing through the sign at 160 mph before the cameras, the right engine sputtered dead. Paper, wood, and other debris splattered around Tallman in the cockpit. The front windscreen was shattered, and bits of glass were everywhere. Tallman radioed the nearby Orange County Airport for an O.K. to make an emergency landing and got in without injury.

That was tough, but zipping through the open hangar was tougher.

Tallman faced two major problems in the hangar stunt. One was wind; no matter what the velocity of the wind outside the building, it wouldn't be the same inside. The slightest difference could easily cause a disastrous crash. "I figured the way to beat that problem," Tallman says, "was to scoot through as fast as I could."

The second problem was clearance: although it would be safer to go through with the wheels down in case the aircraft touched the ground during the stunt, the vertical clearance wouldn't allow it. So Tallman simply zipped through the hangar, wheels up, at a wide-throttle 160 miles an hour.

Another type of trouble, which Tallman now recalls with a shudder, occurred during the filming of *The Kamchatka Incident*. According to the script, an American transport plane with a Soviet defector aboard is suddenly challenged by a Russian MIG off the coast of Siberia. Not wanting the defector to fall into Soviet hands, the transport pilot takes evasive action but is unsuccessful, and is shot down.

Tallman's job: Fly the MIG.

For authenticity, he selected a British DeHavilland Vampire jet fighter —his own—and had it repainted gray, with the Soviet red star plainly visible on the fuselage. When the conversion was completed, Tallman's "British MIG" could have fooled even a Red Air Force marshal. "And that," he remembers, "was precisely the trouble."

All went well with the filming over the Pacific a few miles southwest of California's Santa Catalina Island,

until Tallman, a smile of satisfaction on his face, pointed his bogus MIG toward the Orange County Airport.

Suddenly, Tallman found himself boxed in by two grim-looking U. S. Marine jet interceptors from the El Toro Marine Air Station, each carrying an equally grim-looking Sidewinded air-to-air missile.

"I had a Sidewinder, too," Tallman says now with a laugh. "But I couldn't for the life of me forget that while mine was fake, their's weren't!"

It was at that moment that "MIG" pilot Tallman discovered his radio had quit. Without it, of course, Tallman couldn't explain himself to the Marines, one of whom now had slipped directly behind him. Tallman could feel the hair on his neck bristle. Unfortunately, American pilots wearing flight helmets and oxygen masks look quite the same as Soviet pilots wearing flight helmets and oxygen masks, and those red stars on Tallman's Soviet gray jet suddenly seemed the size of football fields.

"At that moment," Tallman relates, "I would have paid anything for a tiny American flag to wave. I could almost feel a Sidewinder sneaking up my afterburner, and it was the first time in my life I was ready to eject from a perfectly normally functioning aircraft."

The radio fortunately snapped back to life; Tallman identified himself and was saved from a long swim home. Still, the suspicious Marines escorted him all the way to Orange County.

For a sequence in *The Carpetbaggers*, Tallman had to fly inches over a parked truck and land a biplane on a narrow street. So close did the wingtips come to hitting the truck that cameramen shooting the sequence ducked.

It was for *Wake Me When It's*

Over that he brought his P-51 Mustang fighter down on one wheel not once but eight times. "I wanted to be sure," he says, "that it looked good." In another film, he flipped a single-engine monoplane on its back upon landing. The stunt almost wiped out the aircraft, but Tallman walked away without a scratch.

Only once in his adult life did Tallman veer away from his love of aviation. Deciding to try another vocation, he got a job in advertising, but the career was brief.

"I was sitting there at my desk, quite happy," he remembers, "when I heard an aircraft pass overhead. I quit my job right there and then."

He started his collection of vintage aircraft, now unquestionably the world's largest, at the Flabob Airport, Riverside, California. Scouting the world for the models he wanted, usually restoring them from mere skeletons, he soon owned a Bleriot, a Farman, a Sopwith Camel, a Canuck, a Nieuport, a Pfalz, a Fokker, and a number of others whose ages predated the Roaring Twenties. Later, Tallman joined with fellow stuntman Paul Mantz and moved the collection to Orange County Airport, where in 1964 the nostalgia-evoking Movieland of the Air was established. Many of the planes were sold at auction last year, but Tallman's collection still numbers around fifty. And many are in flying condition.

"Working for Frank Tallman," says a longtime Tallmantz employee, "is like working for the Keystone Kops. It's a ball around here."

Although his real love obviously is aircraft that predate the jet era, Tallman is a proficient jet aviator and will fly anything, or do most anything, that movies or television call for.

Typically, on one recent day, Tallman flew around Orange County in his 1909 Bleriot in the morning, test-hopped a 1917 French Nieuport before noon, digested his lunch by flying maneuvers in the only 1918 German Pfalz in existence, and then took off in his DeHavilland Vampire jet to film a TV sequence in late afternoon. Later, he commuted to his plush Palos Verdes home, thirty miles away, in his Cessna 310.

To support his belief that early aviation tradition must be preserved. Tallman jumps at any chance to demonstrate one of his vintage planes. Provide any excuse—an aviation anniversary date, a movie, an air race—and Tallman starts pulling on his leather helmet and goggles.

In 1961, for instance, he decided to duplicate French aircraft designer-pilot Louis Bleriot's history-making 1909 flight from Calais, France, to Dover, England, in the plane bearing Bleriot's name. Bleriot made the hop across the English Channel in thirty-seven minutes, in a rainstorm, without a compass, and with an overheated engine.

It took Tallman fifty-eight minutes to make the duplicate flight from Avalon, Santa Catalina Island, to Long Beach, California, fifty-two years later. The mercury that day soared to 110 degrees, the Bleriot's engine functioned normally, and a Coast Guard helicopter and private plane escorted him. But in all other respects, Tallman very nearly paralleled the historic flight of more than a half century earlier.

"In many ways, my flight was tougher," Tallman recalls. "The downwash from the chopper almost knocked me out of the sky!"

Tallman has warm admiration for the pilots who flew World War I craft regularly. "Let no pilot of today look at these handsome, small aircraft of an earlier day," he once wrote in describing a Nieuport 28 C-1 in flight, "and not appreciate the fact that under certain conditions they can be holy terrors."

Scott Crossfield, first pilot of the supersonic X-15 rocket plane, agrees, "I've got nothing but respect for people who fly these old birds. And Frank Tallman is tops, a pro's pro."

It was Tallman's firm that put together a flying replica of the *Spirit of St. Louis,* the plane in which Charles Lindbergh, "the Lone Eagle," flew across the Atlantic in 1927. Tallman built the new *Spirit* to be flown in Paris in a 1967 ceremony commemorating Lindy's epic conquest of the sky. When agreeing to build it, Tallman made one strict condition: "It's got to be authentic," he insisted, "right down to the last tiny fastening." At a cost of forty thousand dollars the original was faithfully duplicated, right down to the periscope device Lindburgh used to see forward out of the cockpit.

"I'm amazed," remarked Lindbergh while inspecting the craft, "at how closely this one resembles the *Spirit* I flew."

Tallman didn't fly the *Spirit* to Paris the way Lindy did, of course: it got there in the belly of a jumbo cargoliner. But he did circle Paris' Eiffel Tower several times on May 21, 1967, and then land at Le Bourget Airport, and the eyes of many a sentimental, middle-aged Frenchman were damp with tears.

Tallman makes no bones about being a sentimentalist himself where old airplanes are concerned.

"Aviation history is damned important," he argues, "and we've got to preserve it somehow, just as we do other history."

His plush, wood-paneled Orange County Airport office contains a bookshelf crammed with volumes that are helping achieve that goal. Other shelves line the walls of his Palos Verdes home.

The office, in fact, is a veritable museum of aviation lore. The rest of the Tallmantz plant is a jungle of machinery and apparent disorder, but entering Tallman's private office is like stepping into another world.

On one wall hangs an oil painting of the Wright Brothers' epic first flight at Kitty Hawk in 1903. At the opposite end hangs a panel of color, autographed portrait photos of American astronauts. Tallman enjoys the contrast, because more than any other man he has lived that evolution of flight.

With the stature his name implies, Frank Tallman puffs constantly on a pipe as he talks, and occasionally twists the tip of the sandy mustache that makes him look like actor David Nivin. He glances occasionally at the gleaming holstered pistols hanging on other walls and speaks of them, as he speaks of airplanes, as if they were human. "I enjoy guns," he says, "just as I enjoy any piece of precision machinery."

Despite his limited education. Tallman is a man of taste and is well read. He owns collections of rare Chippendale furniture, collects primitive Latin American art and, until recently at least, drove a 1950 model Rolls-Royce Silver Cloud with a "one off" body.

Few heavy drinkers survive in Tallman's steel-nerved business, and his idea of a liquid tranquilizer after a particularly hairy flight is a glass of milk laced with brandy. If the thought of such a mixture makes you reach for the milk of magnesia, Tallman says he drinks it "because that's what World War I pilots used as a stomach settler, and to get the smell of castor oil (used to lubricate World War I engines) out of their system."

19

The telephone on his desk jingles constantly. Sometimes it's a business matter; often it's a movie studio seeking reliable advice on aviation authenticity. A typical question: what kind of planes were flown in the Mexican revolution of 1916–17? Answer: Curtiss Pushers.

Or it's someone looking for a hard-to-find aircraft.

"You need a Messerschmitt Me-109?" Tallman answers. "No, haven't got one. But I know where there's a beautiful Me-108, and if you can wait a few days I just might locate a 109. . . ."

Tallman's uncanny ability to find rare airplanes never ceases to amaze those who know him. They're even more amazed at the way he lovingly puts them back in flying shape again.

Not long ago, he showed a Tallmantz visitor the bare bones of a World War I Spad tucked away in a remote corner of his Movieland of the Air. It was, literally, a piece of junk. The fabric had long since disintegrated, the wood showed the work of the elements in lying half a century in some French farm pasture. "See that beauty?" Tallman said proudly. "I'll be flying that Spad in a few months." Those who know him don't doubt it.

When Tallman lines up a film contract, he allows nothing to interfere with his work. For instance, one night in Florida, where he had stopped off en route to Venezuela for the filming of *Murphy's War*, he prepared for a full night's sleep before the grueling island-hopping trip across the Caribbean, which was to begin the next day. He was dead tired, having pushed the lumbering little "Duck" all the way across country, from California.

The details of how it happened are still somewhat hazy, but Tallman re-members unstrapping his artificial leg and preparing to go to bed; then, without the support of the limb, he stumbled suddenly at the top of a flight of stairs, and fell. Tallman was knocked unconscious by the fall, and when he was revived, the pain was excruciating.

A doctor was summoned and hospitalization recommended, but Tallman would have none of it. Shot full of drugs to ease the tremendous pain, he climbed aboard the Grumman the next morning and flew—without further rest—to South America.

"To this day," he remembers with a wince, "I don't know how I got there. Everything was just a blur. Instinct, I guess."

After he nearly wiped out the Duck in the crash in the river described earlier, it appeared that the filming of *Murphy's War* might have to be suspended. After all, parts for an aircraft nearly forty years old aren't exactly the easiest things to come by in the Venezuelan jungle. But Tallman, as usual, was far from licked.

A local Venezuelan Indian fashioned the spar to replace the damaged one, and Tallman by chance located a former German U-boat commander who operated a small machine shop who jury-rigged replacements for struts out of tubing, and carved fittings out of a scrap propeller.

Of all his years in flying, however, Tallman insists that his work in *Catch-22* presented perhaps the thorniest problems—and the greatest risks—of all.

Finding the desired number of B-25's, the crews, and training them was tough enough, but the logistics problems of building and maintaining a complete air base in a Mexican location were staggering. Everything that existed on a World War II base, including such backup and support facilities as supply and hospitals, had to be authentically re-created. And each morning before the cameras began rolling for the day, air crews underwent briefings as real-life as those in wartime.

One scene, shot at 4 A.M., nearly proved Tallman's undoing. In the sequence, Tallman was to fly his B-25 directly over the cameras, at nearly ground level, and straight toward blazing arc lights, which provided illumination for the shot. Not far past the brilliant lights, a small chain of mountains ringed the location. This was at the inland end of the runway; at the other lay the Gulf of Curtez.

Tallman sucked in his breath and came roaring in on the pass; beyond the blazing lights was inky blackness. Suddenly, the lights dazzled his eyes so intensely it became impossible to read instruments. Then the B-25 roared past the lights and was instantly enveloped in pitch blackness. The feeling was much like stepping into a darkened movie theater from a brightly lit lobby.

"For the first time in my life," Tallman recalls, "I suffered vertigo. I was literally flying blind."

Fortunately, Tallman had prepared himself well for the scene and had studied the geography many times during the daylight. He banked the B-25 hard, and wheeled past the clutches of the mountains.

Flying of this kind doesn't come cheap for any movie company, and although Tallman doesn't talk much about it, his is obviously a wallet-fattening business. But when you get to know Tallman well, you soon realize he isn't a man driven by money alone, nor the lure of trophies, personal adulation, or fame. It is as

if he is driven compulsively to fly, not so much in the swift, safe, antiseptically and aerodynamically clean jets of today, but in the nostalgic birds of other eras of flight as well. Perhaps as no other man, Frank Gifford Tallman has personally spanned the golden age of aviation.

It seems that there are few fields left for Tallman to conquer, but he reminds his visitors, whom he greets with the warmest hospitality, that there still is outer space.

"If I'd been able to fly in space," he says, peering over the memento-strewn desk with a faraway stare, "I'd be the only man in history to fly everything man has put in the air since the dawn of aviation. I don't mean just going along as a passenger; hell, I'll probably be able to do that in another fifteen years or so. I mean to *fly* the thing."

The space agency, of course, has never gone beating the bushes for one-legged astronauts, and Tallman acknowledges a little sadly that his freak accident has knocked him out of the running.

This kind of conversation usually brings him around to the subject of his son, Frank Gifford IV, who is now sixteen. (Tallman also has a married daughter, and is a grandfather.)

"My dad was a naval aviator and so was I," he says. "If Frank became one, it would be the first time that three generations have served. But I'm not pushing him; I want Frank to do what he *wants* to do."

But undoubtedly, nothing would please Frank Tallman more than to add another autographed portrait to the astronaut panel behind his desk. One, naturally, which would be inscribed, "To Dad . . ."

1909 Bleriot

Specifications

ENGINE	Fan or Y-type Anzani
	65-hp Continental
SPAN	29 ft., 2 in.
LENGTH	25 ft., 7 in.
HEIGHT	8 ft.
CREW	1
EMPTY WEIGHT	580 lbs.
USEFUL LOAD	284 lbs.
GROSS WEIGHT	864 lbs.
FUEL CAPACITY	14 gals.

Performance

MAXIMUM SPEED	58 mph
RATE OF CLIMB	375 fpm
STALL SPEED	26 mph
ENDURANCE	2 hrs.
SERVICE CEILING	7500 ft.

1909 Bleriot

OUR 1909 BLERIOT is a frail spindly looking monoplane, which has led a most adventurous life. The Bleriot in my life has flown the English Channel in both directions; the Catalina Channel; over the San Francisco–Oakland Transbay Bridge; in England, Canada, France, and about half of the states in the United States.

Over the years it has served me in much the same reliable way as our versatile present-day aircraft, although I am sure it is responsible for giving me more gray hairs than all the business planes in the alphabet, from Alpha to Zebra.

Louis Bleriot was in many ways as interesting as the airplane. The son of a successful fabric manufacturer, he became a wealthy man in his own right and financed his experiments in aviation by the invention of a successful automobile headlight. Before the advanced design (for its day) that carried Bleriot across the Channel, there were some eight other largely unsuccessful experimental craft, ranging from cellular winged gliders to canard aircraft, most of which crashed, burned, or scattered themselves over the landscape. Until the advent of the 1909 model, Louis Bleriot's major claim to fame seemed to be his ability to survive any and all accidents.

Bleriot was not only the originator

In the cockpit with my hand on the spade-type control
stick. Up ahead, the fuel tank.

of the monoplane design that is basic
to every business aircraft manufactured today, but he also originated
streamlining of the fuselage; the engine placed forward, with the single
tractor propeller; the rudder, elevator,
and stabilizer placed on the aft part
of the fuselage; and even a partially
swiveling landing gear with a capability for crosswinds.

The 1909 Bleriot, along with the
rear-elevator Curtiss, were undoubtedly the two most widely copied aircraft prior to 1914. Literally hundreds
of airplanes were built on farms and
in backyards with nothing more to go
on than photographs, the materials
often being banana oil, mothers' bed
sheets, and slats from the fence. Because of the popularity of the Bleriot
design and its very remarkable im-

pact on the world (for it received as
much publicity in its day as Lindbergh's flight twenty years later),
many wealthy sportsmen bought
them to use for business and pleasure.
Adventurous barnstormers flew them
all over the known world, even as far
as China and Tibet!

The basic Bleriot design was light
and simple to maintain, as well as
easy to take apart or set up for flight.
From the standpoint of the early exhibition pilots these were important
factors, for the Bleriot could be made
ready for flight in thirty minutes, as
against six to eight hours for a Curtiss
or Wright. Another factor was the
advent of the 50-hp Gnome Rotary,
which gave the Bleriot a tremendous
edge because of its general reliability
and low weight per horsepower.

24

The fragile-looking landing gear had a crosswind capability. Note the heavy elastic shock cords.

The warp cable walking beam suspended beneath the fuselage. Warping the wing performed the same function as the ailerons, which were a later development.

FLYING THE OLD PLANES

It's hard to put in words readily explainable to the modern pilot how perfectly awful it really is to fly the Bleriot and what a great admiration I have for the pilots whose raw courage often outstripped their piloting skills and knowledge. Of the 120-odd flying hours I have spent in Bleriots, I am sure no five minutes have gone by without adding a deepening color tone to that streak down my back. My first attempted flight in a Bleriot ended ignominiously in a ground loop when the mighty airflow of a two-cylinder Aeronca engine wasn't sufficient to lift the tail—or, in fact, to control the rudder at all! This same airplane, alter powered by a 65-hp Continental, came within an ace of wiping out a portion of the U. S. Air Force's new (at that time) Delta Convair interceptors. The Bleriot broke ground nicely for the Air Force show; then, at an altitude of about a hundred feet, the realization suddenly came upon one very startled pilot that full deflection of the cloche wheel apparently had no effect at all on the wing warp, and with a very sick feeling, I slanted in toward the line of parked interceptors, out of control. By skidding rudder and dropping the nose, I managed, at the last possible second, to ditch in a parking area without damage, except to my shattered nerves.

The Bleriot that is of our present concern fortunately has somewhat more positive control, but still not more than 10 percent of the aileron control of any modern aircraft; the rudder isn't more than 30 percent to 40 percent as effective, while the elevators are approximately equal, although slower in action.

This Bleriot is the superb workmanship of the Calgary Institute in Alberta, Canada, and was built up as a school project. It was flown several times in Alberta and shipped to England, where it made "flights" across the English Channel in both directions under the capable hands of Mr. Jean de la Bruyere. I bought the aircraft for a motion picture and had it shipped to Hollywood. Then the fun began!

Having nothing except the experience of the other Bleriot to go by, I approached the idea of flying ours with about the same enthusiasm as a soldier walking through a minefield. But I flew it successfully in the motion picture and for the next several years in air shows; into strange, out-of-the-way fields; at night; and over sizable distances of water.

Its Continental always ran beautifully. Thank heaven I did not have to use the original fan or Y-type Anzani —their lack of power must have been appalling. Our Bleriot now uses the original mahogany scimitar-shaped prop, which has been cut and reshaped for the proper rpm; as a consequence it can make a decent circuit of the field and a respectable landing. Previously, every time the Bleriot turned downwind it began to sink, and it became simply a choice of where to stack it. Some twelve different propellers were tried, and only the old style gave the thrust needed.

We completely recovered the Bleriot at our Movieland of the Air Museum at Orange County Airport, Santa Ana, California. This being the aircraft's third recovering, we used a synthetic fiber fabric in hopes it would last. The previous fabric had about the strength and toughness of a rotting window shade.

Pushing the Bleriot to the flight line requires two strong men, in spite of the lightness of the aircraft (some 580 pounds). All of its weight reposes in the tail—both on the ground and in flight. Just before going to takeoff

The graceful, mahogany scimitar-shaped prop, and just above the "A" frames and wing wires.

position, a real preflight of the aircraft is important. The Bleriot is a wire airplane, and without each wire properly attached and safe-tied, it has about the strength of a fifteen-cent grocery store kite. You carefully check your flying cables, both at the bedstead (front fuselage frame) and at the wing, as well as your warp cables through the bottom walking beam and the wing and above on the A frame. Then you check fuselage alignment by eye, including the landing gear sulky wheels and tires, tail surfaces, and control cables. With the aircraft ready for takeoff, the engine idling nicely, and its lone instrument —the oil pressure gauge—showing fifty pounds, I grasp the spade-type grip and shove the throttle forward. The tail is up in about 20 feet; the

wind is a steady twelve knots; temperature, 79 degrees; field elevation, 54 feet. I am airborne in about 170 feet.

As I broke ground, a particularly nasty gust of wind dropped a wing, and for several seconds, full opposite stick, rudder, and elevator were necessary to pick it up. I had forgotten what a job it was to always maintain the wings in a level attitude and the necessity of making only very flat skidding turns, mostly with rudder. In spite of a slow actual ground speed (about 44 to 48 mph), there is still no experience in my years of flying to equal the sick feeling you have when a wing goes down in gusty air and you head for the ground unable to pick up the wing in spite of full opposite control. A good deal of forward

A flight in the rough air around the Golden Gate Bridge
in San Francisco.

pressure is also required on the stick, for the Bleriots I have flown are all tail-heavy, and if one flies for more than ten minutes at a time, he has to keep shifting tired arms.

Flying with the camera ship required some prethought, for if the slipstream ever hit the Bleriot, it could go over on its back—which it did once with me. At the time I could only think of Adolph Pegoud, the Frenchman who made the world's first loop in a Bleriot, and wonder why he didn't suffer a coronary, for I am sure my heart missed a sizable number of beats.

After we finished taking the aerial photographs, I checked the Bleriot on stalls, which are deceptive, since it pays off with absolutely no warning, dropping a wing and forcing one to turn into the dropped wing to pick it up. the stall appears to be at about 25 to 27 mph. Beyond gentle turns, one is quite content to just fly along at about 40-odd mph and enjoy the air-conditioned ride. There is no windshield for protection from the direct prop blast.

Landing can be either power on or power off. My choice is power off, with an extremely steep approach of about 30 percent nose down. One has only a very short flare-out, because there is no float with the inborn drag of a Bleriot. It lands smoothly and rolls to a stop on grass in about fifty feet. One must be very careful to land directly into the wind and pray for no sudden gusty crosswinds; the lat-

ter happened to me once, and one of the very weak main wheels collapsed under the side load. As the Bleriot ground to a stop, the windward wing rose into the air. I jumped out of the cockpit and grabbed the flying wires and promptly rose into the air with the wing. Only the additional weight of a startled airport attendant hanging on my feet brought both the Bleriot and me back to the ground again.

Louis Bleriot, with a typical French statement, once said before his famous Channel flight, "If I cannot walk, I'll show the world I can fly." But this pilot is not so sure—if he had to fly a Bleriot very often, he might prefer to walk!

The Bleriot's cambered wing, with its sharply drooped leading edge, was a forerunner of the current crop of STOL aircraft.

One of the few races between a Curtiss Pusher and a Bleriot since the 1910 period. Palm Springs, California, 1966. The Curtiss Pusher was the winner.

Curtiss Pusher

THE PRE-WORLD WAR I era of aerial barnstorming, racing, and exhibition is epitomized by the Wright and Curtiss biplanes. This era opened in America, a Pandora's Box eye view of the great and busy and dangerous air age to come.

For risks on the order of lion taming or a tight-wire walk across Niagara Falls, few professions offered the challenge of flying in those dear dead days. The Wright and Curtiss pilots flew, loved, and died with all the dispatch and regularity of moths around a candle flame.

Aircraft construction, while none too sturdy in the Curtiss models, verged on strength factors somewhat weaker than wet tissue paper on some of the Wright airplanes. Bamboo from the local Hawaiian bar, muslin, buggy wheels, light wire, and fishing line from the aircraft constructors' tackle boxes were only some of the many materials actually used to build flying powered aircraft.

I have enjoyed flying a number of different early airplanes, such as the Curtiss Pushers, Bleriots, Farmans, and even a Chanute glider, which barely got airborne with yours truly aboard before my launching crew fell over one another with laughter at my attempt to control it. Only in the Maurice Farman was there enough actual, slow-turning, Renault-engined power to give one a secure enough feeling so that you weren't forever biting washers out of the wing and looking for a place to crash in.

The initial reaction of today's aviators to any of the 1910-vintage Pusher aircraft is one of complete disbelief that the squirrel cage of wings, weak fittings, and wires could get anyone airborne and back down again without a call to your friendly mortuary.

Delving into the history of Glenn Curtiss, we find that his first successful flights in the *June Bug*, a joint endeavor of the Aerial Experiment Association in 1908, followed literally years after the Wrights' epic ascension in 1903. Curtiss borrowed liberally from whatever sources of information he and his associates could find, including the Wrights' experiences and know-how, and he brought imagination, engineering skill, and great personal daring into all of his flying.

Side view of the wing section and the midwing allerons, a Curtiss innovation. The boards on the inboard struts were a temporary mount for a camera.

The intrepid aviator, my one hand on the wooden control wheel, the other on the trottle.

In flight in an exact replica of the historic 1910 Curtiss
Pusher.

Curtiss Pusher

Specifications

ENGINE	85-hp Continental
SPAN	27 ft., 9 in.
LENGTH	20 ft., 7 in.
HEIGHT	6 ft., 7 in.
CREW	1
EMPTY WEIGHT	675 lbs.
USEFUL LOAD	310 lbs.
GROSS WEIGHT	985 lbs.
FUEL CAPACITY	14 gals.

Performance

MAXIMUM SPEED	59 mph
RATE OF CLIMB	200 fpm
STALL SPEED	41 mph
ENDURANCE	2½ hrs.
SERVICE CEILING	8000 ft.

Curtiss engines were as far in advance of the Wright power plants as a modern jet is for a World War II reciprocating engine. Glenn Curtiss raced motorcycles, using for power relatively lightweight air-cooled engines of his own design and manufacture. These engines were also used by Capt. Thomas Baldwin and Lincoln Beachey in powered dirigible balloons.

Innovations in design also credited to Curtiss include real ailerons between the wings, and not just wing warping, as in the Wrights' planes; the first successful tricycle landing gear, now such a part of today's aviation; metal structure running gear instead of spruce and bamboo; single-propeller and direct-drive engine, unlike the Wrights' complicated bicycle-chain twin propeller, with its weak hub and keying system.

Actually, prior to Curtiss' successful flights in the *June Bug*, the Aerial Experiment Association, of which Curtiss was a member along with Alexander Graham Bell, had approached the Wrights, hoping that they could save themselves many faltering steps. The Wrights, busily protecting their own interests and establishing patents on their "machine," were quite sparing in their advice and information. The Wrights believed that they had cornered the market and that all future aircraft builders must pay them a royalty for use of their designs and for use of airplanes for commercial gain. Nevertheless, the Aerial Experiment Association went ahead on its own. In a series of letters between Curtiss and the Wrights, Curtiss wrote that he did not intend to either sell aircraft or do exhibitions for money. When Curtiss became more and more successful in both building and flying aircraft, the Wrights brought a lawsuit against

him for infringement of patents. It was a long, drawn-out legal struggle, and there was much bitterness between the parties. Ultimately, the great Curtiss Wright complex that exists even to this day was formed, but by then Wilbur Wright had died and Orville Wright and Glenn Curtiss had long been inactive in aeronautical affairs.

Copies of everything from dueling pistols to the winged victory of Samothrace have existed seemingly since time began, but in aviation probably no airplane has ever been copied more often than the Curtiss (type) biplane, and some were built as late as 1916, in spite of the fact that the first Jennies were on their way. Because of the strength and relative simplicity of the basic Curtiss design, a number of flying replicas or copies of the Curtiss airplanes have been built in recent years.

Ruth Law, the great American woman pilot, had a Curtiss modified with Wright-type controls instead of a wheel, because she had learned in a Wright. Curtiss must have swallowed a sizable dose of wormwood to convert her airplane for Wright controls.

During the exhibition racing and state fair era that existed roughly between 1909 and 1914, some pilots flying for Curtiss and Wright managed to put away sizable amounts of money even by today's standards. Air show fees ran as high as five to eight thousand dollars an afternoon. One such afternoon's earning brought a pretty substantial house, servants, and a dapply gray and carriage to move about town in style.

Lincoln Beachey, whose loops and dives brought America to its toes, was perhaps in his period the best-known and most daring of all the exhibition pilots. He had early in his dirigible balloon days indicated his disdain for the hazards of flight. Later, in a biplane roughly patterned after the Curtiss—but smaller, stronger, and more maneuverable—he raced immortals like the great Barney Oldfield around state fair grounds. Why in his multitude of such exhibition flights he never wound up wearing a copper wire necktie I can't hazard a guess, because in many of the photos of that day, the telephone and electric power wires ringing and crossing the fair grounds look like the leavings from a spaghetti factory.

Beachey, like a few of the more knowledgeable of his contemporaries, learned quickly that the Roberts, Curtiss, and other American engines were overweight and undersized when compared with the French Gnome rotary engine. As expensive and hard to get as were the Gnomes, their performance at altitude and their weight per horsepower more than justified the cost and the change. Throughout Beachey's life and up until his death, he used 50-hp Gnomes and later the more powerful 80-hp.

With a pusher using a rotary, one does not suffer that dread looseness in the lower gut experienced by so many fighter pilots flying rotaries in World War I. As most of my readers probably know, a rotary has all the cleanliness of a sow in a mud wallow. Besides its emetic fumes, it is an engine that has for lubrication pure castor oil, which is used instead of mineral oil, because oil and fuel are introduced down the hollow crank shaft together, and a vegetable-base oil does not break down when exposed to fuel. Whatever oil is not burned goes out the valves in a fine spray that coats everything with a gluey coating quite the equal of some of the current epoxies. One of the reasons rotaries are being found even

now, fifty years later, in respectable condition is because of the permanence and lasting protection of castor oil.

One factor in performance of some of the early pusher aircraft is that a 50-hp Gnome engine turned a huge propeller at only 1000 to 1200 rpm. Today some of the people who are building copies of historic aircraft have forgotten that a modern 50-hp developed at 3000 rpm swinging a toothbrush-sized propeller does not in any way equal the earlier rotary. If you measured actual slow speed thrust with a modern engine in competition you would need horsepower on the order of at least 200 to 250 hp to equal the rotary.

With some hundred-odd hours in several different Bleriots, I was beginning to consider myself an expert on how scared one can get in the early birds, for I had settled out of the sky with full power, ditched in berry patches and backyards, and generally came to the conclusion that wing warping and the strange Bleriot wing curve were specially designed invitations to trouble. A Pusher, I thought, should be more fun and certainly easier to fly.

My interests in aircraft being predominantly early, I avidly looked over the aviation ads for sales of the unusual birds. My Curtiss pusher turned up in Louisiana and was hand built by a fine craftsman whose interest in wood perhaps came from gainful employment with one of the largest lumber producers in the South. A phone call to Louisiana was followed by an agreed price based on eyeball inspection, and I was on my way to New Orleans in a jet.

The flight from New Orleans to Crosby was a step into yesterday, and the field in the middle of the Louisiana pine forests was even more of

The Continental 75 on this Curtiss Pusher is not quite the original goods, but a "h" of a lot more reliable. The ground-adjustable prop gives it additional push.

The "perch" (the padded seat and seat back are a bit more comfortable than the original wicker) and the simple instruments.

the past. Crosby was a lumber town in the South, and in its own way a part of Americana I had never seen. The entire town of about six hundred inhabitants depended for its very existence on the lumber forests and the mill, and the peaceful way of life was a revelation to an ex-New Yorker.

The Pusher that I bought from John Pruett was a product of a romance on John's part for the wonderful dear dead days of the 1910 period.

In spite of my having seen photographs of the Curtiss Pusher replica, I was surprised at its authenticity. The wing section was a dead-ringer of the original, the wire-braced steel tail booms had been painted to look like bamboo, the seat was made of wicker; only the doughnut tires and Continental engine were there to make it look less than a Glenn Curtiss 1910 beauty.

Sitting down in the wicker seat, I felt about as exposed as a stark naked first-nighter at the Metropolitan Opera. I promptly got back out of the wicker morris chair, and with John as a professional guide, we did a walk-around inspection on the Curtiss, which primarily concerned looking at wires, wires, wires, and more wires. The Curtiss is a rigger's nightmare, but if you follow a clockwise path around the aircraft and are careful, you can see any loose items that might make you vulture bait.

With the tank on the upper wing you need a stepladder to check the gas level and to be sure your gas cap is secure. Enough Cessnas and Aero Commanders have bitten the dust because of a loose cap to make it à must check on all preflight inspections, no matter what the vintage of the aircraft.

Sitting in the Pusher, I fired up the Continental, with admonitions from John about the ability of the Continental carburetor to make more ice than the Greenland icecap. There are no brakes, and only the wheel chocks restrained my box-kite airplane.

Taxiing out, I located neutral elevator point by looking back at the tail surfaces. With no nose point to check horizon on, you need actually on the first flight a location of this neutral position related to your legs! I pushed forward on the throttle and started down the runway, lifting off in about two hundred feet, with a speed of about 42 mph. I leveled off about three feet high and checked the ailerons, which are slow-reacting but surprisingly large in area. Fore and aft on the yoke produced a sort of rubbery up-and-down feeling.

After flying about a minute, straight and level, I eased the throttle back and settled on the doughnut wheels. With the engine idling I got out, lifted the nose wheel, walked it around 180 degrees, and then taxiied the Pusher back in the dwindling daylight of a Louisiana evening.

After a pleasant evening, with sleep occasionally interrupted by the unusual sound of wild animals and birds, morning dawned, and with a great ranch-type breakfast under our vests, we were on our way back to the field. Today I faced the prospects of going around the field. Certain aspects of circling the field were none too pleasant, for the tall pine trees left no openings, and in case of a forced landing the pilot was bound to wind up with a face full of pine cones or worse.

After inspecting the Pusher, I got aboard. The Continental fired nicely, and after warmup I pushed my goggles down, and throwing caution to the wind, I let the Pusher have all seventy-five mighty horsepower as I rocketed down the field.

Front view showing why the Pusher is called a rigger's nightmare. Note the fuel tanks behind my back, as compared with the above-the-wing type shown earlier.

Once airborne and settled in a gentle climb, I went out about a half mile over the green deck of pines. I started a turn at an estimated five hundred feet (for there is no air speed nor altimeter). Immediately I felt the kind of queasy feeling of my fanny slipping away. In this respect, the Curtiss is not unlike the Bleriot. In any turn you must use the rudder, because without flat plate fuselage area the Pusher can literally be skidded 90 degrees off heading.

Billy Parker, a great aviator and one who built and flew Pushers in 1910, told me that he had an air show maneuver in which in a climbing turn the Pusher reversed direction as he pushed the rudder in. Billy wound up

flying backward till it stalled; then he would recover! And this was in the day before parachutes!

The ailerons in a turn seem to act more like flaps unless you keep the corrections small. After the turn I settled down to enjoy myself, because with about a 50 to 55 mph speed and sunshine, you really feel like you need only feathers to become a true birdman.

Stall, as in all early high-drag aircraft, is almost instantaneous and without much warning. It takes some time to recover because of the high drag.

Landings are easy, and you can drift along two or three feet high till you get ready and then touch down slightly tail low at about 39 mph (checked by a car running alongside). John enjoined me not to do anything but fly it into the landing spot with power, but I found that like the Bleriot, you can dive it very steeply, as did Lincoln Beachey. This scares hell out of both you and the crowd initially, but you have, as with the later and much-maligned Sea Bee amphibian, a quick and responsive pullout, an easy flare, and a gentle touchdown.

One of the strangest aspects of the configuration of the Pusher is that the higher you are, the less comfortable you feel, which is the reverse of what has been taught to pilots from time immemorial. Two examples of this came to mind. At one time we were doing some promotional filming for the Goodyear people with their blimp, which necessitated circling close to it in the Pusher at twenty-five hundred feet over Long Beach Harbor. I really had to talk to myself like a Dutch uncle, for the height, the up-front exposures, and the huge bulk of the blimp made me feel like a mouse trying to make friends with an angry elephant. At another time I met a DC-7 for photographs in the air at five thousand feet and lived in terror that I would hit his prop wash, for I would have been flung about like a postage stamp in a hurricane.

I have had experience with other replica Curtiss Pusher types, and all have a number of less than desirable features in common. All are built too heavily. For example, the 75-hp Continental engine on one that I flew weighed three hundred pounds more than an original Curtiss, with its very heavy V8 OX5 water-cooled engine. The disparity of weight and the poor push of the small opposed engines are the basic reasons why the replicas do not fly as well as the originals did. Wing sections that worked well for Curtiss are not often copied. To my

knowledge, the rotaries that had such enormous thrust and flew so well for Beachey have only been used on two replicas.

Two Pusher flights are engraved in my memory.

Being asked to fly the Pusher belonging to a friend, I got a real lesson in supersensitivity. The tiniest movement of the yoke caused a sudden pitch up or nose down, and only the landing saved a roller-coaster ride that would make Coney Island pale by comparison. This was the most sensitive of the five hundred-odd airplanes I have flown, and it was a great relief to switch off its engine.

Doing an air show in another Pusher at Palmdale, California, I took off in the high, hot desert air and flew fifteen miles before I could get high enough to turn around! Coming back to the field, the Pusher settled downwind in a stalled altitude, with wide-open throttles and with one wing down and on the wrong side of the power curve.

Coming down like a runaway elevator, I was sure I was going to dig more holes in the desert floor than a family of gophers. I couldn't trade altitude for speed, so just before I hit, I picked the wing up with the rudder and hit hard enough to spread the gear and scare the living "h" out of yours truly.

Over the years I have flown many, many hours in the Pusher, appearing in such movies as *The Great Race*, where I carried a dummy dangling fifteen feet behind and twenty feet below, and tossed the top-hat-clad mannequin into the hay loft of a barn. The Pusher has also done air shows, TV commercials, and some in-house films. I love the open air of the Pushers, but the never-to-be-forgotten sensation of the airplane under full power sinking into the obstacles ahead is one that you would hesitate giving even to your worst enemy.

Fokker E III

THE FOKKER "Scourge," or Fokker Terror, as it was known in the British wartime press of 1915, is just that as far as this World War II aviator is concerned.

The background of the Fokker III Eindecker (single-wing or monoplane in German) is inextricably bound up with the burgeoning career of Anthony Fokker, a Dutch pilot-designer of great ability and skill who had been an important part of the German military master plan since 1912.

His school at Schwerin, where he trained some of Germany's aces, was also the home of some of his early engineering developments, starting with his "Spin" monoplane, which because of its extraordinary dihedral did not need either wing warping or aileron for control.

For the rapidly increasing horde of World War I aviation fans, I hardly need to point out that the Eindecker started war in the air as we know it today. Up until the development of the E III an extraordinary variety of weapons had been used. Bricks, Webley and Luger pistols, Mauser and Lee Enfield rifles, Flechette darts, hand grenades, nets, anchors on the end of chains, and occasionally, machine guns (if they were light enough to be carried in the air by the underpowered World War I aircraft). In short, anything that could be lifted into the cockpit—except chain mail and crossbows—was taken aloft to be thrown, projected, or dropped on the enemy.

In April 1915 a secret of great price and value to the Allies was lost when the Germans captured a Morane-Saulnier monoplane flown by the great French prewar record-holding pilot, Roland Garros. Garros and his Morane had previously destroyed a number of German aircraft in one-sided combat. This fighting edge came from the machine guns, which were mounted to fire forward through the propeller, which was protected from the gunfire by steel deflector plates.

Upon the capture of the Morane, the German high command immediately put the problem of a forward-firing synchronized machine gun for aircraft in the hands of the brilliant Anthony Fokker. In three days he had the solution, and for nearly a year following the arrival of the E series Fokkers, equipped variously with Parebellum-Maxim and Spandau machine guns, no Allied aircraft was safe. In at least one instance, it is reported that twelve Allied fighter aircraft escorted one observation plane in order to protect it from the Fokker Eindecker.

Hauptmann Oswald Boecke, one of the great instructors, as well as one of Germany's greater aces, made all of his early record on Eindeckers. Other aces, such as Wintgens and Immelman, also flew E III's. Immelman is perhaps best remembered for the maneuver that is characterized by a roll on top of a loop.

Both Boecke and Immelmann received the *Pour le Mérite* flying E III's. This was Germany's highest honor, and as far as this slightly chicken aviator is concerned, anyone who would loop the E III and then half roll on top assuredly deserves this decoration, as well as the Victoria Cross and the Medal of Honor.

The E III Eindecker in our collection is the extraordinary achievement of an extremely dedicated and talented ex-U. S. Air Force officer, Maj. James Appleby. It all started with a photograph, followed by careful drawings and research and painstaking, nonswerving attention to detail. The airplane has traveled in pieces over much of the United States and even to Japan during Major Appleby's various service transfers. Five difficult years saw it completed and flying.

After some lengthy negotiations, we bought this magnificent plane and added it to the collection at Movieland of the Air in Orange County Airport, Santa Ana, California.

Inspecting the aircraft for flight is, in some respects, similar to inspecting the Bleriot, for the Eindecker shares its wing-warping control system and has no ailerons. It makes good sense to be careful in checking the flying and warping attaching fittings. Following these checks you are faced with the problem of climbing into the cockpit. You must be either exceptionally long-legged to manage this easily or use a rather unglamorous stepladder, as we see the German aviators doing in those old photographs of World War I.

The cockpit is in the center of a rather wide-chorded wing and is comfortable with a protective windshield. The flight instruments include tachometer, air speed, oil pulsator, and altimeter. In addition to the mixture and throttle controls there is the characteristic German control stick with its dual handles, which is certainly most necessary in this aircraft.

The tail is light, and it's an easy job for one man, with the skid on his shoulder, to wheel it out to takeoff position.

Starting the Le Rhone engine is much the same as with other rotaries, except that the 80-hp Le Rhone is an easy-starting, delightfully smooth-running engine. You prime each cylinder with gas from a squirt can after bleeding the oil pump (by removing the cap), then turn the gas valve on, and push both throttle and mixture

The 80-hp Le Rhone in its distinctive horseshoe cowling.

Herr Tallman in an authentic World War I German pilot's uniform, with its original *Pour le Mérite* at his throat.

controls on full until the fuel runs out the overflow. This fulfills the pre-starting check. Usually one pull will start the engine. With both air-mixture and throttle back, the engine idles smoothly and you feel a great deal of thrust from its high-pitch wood propeller. Checking the coupé (cut-out) button on the stick and having the mechanic check that the engine is oiling properly (in other words, throwing the castor oil all over the place) is all that remains to check before takeoff.

The temperature was sixty-five degrees and the wind steady at twelve knots at Orange County Airport on the day I took my first flight in the Eindecker. With throttle and air-mixture controls pushed forward, the Le Rhone revved up and the Eindecker began to roll. The tail was up almost instantly, and we lifted in 290 feet.

The immediate reaction when airborne is, "How in hades did an inexperienced pilot ever fly this bucking broncho?" Climb is at the rate of about 600 feet a minute.

The warp is extremely stiff on the wings, but slight pressure and almost no apparent movement of the stick is enough to drop a wing in normal turn.

The synchronized single Spandau.

Closeup of the 80-hp Le Rhone. Note the front push rod
and the delicate ignition wire to the spark plug.

Because I overcontrol on the rudder,
I lock my heels on the shock cord for
the landing gear, which is directly
under the rudder bar.

The tendency, as you level out, is to
want to get both hands on the stick,
for, as you pick up speed, it gets very
sensitive fore and aft, and you have
some difficulty not porpoising.

My two favorite types of rotary
engines are the 160-hp Gnome and
the 80-hp Le Rhone, and this particular 80 Le Rhone runs like a lovely
watch.

I settled down at 1000 feet, indicating 75 mph, and had completely
run away from my Stinson L I camera
plane. With the engine idled back and
with a 360-degree turn, I come up on
the camera plane and slide into position on his wing with slight rudder.
For the picture session I am in period
costume.

Strangely, the downwash from the
slots, or ailerons on the Stinson,
seems to adversely affect the Eindecker and draw it in toward the other
plane like a magnet. Only by drop-

45

The full flying rudder and elevator nibbles endlessly at
one's hands and feet in flight.

ping sharply away from the camera
plane can I solve this problem, but at
the same time it rather obviously dis-
gusts the photographer, who was all
set to shoot.

Later, when the photographing is
finished, the Eindecker gets its chance
to really prove itself as an aircraft.

Unlike my experience with the SE5,
there is no desire on my part to even
attempt aerobatics with the Eindecker.
I can't forget its well-deserved repu-

tation for structural failures when it
first appeared at the front in 1915.

The pearl of information that I
have saved until now is that the Eindecker series, like our modern jets,
had full flying elevator and full flying
rudder—in short, no fixed surfaces.
Perhaps because of lack of aerodynamic knowledge in the early days,
the elevator and rudder are perpetually hunting and feeding the attendant change back through the control

The landing gear doesn't look like much, but it did the job. The gear shock cord is inside the fuselage above the main gear strut.

system to the pilot. I found this same feedback in the early Bleriot but it was nothing like the constant heavy pressure present in the E III.

Perhaps the major flight characteristic ever present is the feeling that if you took your hands off the stick or your feet off the rudders, the Eindecker would turn itself inside out or literally swap ends. It stalls rather gently at 43 mph, and as the right wing drops, I make no attempt to pick it up. I just turn into the downwing.

Steep turns at altitude, climbs, glides, shallow dives, chandelles, and lazy 8's, all of which it does nicely except for the uncomfortable control feedback, complete our flight check.

Coming in to land on our busy airport has its problems. Aircraft are parked on the edge of our grass strip, which is about 100 feet wide and 800 feet long.

As I turn into final at 300 feet, the Le Rhone is barely ticking over and holding about 50 airspeed. The E III settles nicely. I have good visibility, and it pays off cleanly, but with adequate time to touch in a three-point attitude at about 38 to 40 mph. Alternating my finger on and off the coupé button, I have more than enough rudder control to taxi back to our display area.

As I climb to the ground, still dressed in an original German World War I pilot's uniform, I have a sudden urge to click my heels and stiffly salute, not the Fokker Eindecker, but the men who had to fly it in combat.

Side view of the delicate Eindecker built by James Appleby.

Aloft with a passenger in our nearly sixty-year-old
Maurice Farman.

Maurice Farman

Specifications

ENGINE	70-hp Renault
SPAN	57 ft.
LENGTH	37 ft., 9 in.
HEIGHT	11 ft.
CREW	2
EMPTY WEIGHT	1280 lbs.
USEFUL LOAD	610 lbs.
GROSS WEIGHT	1890 lbs.
FUEL CAPACITY	28 gals.
ARMAMENT	Occasionally Ground Lewis .303

Performance

MAXIMUM SPEED	56 mph
RATE OF CLIMB	250 fpm
STALL SPEED	32 mph
ENDURANCE	2 hrs.
SERVICE CEILING	8000 ft.

Checking out the smoothness of the Renault engines.

Maurice Farman

THE SOCIETE HENRI ET Maurice Farman Ateliers du Aviation was one of
the pioneer airplane manufacturing
companies in Europe. The English
brothers, Henry and Maurice, had
joined with a third brother Dick and
established the firm in 1912 in France.
With extraordinary foresight, they
had designed their factory for mass
production and were probably the
only aircraft firm in the world capable
of sizable contracts on that warm
June day in 1914 that the fatal shots
were fired at Sarajevo.

The Farman brothers seemed only
too satisfied with the basic Vosin design, stability, climb, and speed, and

were content to leave ideas and
imagination status quo while truly
great designers like Sopwith, Junker,
Dornier, Koolhaven, and others
leaped ahead in World War I. By the
end of that war the gentle old pigeon
roost was as much a part of the past
as the pterodactyl.

It is perhaps worthwhile to tell a bit
about the history of *our* Maurice Farman. As nearly as known, it was built
in the early war years, flown for a
time in England, and then sent to
Australia, to serve as a trainer in the
Royal Australian Flying Corps. Following the war it was registered by
the Civil Aviation Department as

In steady flight at 58 mph over the fields of Southern
California.

VH-UBC and was the second aircraft on the Australian civil register.

It was purchased complete with spares by a Mr. Graham Carey of Melbourne, who used it for aerial cargo, advertising, and a host of other purposes. Sometime in the late 1920s it was stored, and it was not returned to daylight till 1952, when it was rebuilt for flight. Fortunately, unlike many historical aircraft that we have rebuilt, due to the hot, dry climate of Australia, the woodwork of the Farman looked like that on an art institute's best Georgian Chippendale highboy. Being close to the ocean, it is not unknown for us at Tallmantz to find a longeron from a Spad or a spar from a Nieuport as full of moisture as a new Du Pont synthetic sponge and consequently as stout.

Our purchase of this rare airplane had high overtones of Operative 007 and the CIA, and was every bit as difficult to get out of Australia as Sputnik's secrets would be out of the Kremlin. After a year of waiting, the Farman arrived after its ocean voyage crated in a box literally just slightly larger than a standard Union Pacific Railroad refrigerator car. The people in Australia had crated it beautifully, and it needed Jimmy Valentine and three ounces of freshly brewed nitro to get into the box. Not knowing how it was packed inside, we went slowly and removed a board, and when we shoved the first flashlight into the crate and could see the wicker seats and the dull gleam of the copper gas tank, it must have been the same heart-stopping thrill that Lord Carnarvon had when he opened the royal treasure room in Tutankhamen's tomb.

Tallmantz Aviation and Shuttleworth Trust in England share the distinction of having rebuilt, flown, and operated more early and historic aircraft longer than any other individuals or groups in the world. Yet, because of the incredible difficulty of the Farman's rigging, without the blowups of the 1917 RAF's rigging diagrams, I am afraid our most experienced people would still, years later, be toiling slowly toward putting the Farman in flight status. (Actually, because of space and hangar limitations, it was nearly three full years before we assembled and flew this fascinating airplane.)

As we opened the crates in our own private "refrigerator car," we found the Farman's basic construction to be wings with wooden spars, built up ribs with trailing edges of wire, (all, of course, wire braced). The long tailbooms were laminated wire braced and carried dual rudders. Because of the Farman's DC-8-type span of fifty-one feet, the wings are in panels, top and bottom, and you join them in cells and put them together like an Erector Set.

Certainly the most interesting part of the airplane, and the part you actually start working on first, is the nacelle, or bathtub. It is made of wood, with longerons covered by plywood. Two leather-rimmed wicker seats support the pilots in Victorian splendor. The seats are in tandem, facing a rather streamlined clear windshield framed in aluminum.

The profusion of instrumentation is not likely to upset an airline captain, but it included electric tachometer, oil pressure indicator, altimeter, and air speed indicator. Unlike any other aviation controls I have seen are the twin spade grip handlebars pivoted to the center of the stick that controls the ailerons. Once in a moment of good balance and derring-do I rode an 1880 high-wheel bicycle that had the same type of handlebar.

The engine is the 80-hp French

Close-up of the two-place commodious nacelle. My left
hand is on the elevator "horn."

Renault, a V8 air-cooled of no incon-
siderable size. Cooling in addition to
the cylinder fins was by a shrouded
fan on the forward section of the
engine. To help feed air to the fan the
lower rear flooring of the fuselage
nacelle was given a concave contour.

The single ignition switch is a
lovely porcelain item on the outside
of the aircraft that looks about the
size of a good paperweight. The only
other item of interest is a tiny throttle,
which seems more fitted to control a
lawn mower than an airplane.

As we slowly assembled the Farman working out from the center
nacelle the maze of wires, even with
the RAF's diagrams, sometimes
looked more like the standing rigging
on a New Bedford whaling ship than
an aircraft. Most of the Farman is put
together with hard wire rather than
1–19 cable, and consequently if you
get it too tight it will snap, and in
rigging the old girl we snapped a
number of wires, which had to be
replaced.

After many weeks' work the Far-

Spinning the great bulk of the Farman as we get ready to takeoff.

man was finally fully assembled. With a large audience of buffs as well as mechanics in attendance, we rolled it out into the sun with its wings shining with silver dope, varnished struts and landing skids glowing, and copper gas tank gleaming. In spite of its very obvious antiquity it was a thing of real beauty.

To climb into the nacelle you need a guide to the maze to wend your way through the multitude of wires, and then a steeplejack's ability to ignore heights. Once in the nacelle you find it comfortable and, except for its size and the unusual controls, you feel right at home.

The Renault engine was as well taken care of as the rest of the airplane. As soon as the tank was filled, and plugs and fittings checked, and

the carburetor flooded (incidently, the carburetor is in a lovely spot hanging below the crankcase and only a couple of inches in front of the turning propeller), the engine was ready to run.

It started on the first pull. Fortunately there wasn't much compression, because the formidable wooden propeller is about the size of one of the five on the *Graf Zeppelin*. The engine runs smoothly but with a most distinctive clatter, which resembles the sound of a grain separator. The engine turns so slowly you can almost count the blades. As with all early birds with skids, we took the Farman out on the grass and faced it into the wind.

Looking at this huge old bird, you realized that weightwise it is no Nieuport II or Sopwith Pup, and you defi-

54

nitely need a ground crew to help in ground movement, for the tail booms dig in and drag like a steer going to branding.

The first takeoff was at Orange County Airport. The wind was eight knots. Ground temperature was sixty-seven degrees, with altitude at fifty-three feet. The tail comes up rather slowly, and while you are hoping this gathering of spare parts stays together you find yourself rather surprisingly in the air. Like all first flights you hold it low, checking on control movements and general aircraft feel. Because we are steaming along at all of forty-four miles per hour, we haven't covered much of the airport's fifty-eight hundred feet, so with no apparent problems we start a climb. The rate of climb, while nothing to excite the astronauts, is still in excess of some of the early Curtiss planes and Bleriots, and with a long, gentle turn, I have about five hundred feet downwind.

It's quite possible to take off the fearless aviator-type goggles, because the windshield comfortably deflects the fifty-five miles per hour cruising airspeed. With time to look around, the rpm of the slow-turning blades still surprise one.

All controls require a measureable time quotient between cockpit movement and aircraft response. This is certainly understandable when you consider the actual distance the various cables travel and the possibility of stretch. Although the response is slow, it has none of the heart-stopping sense of control loss that seems to be part of flying of the early Pushers and Bleriots.

There is a sudden bump, and I see a tremor start at one wingtip and run across underneath the Nacelle and out the other wingtip! Along with the wings, the tail booms also have this slightly disconcerting Jello-like quality.

In all fairness to the Farman, there is in spite of the wobbles a feeling of security and a complete enjoyment of the slow Noah's Ark type of flying. The visibility is perhaps the finest of any aircraft ever built, and it's no wonder the Farman was great as an observation plane.

With the snaillike flying speed of the Farman, the only flying machines I can keep in a compatible traffic pattern with are a blimp and a helicopter. Airspeed on my crosswind is about fifty, and over-the-fence speed is about forty-five. Like any aircraft with great drag, I get just inches off before flare out, and it sets down as gently as a mother hen at thirty-three miles per hour. The shock cord sprung double truck wheeled gear makes a lovely pleasant rumble, and I roll to a stop in about the length of a tennis court and a half.

I must admit to one "boo-boo" with the Farman. We were shooting some film, and I started a running takeoff from ninety degrees out of the wind, figuring the rudder would be adequate as I turned into the wind. Such was not the case, and I made a handsome ground-loop. I waited for that cracking noise that would let me know that I would be picking up splinters. All I did was turn over the double truck wheels, which are attached to the landing skids with a kind of swiveling steel "A" frame.

I never did completely stall the Farman and rather obviously never stunted it, even to the point of doing little more than gentle turns.

The Farman is a gracious, tractable old crock, and in successive flights with her I was content to fly quietly around in the sunshine and enjoy an old-fashioned railroad observation car-type ride.

Front view of the agile Nieuport 28, with its lovely race-horse lines and the clear cowling of the 160-hp Gnome.

Nieuport 28C-1

CERTAINLY THE LOVELIEST race horse lines of all the World War I aircraft belonged to the French Nieuport 28, and like the beautiful thoroughbred it resembles, it also had real speed and agility. I share the feeling of others lucky enough to fly the "28" that it certainly is the epitome of World War I flying. After you have flown this beauty you are ready to throw old rusty water-cooled engines at other much better publicized Allied and German aircraft.

Strangely enough, all of the successful designs of the Nieuport factory (Société Anonyme des Establishments Nieuport) in World War I were biplanes. Yet the prewar Nieuports that established many racing records were all monoplanes, graceful and well-designed for their time. Possibly, if the same amount of engineering had been spent on monoplanes in World War I that was spent on biplanes with their inborn drag, we might have seen level flight speeds approaching two hundred miles an hour by the end of the first global conflict.

Gustave Delage, a former naval engineer, was chief designer of the extensive series of Nieuport World War I aircraft. In spite of the rather efficient biplane design of most World War I Nieuport aircraft, many of the different models seemed to be constructed in a manner most likely to hospitalize their pilots due to a structural or manufacturing failure of some kind. The "28" was no exception. As the story goes, the sometimes parsimonious French designed a lovely, graceful airplane but added to it a wing cover carefully conceived by a demented seamstress.

The sewn cover seam lay so spanwise, approximately ten inches back on the upper surface of the wing. Even in those relatively early years of aviation the areas of life on a wing were known, and this major error in manufacturing, tied to an airplane quite capable of exceeding two hundred miles per hour in a dive, culmi-

nated in many an accident looking for a place to happen. Consequently, the "28" series were never as popular as the Spads because of this ability to lose the laundry on the upper wing.

Construction of the "28" was pretty standard for World War I, with the exception that it included a conglomeration of different materials that would turn a post-World War I junk dealer pink with envy: wood spars with built-up wood ribs; plywood leading edge; turn buckles by the cracker barrelful; streamline tubing for the landing gear; "l"-beam steel tubing in the cockpit section and center section, paired with light aluminum and wooden outer wing struts; and a pressed-cardboard cover from the engine cowling to the rear of the cockpit area. Added to all this was a cockpit just large enough for a thin ten-year-old boy in a bathing suit.

America's first air victories in World War I fell on April 14, 1918, when Lt. Douglas Campbell and Lt. Alan Winslow of the newly formed "Hat in the Ring" 94th Pursuit

The "Ace" in the cockpit of his mount.

Squadron shot down Pfalz single-seat fighters.

So much unutterable garbage has been written about rotary engines that many of our current pilots approach them with severe palpitations and vibrations in the area of the backbone. Actually, the characteristics of the 160-hp Gnome as I know them are delightful. Unlike most rotaries, this engine has dual ignition. Few of our pilots of today have become acquainted with that so-well-remembered silence that occurs when the lone ignition system folds its tent and steals silently away. A rather common occurrence with magnetos on rotary engines aging now for half a century is that when they are actually turned up and flown, the very

old winding on the armature can often swell, then drag, and finally shear the rotor shaft key, which promptly cancels your current flight plan. A rather competent aviator of the Old School said, "Two magnetos can be as comforting as the difference between a fifth and a quart."

The mixed construction of the Nieuport 28 made inspection a real necessity. When you walk up to the graceful, slender bird, it's a question of whether to start at the tail or the camouflaged cowling. Having once found a broken fitting on the short strut bracing the underside of the Nieuport's horizontal tail, I begin here. I move forward checking the fabric for wrinkles, which might indicate a broken longeron or former,

Side view of the Nieuport, dressed in the colors and wearing the insignia of the 94th "Hat in the Ring" Pursuit Squadron. The graceful rudder evident in this view gave the 28 more ground control than any other World War I fighter I have flown.

then the wings, the wires, the security of cowling and propeller, the inflation of the tires, and the soundness of the shock cord. As you finish your inspection and climb into the cockpit, you hope that your trouser size, which usually increases with age, hasn't exceeded the sylphlike proportions of the basket-weave plywood seat.

We are shy some instruments that usually were carried by the 28, but presently we mount an airspeed indicator, oil pressure gauge, and altimeter. Missing also is the infamous cut-out switch, with which you could ground out three, six, or nine cylinders. According to legend, if you grounded out three or six, the distinctive sound was the signal for the pyrene-equipped World War I fire crews to run out on the field to greet the 28 as it landed in flames.

We face the little bird into the wind with a clear area ahead, and chock it.

The single level controlling fuel air mixture is retarded while the gas is on and the propeller is pulled through. The dual ignition switch is off, and the coupé (cut-out) button on the top of the stick is depressed for added safety.

There is pretty fair compression, necessitating a mechanic selected primarily for fine muscle tone and body structure to pull the prop through.

The Gnome starts without priming (unlike other rotaries), and with a real bark. As the little lady tugs at the chocks you are sure you really have a tiger in the cowling, even if the spots don't match the camouflage. With the appearance of spattered castor oil on the leading edge of the wing we know we are oiling and consequently ready for takeoff. The temperature is 63 degrees, the altitude is 53 feet, and the wind on our nose of 11 knots. With the chocks pulled and the Gnome winding up, it's like a Clydesdale or Percheron pulling, for there is no doubt as to the old engine's raw horsepower.

I know of no other aircraft except the Boeing F4BI (P-12) that has such complete and instant response. The tail is up in 15 feet of forward roll, and rudder is needed to overcome torque, though the actual torque is nothing like the hair-raising fables of the World War I-type pulp magazines.

With its short wingspan, it bounces off over several Jack Rabbit burrows in about 220 feet. Wow! The climb is spectacular, and the steep-climbing turn gives not the tiniest evidence of payoff. Unfortunately, as I level off in the pattern with essentially no throttle control, I am going by the modern civilian aircraft like they were at anchor.

In flight, the most noticeable fact of the 28 is that the big Gnome gives off heat like a cast-iron stove in a New England country store in winter. It's so d--- hot you're sure the ship is afire.

Climb is on the order of 1300 feet a minute, and stalls are straightforward unless one uses full back elevator.

In our present state of aircraft design, it's easy to forget that many aircraft of earlier vintage had enormous control throws on the order of two feet (elevators) instead of several inches. This excess of control is desirable in the hands of a professional but often deadly dangerous in the hands of an amateur. Certainly many of our World War I pilots who arrived at the front with great gallantry and noble purpose could only qualify today as beginners.

In flight, apart from the stovelike heat and the more than adequate control throw, the most noticeable sensation is the overwhelming castor oil

The twin Vickers were staggered so that the ammunition boxes inside the cockpit could be arranged to conserve space.

smell. Having flown many rotary-powered aircraft, I rather look forward as something of an aficionado to the castor oil. Not so in the 28, however; for the comfort of the driver, one needs a nice tight pressure-type oxygen mask.

Not having to outdive some leathercoated Prussian preparing to ventilate my coat tails with a pair of Spandaus, most of my aerobatics are done with "G" loads on the order of 2½, and with some timidity on my part.

The 28 loops beautifully, and with the exception of offset rudder at the top (to counteract torque), it might as well be on rails. I start the loop at 120 mph, and there is an immense sense of thrust from the big Gnome as it pulls you up and over.

Slow rolls are smooth, and you don't need forward stick to hold the nose up, just unshakable faith, for the engine quits and doesn't come back again for about 15 seconds. You would be surprised how much landscape and real estate you can assess for a forced landing in this time.

No other aerobatics were tried, but the plane picks up speed like a pig on a greased slide, and you can comfortably get 200 mph without too much of a dive.

Like almost all World War I planes, a nose-high forward slip with this plane can kill off speed and yet give you some idea of clearance in your landing area. In the 28 this is even more necessary, because with the Vickers guns in the staggered position (because of ammunition boxes inside the fuselage), your vision is restricted in a standard field pattern in a left turn.

With its short wings the Nieuport pays off fast, and you better be close to the ground in any three-point attitude. But thanks to the graceful and generous rudder, you don't have to make the rudder correction on landing that you do with both the Spad and the Fokker DVIII. The apparent touchdown speed is between 48 and 50 mph. The skid takes hold quickly,

and you drag to a stop in about 300 feet.

As I taxi in, with bursts of power from the big Gnome, I feel like I could use a brandy and milk, which seems to have been World War I's favorite stomach settler after an hour of concentrated atomized castor oil.

Flying formation with a Pfalz DXII during a filming session. The 28 could—and did this day—lick the DXII hands down.

Tail up—take off.

Sopwith F1 Camel

NOT HAVING ANY Arab forebears in my heritage, the care and grooming of a Camel came as something of an exercise in patience and understanding.

The genealogy of this famous fighting plane of World War I traces back to a Wright biplane. Thomas Octave Murdock Sopwith, a wealthy English sportsman and pilot, and holder of a number of courageously earned flying records, decided in the year 1911 to erect an aircraft factory whose major purpose was to rebuild and refit wrecked English aircraft, primarily Howard-Wright biplanes, which by then were beginning to litter the British countryside like confetti.

A deserted skating rink at Kingston on the Thames was chosen as the plant, and thanks to the brilliant designs and magnificent fighting records of Sopwith World War I products, it came in time to be one of the best-known factory locations in the world.

Harry Hawker, an engineer and test pilot and son of an Australian blacksmith, and Fred Sigrist, plant manager, were along with Sopwith to become a triumvirate that accomplished much for British aviation in World War I.

Long before the Camel scared both its pilots and the enemy, Sopwith came out with what for their day were a number of brilliant, practical aircraft designs.

The bat boat was perhaps the first really successful amphibian, and while it followed Glenn Curtiss's earlier experiments, it certainly saved a lot of wet clothing, for the pilot sat in an enclosed boat hull instead of on the leading edge of the wing, as in the Curtiss design.

Following in short order came the Torpedo float plane; the Gnome seaplane, and the lovely, all-white Tabloid. Because of its speed, strength, and performance, the Tabloid quickly reversed the prewar leaning toward monoplanes.

Innovations in aircraft design and performance were to be as much a part of the Sopwith mystique as feathers to a bird, and the Tabloid was no exception. It had side-by-side seating, a 1200 feet-a-minute rate of climb, and fuel for 2½ hours. All this in 1913.

Sopwith's first contribution to war in the air was initiated on October 8, 1914, when two Tabloids attached to the Royal Naval Air Service took off from beleaguered Antwerp carrying a few 20-pound bombs. *Tabloid 167*, flown with supreme skill and daring by Flight Lieutenant Marix, managed to zero in on target so well that Count von Zeppelin's newest airship XIX went up in flames in its hangar at Dusseldorf.

The next ancestor in the Camel's proud heritage was the Sopwith 1½ Strutter, and though rather stable and stiff, it became the first tractor two-seat fighter. Operationally, it mounted a synchronized Vickers gun firing through the propeller and a rear-

The original Camel without its fabric. Checking out the construction of this all-wood fighter before putting on new covering.

mounted Lewis, which used the first of the fine flexible Scarff rings.

Various engines, Gnomes and Le Rhones, were fitted to the 1½ Strutter, from 80 to 135 hp. Of design note, the aircraft had the first variable-incidence horizontal tail plane in production and the first operational wing flaps, which predated by nearly twenty years Donald Douglas's fabulous twin-engine DC-1 and 1-2, the first large production aircraft with wing flaps.

The father of the Camel was the Sopwith Pup, considered by all lucky enough to fly her as World War I's most viceless and lovely airplane. Power was the 80-hp Le Rhone rotary, which, in this writer's opinion, is the nicest of all rotaries: sweet-running, smooth as a dynamo, and as reliable as a Rolls-Royce.

Pups that officially came in service in February 1916 were a godsend to the hard-pressed Allies, and in spite of only a single forward-firing Vickers, were more than a match for the German Albatros.

Because of the Pup's light weight (787 pounds) and its rate of climb and short takeoff capabilities, it pioneered many of the early deck-landing experiments, which led to the mighty aircraft carriers of today.

One of the Pup's most interesting features is a windshield about the size of a small porthole attached to the back of the Vickers gun. It is framed in a heavy leather-padded cover, which was apparently carefully designed to prevent heavy dental bills in case of a crash.

Because of a father who was a naval aviator in World War 1, and an uncle who flew Salmsons in the 91st Squadron in France, my interests in historical airplanes have always been with the glamorous and exciting

Once again in full dress and looking sassy.

Climbing for altitude in our original Sopwith Camel.

Sopwith F1 Camel

Specifications

ENGINE	110-hp Le Rhone, Type J
SPAN	28 ft.
LENGTH	18 ft., 8 in.
HEIGHT	8 ft., 6 in.
CREW	1
EMPTY WEIGHT	889 lbs.
USEFUL LOAD	530 lbs.
GROSS WEIGHT	1419 lbs.
FUEL CAPACITY	35 gals.
ARMAMENT	2 .303 Vickers

Performance

MAXIMUM SPEED	108 mph
RATE OF CLIMB	1100 fpm
STALL SPEED	35 mph
ENDURANCE	2¾ hrs.
SERVICE CEILING	21,000 ft.

Nieuport 28C-1

Specifications

ENGINE	160-hp Gnome dual ignitions
SPAN	26 ft., 9 in.
LENGTH	21 ft.
HEIGHT	8 ft., 1 in.
CREW	1
EMPTY WEIGHT	961 lbs.
USEFUL LOAD	578 lbs.
GROSS WEIGHT	1539 lbs.
FUEL CAPACITY	36 gals.
ARMAMENT	2 Vickers .303

Performance

MAXIMUM SPEED	138 mph
RATE OF CLIMB	1200 fpm
STALL SPEED	49 mph
ENDURANCE	2 hrs., 20 min.
SERVICE CEILING	19,685 ft.

Overleaf: Piloting my Nieuport 28 in a mock dog fight with a persistent Fokker DVII.

aircraft of 1914 to 1918. As a pilot with one-third of a century experience, I love anything that flies, be it hang glider or jet, but like many of my contemporaries, I was weaned on the World War I aviation pulp magazines, such as, *War Birds* and *Battle Aces*. The names and exploits of McCudden, Richthofen, Ball, Rickenbacker, and Guynemer were as familiar and romantic to me as Babe Ruth and Lou Gehrig were to others of my generation.

My Sopwith F1 Camel, which was, as far as I know, the only original World War I Camel ever brought back to flying condition, was acquired under a set of circumstances sounding as fictional as incidents in *Gulliver's Travels*.

Having been interested in weapons of war all my life, I acquired in one of many exchanges and trades an early wide-jacket Parabellum German aircraft machine gun, and during a visit to the Jarrett War Museum on the old Steel Pier in Atlantic City in the middle thirties, I had a chance to make a trade for something else in the gun line. In the process I saw what will always be the best museum of World War I equipment ever assembled, including the Belgian War Museum in Brussels.

Colonel Jarrett starting as a young man and had built a museum of hundreds of thousands of items from every warring nation and comprising everything from field kitchens to airplanes.

At this time, due to outdoor exposure on the pier, with inclement weather and salt air, Jarrett's aircraft were beginning to show the ravages of their second decade. The airplanes included a Sopwith F1 Camel, a Nieuport 28C, a Thomas Morse S4B, a German Pfalz DXII, and the majority of a Fokker DVII.

Years elapsed, the excitement and enormous changes brought about by World War II came and went, and another generation was supposedly made safe and secure for all time, thanks to the lives and fortunes sacrificed again to the gods of war.

Never forgetting an early dream of owning a World War I aircraft, and with some leisure and my mustering-out pay from the service, I contacted Colonel Jarrett, and for a sum small in comparison to today's incredibly inflated market, I purchased several antique aircraft, which included the Camel and a Nieuport 28, a Pfalz DXII, and a Spad VII.

The war and a variety of reasons had forced Colonel Jarrett to remove his huge collection from the Steel Pier to a farm in Maryland. Journeying there and seeing my future airplanes dilapidated, rusty, and sagging in their shed, was a sobering dash of cold water to my enthusiastic but inconclusive plans.

The Camel was the only airplane of the four that appeared to be most complete, and without any better motivation than having most of its pieces intact, I chose it as No. 1 for rebuilding.

It was necessary to move all the aircraft from Maryland to Biggs Field in New Castle, Delaware, and not being rich as Croesus or having a hauling company, I got checked out as senior pilot on a large rented stakebed GMC truck.

With the aid of my brother, some well-muscled pals, and a patient but interested state police, we moved the bulky group of aircraft more than a hundred miles. We were followed the entire way by the stares of thousands of surprised motorists who paced our Camel caravan.

The small grass airport in New Castle where we stored the planes, with its pleasant trees and contented cows, was a perfect setting for the reconstruction of our World War I aircraft, but ultimately all the airplanes were to be both miles and years away from this location before they were rebuilt.

Had I known the problems and vicissitudes accompanying the rebuilding of my humped friend, I am sure I would happily have used the necessary cubic footage of the public gas company's best product and ended it all.

Traveling the world like the Ancient Mariner, my Camel's first stop was in New England, where I had interested an aircraft school in the project. Fortunately, in those dear dead days, aircraft schools still believed that wood was used not only in matchsticks and Chippendale furniture, but in aircraft construction as well. However, with what appeared to me to be snaillike progress, only a lower wing and the center section had been finished in a year and a half, and seemingly the school's flamelike enthusiasm had lessened to a tiny flicker. My old friend Paul Poberzney of the Experimental Aircraft Association came to the rescue and furnished aerial transportation for the Camel from Boston to Peoria, where it was off-loaded into the capable and dedicated hands of an old airplane buff by the name of Ned Kensinger.

Two and one-half years of delays, expenses, and unforeseen problems had somewhat dulled my earlier dreams, but Ned Kensinger's progress on the Camel made the dream come rapidly alive in glowing Technicolor. In short order, the wings took shape. The spruce spars that were unusable were given back to the termites. All new ribs were sawed and glued into place with the necessary new spars. The original hardware, such as

plates and cluster fittings, were found to be safe and, after stripping and magnafluxing, they were used.

The same general rule of thumb was followed in all stages of the Camel's reconstruction, and that was to use every possible original piece of the Camel and only replace it with an identical item of the same shape and material if the original piece was unairworthy.

Three spars of the original eight were used, as well as the wood interplane and outer struts. The rear longerons were new and were spliced into the forward longerons just aft of the pilot's seat.

Bending the rear longerons required the services of the local sauna bath, and one of the longerons split anyway, accompanied not only by the noise of the breaking wood, but by the curses and lamentations of my master mechanic.

Construction plans (compliments of the Hawker Siddeley Group) being what they are and nearly half a century old, as each of the Camel's wooden structures were completed, they were very wisely assembled without cover. I finally flew down to Peoria one sunny pleasant day to see a completed Sopwith F1 Camel in the hangar, gleaming in spar varnish but without any more covering than there is in the local nudist colony.

Acquisition of engine, wheels, tires, and instruments all proved to be formidable. My knowledge of rotaries was confined to having seen a photograph of one in a book, and the outside appearance of the Camel's engine was horrible.

Fortunately, thanks to the rocklike varnish of dried castor oil, the cylinder wall rods, pins, and valves were silver bright, but the huge main bearing races and balls were rusty and had to be removed. A new commer-

Closeup of the 110-hp Le Rhone J, with the F1 muzzles of
the twin Vickers above.

cial bearing race was ground into and
reset in the master rod.

The block tube cheese-boxlike carburetor was overhauled, as was the
single Lavallette and Sons-Paris magneto. Though the winding on the mag
looked pretty moth-eaten, we decided
to use it, and this proved later to be
an error of the magnitude of the
sinking of the *Titanic*.

The original propeller had degener-
ated to the consistency and strength
of wet balsa, so without anyone's
knowledge to lean on, I used horse
sense gleaned from the old barnstormers in replacing the propeller.

The 110-hp Le Rhone turns a top
1200 rpm, and in my travels I found
a handsome though dusty Hisso prop
gracing the doorway of a garage in
my hometown. The stamping on the

hub of this prop indicated that the
150-hp Hispano was designed for
1450 rpm. By a rule of thumb I estimated that the lower-horsepower Le
Rhone might turn this Hiss propeller
at nearly the right rpm, and so it
turned out, and for many years the
Camel was flown with a Hisso prop.

Wheels and particularly tires were
a problem. One day when I had a
welding job done in a small airport
in Illinois, I suddenly noticed early
airplane wire wheels and fine tires on
the welding cart. Measuring them
with my ever-present tape measure, I
found they were perfect! Some fairly
heavily marked lettuce changed
hands, and the Camel had wheels.

Early instruments, sketchy as they
were, came from a variety of sources.

Covering was not Irish linen, as in

Adjusting one of the Vickers, but note the closeness of the engine to the cockpit.

World War I, but Grade A, and not doped with flammable nitrate, but with flame-resistant butyrate.

Unfortunately, I decided because of the fire potential and the lack of a wind-driven pressure pump to eliminate the pressure fuel system in the Camel and just work from gravity and the small emergency tank behind the pilot's shoulders.

One Friday the long-awaited call came from Ned Kensinger. The Camel was finished and only awaiting her driver. After years of waiting and the expenditure of thousands of dollars, I was on my way to the Camel flying a Navy JRB Twin Beechcraft down from the Glenview Naval Air Station to Peoria.

With a lovely day, and with a co-pilot doing most of the flying, I had time to muse about the extraordinary history of the Camel series of airplanes and the history of this particular Camel before I became its owner.

No airplane built during World War I could stunt or stay with a well-flown Camel. Consequently, in its relatively short space of service, between July 1917 and the end of World War I, the Camel accounted for 1294 enemy aircraft. This record was not equal until the Battle of Britain, when the Hurricane exceeded the figure.

Among design innovations, the Camel's Vickers guns were equipped for the first time with the Hawker Kauper gear, which allowed full rather than interrupted fire. This was a very material improvement.

Thousands of Camels were turned out not only by Sopwith but by other contractors as well, and naturally enough new ideas and new operational jobs fell to the versatile airplane. Trench strafing, which the Camel helped to pioneer, was about as eagerly sought after by Allied pilots as skinny dipping in shark-infested waters. And how anyone could get into the Camel's crowded cockpit with the addition of the extra Lewis guns, which fired through the floor, is a mystery. The fact that the missions were sometimes flown as low as ten feet and could literally be ended with a well-placed slingshot didn't make the planes any more popular.

Other unusual flying jobs handled by planes in the Camel series included open-sea landings for flotation tests, drop trials in flight from a British airship, pioneering deck landings for the Royal Navy, and the incomparable interception of the German Zeppelin *L53* (the last to be shot down in the war) by Lieut. S. D. Culley, flying a Camel that had taken off from a sea sled towed by a destroyer. He climbed to nineteen thousand feet before the Camel stalled out nose high. With only one Vickers firing, he still set the Zeppelin alight, and it broke in half in flames and fell into the sea.

The Camel was also used in a night-flying role. This is to me perhaps its most interesting assignment, because my Camel had been a night aircraft. On the broken panel, before reconstruction, we found primitive wiring and a small hooded socket over each instrument location.

Cecil Lewis writes in his lovely book, 'Farewell to Wings,' about his fear and reluctance to take off, Zeppelin or Gotha hunting, when his Camel's only night-flying equipment consisted of a flashlight, and the only illumination for the runaway was a paraffin flare path. Once airborne, he writes lyrically about the silver Thames and moonlit London. I must confess, on reading this, that the thought of flying over London at any time, day or night, behind a 110-hp Le Rhone, Type 9J, which I consider without peer the most unpleasant, cranky, and treacherous of all rotaries, simply leaves me breathless.

In time I came to consider any flight in my F1 Camel, because of the unpredictability of the Le Rhone, as I would a sailplane or glider, and flew it from one possible dead-stick landing point to another.

I put my airborne reflections of the Camel's past to rest as we circled for a landing at Peoria. Then my first shock of the day arrived with a bang. The Twin Beech's motorized chain-driven landing gear refused to swing down, and the warning horn began to blare. Because this was the admiral's personally assigned airplane, considerably more rode on getting the gear down than with a normal Navy aircraft.

We dug into the airplane's vitals like the Seven Dwarfs in their mine, and in minutes had the clutch released and the gear down, with green light showing and the horn silent. Palpitations subsiding somewhat, I gingerly made a wheel landing and taxied up to where the Camel sat on the grass looking fresh and new, and quite the most exciting-looking airplane I had ever seen.

The Camel's appearance contrasted strongly with that of its crew, who were laid out on the grass in every possible position and attitude, as though cast by a giant explosion. A more somber, unhappy, and dismal group I had never seen. The reason for the gloom and the supine attitudes was that since 8 A.M., some six hours earlier, relays of well-muscled prop-twirler types had worked increasingly on the Le Rhone without one rewarding bark.

All the knowledge any of us had about rotaries could have been contained in a contact lens and the pressure not even felt against the eye. Did we have spark? Yes. Was the mag set? Yes. Had the commutator ring been wiped off? Yes. Had we primed it? Only every other cylinder. Did we have gas to the Block tube? We weren't sure.

With a quick walk around the airplane, I settled in the wicker seat minus a chute, for the Navy chute is too large to squeeze into the small cockpit and I didn't expect to fly anyway. Anyone expecting to fly a Camel better take the long course at the local reducing salon, for substantial girth

My brother, Foster, swinging the Camel's prop at the Andrews Air Force Base Air Show a few years back.

Closeup of the Camel's Vickers, and the windshield with its sighting tube.

Runup with our Fokker DVII *Lo!* in the background. Note the blur of the Camel's 110 turning at speed.

was never considered by the Camel's designers.

The cord-wrapped Spade stick, the Block tube, carburetors next to one's knees, the flexible air intake to the outside air scoops, the wood wire brace longerons, the instrument panel with its clutter, and the dual control cables to the wooden rudder bar all seemed as strange and antiquated as a covered wagon.

At my wish, the crew forced open the intake valves as the engine was pulled through (switch off) and shot a charge of fuel in each cylinder, as the cylinder came in front of the hole in the cowling. By accident, rather than knowledge, I advanced the long lever controlling the air, and in push-

ing the manet (a small wheel knob on the miniature control quadrant) forward and then returning it, I had hit on the correct starting procedure.

Wonder of wonders, as I flipped the porcelain-mounted switch up and called for contact, the Le Rhone started with a full-throated bellow, scaring both me and the crew.

By shoving the fuel-controlling lever forward and using the coupé (cut-out) button on the stick, I was able to keep the engine running. Soon the never-to-be-forgotten smell of castor oil infused our area, and the sight of oil spattering the leading edge of the low wings indicated that the engine was lubricating properly.

Taxiing practice ended rather ignominiously a hundred feet from the starting point, when my newfound knowledge wasn't equal to the delicate adjustment of fuel and air, and the Le Rhone quit.

The revitalized ground crew hauled the nine hundred-pound airplane over to the grass and faced me into the wind. For safety's sake we changed plugs, and the engine started on the first pull. Signaling the crew to let go of the wings (brakes in this day being relegated to stagecoaches, bicycles, and cars), I headed down the field with the throttle wide open. The tail came up almost instantly, and visibility was good, except for the Aldis telescopic sight and the twin Vickers.

Having no anticipation of flight, it came as something of a shock to find the Camel airborne at about 35 mph after a ground run of barely 150 feet. Being afraid of jockeying with my ticklish fuel and air controls, I climbed into the traffic pattern enjoying the Camel's sensitive ailerons, elevators, and rudder.

I circled the field once, got into position, shut fuel air and switch off, and made a light forward slip, touching down gently on three points in the green grass bordering the runway. Total landing runout couldn't have been much more than the takeoff run.

In the few sentences contained above are culmination of years of work, worry, and money, all in large doses and all riding on skills forgotten since World War I. But this Sopwith F1 Camel has since afforded me the most flying hours that I have accumulated in World War I aircraft, as well as more forced landings than all the rest of the historical planes put together.

A week following the test flight, I flew the Camel back to Chicago, some 150 miles. This was to prove to be the longest flight I have ever made in the pugnacious World War I fighter.

Of the many military shows and civilian events that the Camel appeared in, I remember best the Philadelphia show where I flew the Camel by the aircraft carrier *Princeton*, in the Delaware River. With only eight cylinders functioning, because the porcelain element of the spark plug had broken and thrown itself away, it was so rough that I had to rest my feet on the tie wires in the fuselage. After this event, I went back happily to using the old World War I Micarta plugs.

Readying the Camel for a TV series at my old base in Riverside, I was flying formation with the camera plane when my engine's main bearing froze and stopped. With nothing but wine grape orchards below me, I chose an unfinished housing project with a tennis-courtlike rear area. Coming in, I deliberately stalled out over high trees, and this was quickly followed by a nose-high forward slip. I stopped unscathed in a littered area that couldn't have been more than a couple of hundred feet across.

The Lavallette and Sons Paris magneto was in time to be responsible for two forced landings. The first occurred some four hours after the first test flight. Due to age, the winding on the mag had swollen, and as the mag turned it created heat, further swelling the winding until finally it dragged so badly that it sheared the key on the shaft, and I ingloriously made an unexpected landing in a plowed farmer's field. The second forced landing came when the hot wire vibrated off the mag, leaving me downwind at about four hundred feet over a newly graded road. Thanks to the Camel's ability to turn on a dime and still give nine cents change, I put it down after bounding over a road grader. I wound up with a broken tail skid and stopped ten feet from the very surprised owner of the local gas station and two surfers in their surfboard-covered Volkswagen.

On this Le Rhone 9J, you cannot adjust either the fuel or air intake without running the risk of a dead-stick landing. You must leave them alone and use your cut-out button for all flight handling.

The takeoff run is easy. In a wind of 10 to 15 knots you are airborne in a couple of plane lengths at 35 mph and climbing out at about 60 mph, with a rate of climb of nearly 1000 feet a minute.

The elevators are sensitive, as is the rudder. Consequently, when flying for any distance I often put the heels of my shoes on the floor tie wires, because the vibration of the Le Rhone through the rudder bar exaggerates the rudder movements.

In level flight at 100 mph indicated, the Camel is delightful, and the structure is rugged enough to feel comfortable in loops. Unfortunately, with the British Spade stick and my 6-foot, 1-inch size, there's little room for aileron movement. The stick contacts my knees and thighs with anything stiffer than a 30-degree bank, and consequently I never rolled the Camel.

In military shows I have ground-strafed, and as soon as the airspeed reaches 130 or 140 mph the nose begins to hunt up and down, and the elevator becomes extremely sensitive. I feel that this action is due largely to the square windshield between the two Vickers guns, causing a substantial burble over the tail surfaces.

Turns with the torque require the top rudder to hold the nose up, and in stalls at 35 to 40 mph the nose drops through frighteningly fast, but you also get control back in a hurry. The loop at 110 is an incredibly small circle in the sky, and, as in most rotaries, as you slow down at the top you must feed in rudder against the torque. I have had the pleasure of limited dog-fighting with other World War I fighters, and there are none that can stay with the Camel in a turn.

Flying around any busy airport is not the Camel's forte because of its propensity to let one down engine-wise. I usually flew it when there wasn't much traffic and I could land at will always into the wind, and I always three-pointed it so as to dig in the tail skid. The skid is steerable within 15 degrees of either side of the center line of the fuselage. The Camel touches down easily but runs out of rudder control almost instantly, and if you bounce your landing at all, you are likely to find yourself in a hairy ground loop looking at a rapidly bending aileron dragging in the grass.

For a wide variety of reasons, the Camel is a fascinating airplane, flight-wise as well as historically. But don't think I ever got out of the Camel after being airborne even in the coldest weather without buckets of perspiration and considerable gratitude that I had gotten the little girl home again without breaking her into splinters!

On the flight line with our Nieuport 28 and Pfalz DXII
in the background.

Spad VII

To a generation of troops brought
up on space flights and moon
launches, the name Spad means a
very superior Douglas low-wing attack plane named the Skyraider,
which is generally considered to be
one of the great airplanes of the Viet-
namese War.

To the old fogeys like myself, Spad
represents the far-famed family of
rugged maneuverable fighters that
helped the Allies in World War I to
re-establish their air war superiority.

The tongue-twisting mouthful of
Société pour Aviation et Ses Dérives
were the manufacturers of the Spad,
and it was Louis Becherau, the designer of the prewar Gordon Bennet-
winning Deperdussin monoplane,
who carried his ideas for speed and
ruggedness into this new concept of
fighter.

The choice of the superb Hispano

Suiza powerplant was an innovation
for its day. The Germans had reverted
back to the heavy but reliable water-
cooled engines following the phasing
out of the Fokker Eindecker and its
loss of air superiority to the Nieuports, but many Allied planes were
still powered by rotaries.

Prewar Europe had been treated to
three really fine reliable cars: They
were, of course, the Mercedes, the
Rolls-Royce and the Hispano-Suiza,
the latter designed by the genius of
Swiss engineer Mark Birkigit. French
designer Becherau, with the farsightedness of Merlin and his crystal ball,
had decided that the days of rotaries
were numbered. Gyroscopic force and
the unreliability of rotaries had combined to make the choice of a Hisso
an imaginative but eminently proper
one. Starting with the 140-hp Hispano-Suiza, Becherau gradually in-

creased the horsepower with different engine models of 150, 180, and finally 200 hp.

In discussing the potential of the famous fighters of World War I and the general reliability of the water-cooled, inline engines, one must keep in mind the importance of the rather temperate climate of Europe. Many a time I have cursed the designer of the Spad, for the radiator capacity was never intended to take care of flight above the sunshiny beaches and admiring crowds of warm California. On many a flight here with the Spad VII, I have spit out enough rust from the boiling radiator to keep any scrap yard happy.

In many hours of pleasant flying with the grand old American Standard J1, riding behind a Wright-manufactured Hisso, I never experienced any radiator boil, even in the long climbs, limited aerobatics, and lazy loops that this airplane does so beautifully. Everything is in the radiator's design, and so with the second original Spad that we are rebuilding now, I may go to a thicker modern core and save my delicate nerves.

Spad VII's were to survive the war in squadron service and to have flown not only on the Western front, but in Mesopotamia as well. Being a French airplane, it went predominantly to French squadrons and especially the famous "Les Cicognes." The Storks punched some truck-sized holes in the German Jasta ranks of that day.

The ruggedness of the Spad was refreshing to the French squadrons, and it could readily make a tiger out of an Escadrille pilot who in flying Nieuports in combat often waited for the weakly designed wing to take French leave. Many great French aces owed victories to the bridgelike strength of the Spad and its nice handling qualities. Aces like René Fonck

and the immortal Guynemer started their one-man crusades against German airpower mounted on the trusty Spad.

The Lafayette Escadrille flew early-model Spad VII's and liked everything but the carburetor on the Hisso, which because of unreliability on several occasions claimed the lives of gallant members of this *escadrille*.

One other glaring fault, later to be corrected with the Spad XIII, was the single Vickers gun. Some of the high-scoring Allied pilots, like René Fonck, perfected their marksmanship with target practice on the ground to implement the lack of firepower. On some RFC Spads a Lewis gun was mounted on the upper wing, as it was on the Nieuport 11's and 17's.

The Spad VII proved to be both successful and well-liked by the pilots, and Great Britain got manufacturing rights and constructed several hundred of them in England. The British Navy had ordered Spads, but due to one of those typical Colonel Blimp decisions, the RFC decided to retain all the Spads and give their newly ordered Sopwith Triplanes to the Navy. The single-gun armament of the Sopwith Triplane paralleled that of the Spad, but its viceless flight characteristics in the hands of virtuosos like the all-Canadian Black Flight of Naval Ten accounted for eighty-seven German airplanes in little over two months and set the stage for German acceptance of the Fokker triplane.

The Spad construction was, of course, predominantly wood, and it never ceases to surprise me that in this First World War period such large quantities of spruce, veneers, and plys were available to both the Allies and the Germans. I'm amazed that there is still a tree left for a happy dog in all of Europe.

Although we are perhaps not the world's expert on Spads, the fact that we are restoring another Spad VII for flight has opened my eyes to the quality of the little airplane.

Being brass, lead, aluminum, and some steel, the radiator weighs enough to require a forklift or nine graduates of a Charles Atlas weightlifting class to get it on the Spad; and, of course, behind it is a water-cooled V8, which, while light for its day, weighs more than most modern-day air-cooled engines of similar size.

At this time it might be wise to mention a fact not generally known, but enormously important to the widening group of World War I aficionados who are copying the lovely airplanes of the first global conflict. All the engines of World War I including in-lines, rotaries, V8's, and V12's, turned huge propellers, with rpm's ranging from about 1100 to 1450. Make no mistake, no modern Continental or Lycoming with its output of 200 hp or more even begins to do the job of an early airplane. Usually the modern props are less than half size of the original, and flight safety is barely marginal. With these halfpint props there are none of the lovely flying characteristics I have been lucky enough to enjoy in the original World War I aircraft.

A case in point: For the motion picture *Blue Max*, a French firm copied three Fokker DVII's meticulously, with utmost care and loving draftmanship, and, because no Mercedes were available, decided to equip them with De Havilland Gypsy engines of 200 hp. With a prop that fell short of touching the ground by more than four feet, it was hard to get the DVII's even airborne. No toothpick propeller hitched to a modern engine whose power is only developed at high rpm's is ever going to be satisfactory in a good World War I flying replica. This, strangely enough, is a hard lesson to learn in a day where we are talking about 400-hp cars that also only develop power at very high rpm's.

When we finish our current restoration, there will be to our knowledge five original Spad VII's in the world, perhaps the most famous being that of Georges Guynemer (Le Vieux Georges); it now resides on an open balcony at the Hotel Des Invalides in Paris.

Like most of the aircraft of the time, the Spad VII had a square longeron fuselage covered in the engine area with aluminum, and the oval-shaped fuselage was formed with light veneer and stringers. The tail surfaces were wooden and used a

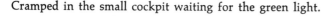

Cramped in the small cockpit waiting for the green light.

comfort-making strut for additional rigidity on the fixed portion of the elevators.

In the 180-hp and the 200-hp Spad VII's, they used a rudder with an additional midsection bulge like the belt line of a beer salesman, and this was supposed to take care of the additional torque of the larger engines. I have always flown our Spad with the smaller straight-sided surface, and have had no rudder problems in the air or on the ground.

The wings of the Spad were a thin French wingsection made with two routed spars and built up ribs. Wings and tailsection all had a typical wire-formed scalloped trailing edge. In our current Spad wing restoration, we found in the yellowed linen (which seemed old and dusty enough to have been the mummy wrappings of Tutankhamon) a linen or flax cord in place of the trailing edge wire.

The Spad has an airfoil that gives a good climb, while the SE5, according to the historians, was better aerobatically. Having flown both the Spad VII and the Spad XIII as well as the SE5, if I were in combat I would choose the Spad VII. With no dihedral and quite light control force, I found that the Spad did not require the high perspiration count to throw it about that the SE5 required.

Like all World War I fighters, size of cockpit must have been based on the Middle ages, when most of our knights of fame and legend stood a good five feet, four inches in their iron-shod footwear. The weight of the engine and radiator required the location of the cockpit aft, and the placement of the pilot's legs in aluminum bulges under the engine block make this a not too comfortable arrangement in a crash.

Instrumentation wandered amiably about the cockpit like a professor hunting butterflies and included Tach airspeed, water temperature, oil pressure compass, and probably a few cutouts from a World War I issue of Gaiety Parisian.

A notable concession to pilot safety and comfort was the straight stick, allowing the French pilot to wear a bearskin flying suit; his British brethren, because of the spade grip and its control restrictions in British-designed aircraft, were lucky if they could get airborne in their undies.

Also, Spads had push-pull rod-controlled ailerons; this was a real innovation, and it gives a Spad a light feel and quick response.

Historically, the Spad VII that I first flew (not our current restoration) was found by Paul Mantz in the basement of a deserted hotel in northern California and was purchased for Men with Wings, a Paramount color release of 1938. A World War I sequence was needed, and all of the World War I aircraft used in such pictures as Wings, Hell's Angels, and Dawn Patrol had scattered to the four winds like small craft in a hurricane. The Spad was restored and, along with our DVII, some Wacos, and some Wichita Fokkers (Travelaires), made a memorable sequence and added immeasurably to the success of the film and to the mystique of this period, with authentic early aircraft that had not previously been filmed in color.

The first time I flew the Spad, our airport was going through one of its periodic upheavals, and an airport group dead set for change was wiping out a lot of the green grass and rabbit tracks. My landing area was restricted to an area of three hundred feet of dirt and grass. With this to look forward to, we wheeled the airplane out to the takeoff point.

Before flight, we had to set the

Spad in level-flight position and fill the header tank first, then the radiator, to eliminate, as much as possible, the steam-provoking air bubbles.

Once in a position for takeoff, I hauled my six-foot, one-inch frame over the exhaust pipe (which extends behind the cockpit and can raise balloonlike blisters if one ever contacts it) and dropped it into a small but comfortable cockpit.

Having satisfied myself in preflight that the struts and wires and cable intersection struts were hanging together, I turned the fuel-on switch off, and we went through the procedure that is necessary to start a Hisso. It includes checking if the fuel pump is operative. We also rock the propeller until fuel spills from the carburetor; then with contact, the pilot madly spins the booster coil and the mechanic flips the prop backward. It kicks forward and catches, and the Hisso rumbles nicely as the pressure and temperature rise. With mechanics holding the wings, I check the mags at full throttle, but like the SE5, because of the long stacks, the engine is making about as much noise as a kitten with a stomachful of cream,

and it just doesn't sound like enough commotion to fly the airplane.

Pointing the Spad into the 15-knot wind at Orange County Airport, I pour the coal on. Instantly the tail is up, and I have complete rudder control. I am off the ground and climbing in about 150 feet. The push-pull ailerons are delightful, and the response is equal to or exceeds that of our present crop of aircraft.

A climb into the afternoon local traffic is at about 60 mph, with a wary eye evenly divided between traffic and a rising water temperature. I am aware that my head is about even with the top wing, and in case of an emergency and a rollover, I could get to be the original flat top!

Because of the closely placed center section struts and the Vickers gun, the Spad is no Cessna 310 or Piper Aztec as far as visibility goes, so I leave the pattern for a session of fun and games.

The Hisso idles beautifully, and power-off stalls occur at 47 mph, with a positive and quick nose drop. Like all World War I planes, dimensions in the Spad VII exterior and interior are small, and claustrophobia better not

Front view of the prop and the shutters on the water radiator, which cooled the Hispano-Suiza engine.

The distinctive wire-scalloped trailing edge of the wing, rudder, and (mismarked) tail denote this as a Spad VII and not a XIII.

be one of the pilot's psychological problem areas. Again, like other early aircraft, the Spad VII control travel is measured by the baker's dozen rule and exceeds anything the modern pilot is familiar with. This could be a boon in combat. If a pilot uses his Mr. America muscles instead of a pianist's feel, he'll probably have a one-way ticket to the marble orchard. I enjoy large control throw, and the challenge of smooth, coordinated flight in the Spad is a real pleasure.

Climbing out with the Spad is a commando operation with one's nerves, watching water temperature rise and oil pressure fall like an old medicine man departing a carnival street. Flying straight and level, I feel like the stilt man in the circus, because my eye level exactly splits the trailing edge of the center section. The balmy California air at 115 mph is deflected by the windshield and the ever-present receiver of the single Vickers gun.

The Spad VII's characteristics in the air, to me at least, most nearly resembles a Great Lakes BG-1 and while they look about as much alike as an impala and a crocodile, they still have a flight responsiveness that makes them, if not brothers, at least relatives.

Rarely do I spin the World War I airplanes. If they are out of rig and you can't recover, having to leave them would be much like the skipper of the *Lusitania* saying goodbye to his pride and joy.

With fly-through maneuvers like the loop, I start at 135 mph, and halfway up I can either quit or go through with ball-bearing facility. It goes over nicely, but you see the flying wires slightly bowing all the way around. Generally, I take a G meter along and try to stay within 2 to 2½ G's in maneuvers with the old girls. Slow rolls are a combination of slow roll and aileron roll and come through nicely at 110 mph without enough altitude loss to upset the most stringent FAA flight examiner.

Cuban 8's are a combination of the above, but aerobatics with the Spad are always leavened by a hawklike view of the water temperature gauge, which can change with the rapidity of a thermometer dropped into boiling water.

With the water temperature again

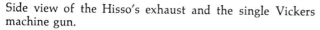

Side view of the Hisso's exhaust and the single Vickers machine gun.

rising like my nerves, I got back in the pattern, let down, and headed for the concrete. A speed of 55 to 65 mph was adequate for the approach, and I touched wheels first on the concrete at about 48 mph. Holding the tail up with just enough power, I rolled onto the grass, immediately sucking the stick back and digging in the tail skid. With blasts from the Hisso over the rudder to keep the course straight, I stopped in about 250 feet.

Just flying these World War I airplanes straight and level isn't enough, so when the opportunity arose to do a special film documentary, I got most of the World War I birds out for flight and evaluation. In limited combat I found the Spad noticeably more maneuverable than the SE5, better than the Pfalz DXII, and better in some respects than the Camel or Nieuport. It is, of course, more limber than anything except the Camel, and with the exclusion of the rust-throwing radiator and heater, the engine is pure reliability, and I would trust it as I do the Continentals in my Cessna 310.

High speed of 115 mph indicated will run away from everything except the Pfalz, and loops and rolls are positive and comfortable.

We had most of the early historical aircraft assembled for this motion picture project, and as I flew into our World War I-type location airfield, I couldn't help comparing this Spad of nearly half a century ago to the plush trouble-free business aircraft of today. Flight freedom, beauty of design, and spirit of adventure are basic and necessary elements that are sadly lacking in today's space-ship environment. Is progress worth it?

Our Spad VII in the colors of the 94th Pursuit Squadron.

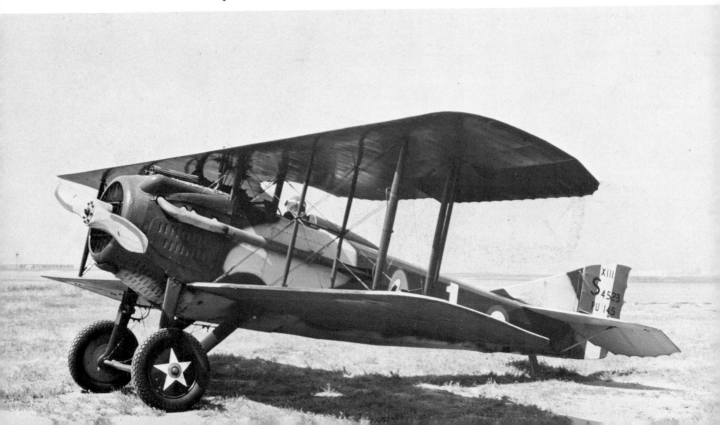

Our Spad VII silhouetted against a darkening sky.

Spad VII

Specifications

ENGINE	180-hp, E Model, Hispano-Suiza
SPAN	25 ft., 6 in.
LENGTH	20 ft., 1 in.
HEIGHT	7 ft., 8½ in.
CREW	1
EMPTY WEIGHT	1100 lbs.
USEFUL LOAD	450 lbs.
GROSS WEIGHT	1550 lbs.
FUEL CAPACITY	28 gals.
ARMAMENT	1 Vickers .303

Performance

MAXIMUM SPEED	119 mph
RATE OF CLIMB	1000 fpm
STALL SPEED	49 mph
ENDURANCE	2½ hrs.
SERVICE CEILING	18,000 ft.

Sopwith Triplane

Specifications

ENGINE	165-hp Warner (130-hp Clerget)
SPAN	26 ft., 6 in.
LENGTH	19 ft., 4 in.
HEIGHT	10 ft., 6 in.
CREW	1
EMPTY WEIGHT	1101 lbs.
USEFUL LOAD	440 lbs.
GROSS WEIGHT	1541 lbs.
FUEL CAPACITY	20 gals.
ARMAMENT	1 Vickers .303

Performance

MAXIMUM SPEED	117 mph
RATE OF CLIMB	1000 fpm
STALL SPEED	44 mph
ENDURANCE	2½ hrs.
SERVICE CEILING	20,500 ft.

In a light bank in our Sopwith Triplane.

Closeup of the flying staircase and its diving board-size interplane struts.

Sopwith Triplane

IN AN AGE when flying has taken some very strange and exotic forms, such as Bell Aircraft's Jet Man and the successful wingless flying body of Martin, which one day may return our astronauts to a Barnum & Bailey-type welcome on Earth, it's perhaps pleasant to remember an airplane that in its brief lifetime was as much of an innovation as either of these Buck Rogers-type flying machines.

The father of the Sopwith Triplane was the Sopwith Pup, and according to Oliver Stewart, one of the most romantic chroniclers of World War I flying, these were the two finest and most widely loved and respected Allied aircraft of that conflict. If one had

the herculean strength to physically turn a Sopwith Tripe over, he could readily see the genealogy inherent in the fuselage lines and the tail surfaces of the Tripe, which obviously both came out of the same mold as the Pup. Although nearly two hundred pounds heavier than the Pup, the addition of the three shallow-chord wings and the 25 percent increased horsepower made the Sopwith Triplane a tiger in its time.

To the surprise of many Royal Flying Corps types whose major experience had been in craft like the Farman and occasionally the Avro, the long step to the operational Sopwith Triplane was not as great as anticipated.

81

The Tripe's lovely flight characteristics and good visibility went a long way toward quieting a Farman pilot's sudden heart tremor on flying a faster, heavier airplane.

Although only about 160-odd Sopwith Triplanes were built and delivered, they had a most profound effect on the German High Command, and after a few combats where the Sopwith Tripe had taken on as many as eight German fighters alone, the Germans began approaching the Triplane with about the same respect as handling a live cobra.

The British sensibly decided to use the Clerget Rotary engine, which, among other qualifications, had dual ignition and was an advanced design over the 110-hp Type 9J Le Rhone. The Le Rhone, because of single ignition and a variety of other faults, has let me down personally so often that the mere mention of it is enough to make my pen shake like a castanet. In a day when climbs were frustratingly slow, the Triplane could make thirteen thousand feet in thirteen minutes— not a climb to be sneezed at, even in our day.

Speed was claimed to be and was recorded at 116 mph on the deck, and in 1916 this must have seemed like an F4H Phantom of today.

Like the Pup, the Tripe borrowed the single Vickers gun for armament, plus the padded porthole-like windscreen on the back of the gun. Clearing a jam on this little dude must have involved a frozen face and fingers over the snow-covered Western front, and the pilot must have needed a high-wire artist's lack of acrophobia to stand up and play armorer on the jammed Vickers. Several Tripes were built with twin Vickers, but by this time Camels were beginning to be delivered in huge quantities, and the Triplane was relegated to second-line

status, to the dismay of its admirers.

Through the history of this unusual airplane runs an aura of very strange dealings and decisions. At the same time that the Sopwith Triplane had been ordered for the Royal Flying Corps, the Admirality had ordered Spad VII's to be built under license in England. Due to a swap never clearly explained, the services changed aircraft, and the Navy wound up with the Triplanes, and except for one that flew in the Near East and another that found itself on skis and fighting for the White Russians in 1919, none was ever flown by the Royal Flying Corps. The area of doubt that still remains is why these fine aircraft were never put into quantity production in spite of their very evident superiority to anything Allied or German in their brief day of glory.

Like the later Fokker Triplane, the Royal Naval Air Service types looked at the single I bracing-type struts and lack of wires as having all the strength of an orange crate. Time was to prove it a strong basic design which, except for rigging problems, gave little reason for structural worries. But to this day the simple I struts and wires look rather weak, and in a time before parachutes, when everything was wire-braced except the pilot's hip flask, it's no wonder that the flying staircase was approached with caution. Many gallant squadrons, both Allied and German, fought over the fields of France, but few had the fighting record and unblemished gallantry of Naval Ten.

Air Marshal Collishaw, one of the highest-scoring aces of the Great War, led the immortal Black Flight or B Flight of Naval Ten. This flight was an all-Canadian group, and their aircraft were named *Black Death, Black Roger, Black Maria, Black Sheep,* and *Black Prince.* In the incredibly short span of two months, they accounted for eighty-seven airplanes. Although perhaps not a record, it was certainly one of the great scoring feats of the war.

Several firms produced the triplane besides Sopwith. Among them were the firms of Clayton and Shuttleworth, and Oakley and Company, one of whose triplanes managed to survive the axes and funeral pyres following the war and was flown as late as 1936 at the RAF Hendon display. This lone triplane still survives in England, while a meticulous master copy built by Carl Swanson is now in the Canadian Air Museum. In the case of this latter extraordinary copy, it is powered by a 110-hp Type 9J Le Rhone, and whether it will ever fly is problematical.

The Sopwith Triplane's fuselage, gear, and tail surfaces are almost dead ringers of the Pup's, so they are simplicity with a capital S, and the Sopwith triplane's wings have two solid spars fifteen inches apart, unlike those on the Fokker Triplanes, which were complicated and difficult to build. Also, though not apparent in most photos, the RAF wires are massive and numerous. There are flying and landing wires, as well as drag wires from the cowling area to the wings, and additional wires from aft of the pilot's seat forward to the wing structure. Pilots had to take a substantial course on a jungle gym to get through to the seat.

The struts, which are of spruce and go through the wings as well as the fuselage in the cockpit areas, are the size and shape of a plank from a hundred-gun ship of the line. Interestingly enough, the trim wheel for the adjustable tail plane is bolted to the center section strut that goes through the cockpit and fastens to the bottom longeron.

The great ace, Baron Manfred von Richthofen, in April of 1917 considered the Sopwith without peer as an antagonist, and felt that in comparison most German aircraft had the fighting qualities of a wounded jellyfish. The German High Command, equally impressed, soon produced a conglomerate group of triplanes and quadruplanes. But none, including the more famous Fokker DRI, was ever to equal the Sopwith Triplane in performance.

Our triplane story is about a California rancher with a dream. While most cattlemen picture an endless herd of longhorns stretching to a grass-covered horizon, rancher Earl Tavan's mirage had the Sopwith Triplanes replacing the cattle-crowded spread.

He approached Lou Stolp, known to many Experimental Aircraft Association members as a master builder and designer of such beautiful biplanes as the Starduster and Starduster 2, and persuaded him to take on the difficult and demanding task of building the Sopwith Triplane.

The first order of business was to consult with the Hawker Siddeley Group in England; many years ago Hawker Siddeley absorbed the Sopwith Company. Unlike our own aviation concerns who throw away valuable historical data without a thought —it clutters their very neat files and takes space—the British in their careful and conservative manner retain everything. Hawker Siddeley were happy to share the treasures of their archives.

One Sopwith Triplane had been previously built for the Canadian Air Museum by another master craftsman, Carl Swanson of Illinois, who had also built a magnificent Nieuport 17 in Air Marshal Billy Bishop's colors for the museum. The Sopwith

The padded windshield covering the butt of the single Vickers.

Closeup of the Warner 165-hp radial, a modern-day substitute for the original Clerget rotary.

Triplane built for the Canadian Museum was exact in every detail and had for power a Clerget rotary engine, original instruments, and a wood built-up fuselage. It is perfectly flyable, but its value is such that it is doubtful it will ever be allowed to get airborne.

But Earl Tavan's Sopwith Tripe was built to be flown. Consequently, certain modernization changes were made that did not spoil the appearance. For power, instead of the cranky and unpredictable rotaries, a Warner 165-hp radial, fortunately with almost identically the same frontal area and appearance, was substituted. A battery, starter, and generator were included to make the old bugaboo of the Armstrong starter unnecessary. Wire wheels of the proper size were designed and beautifully built, with a brake inside the hub and completely unseen.

The basic fuselage was constructed out of square steel tubing of the same dimension and greater strength than the original wire-braced wood longeron. The cockpit layout was made identical to the original, including the handsome brass plates bearing the name of the manufacturer, Sopwith Kingston on the Thames, and one stating that the Vickers gun had a Scarff-patented interrupter gear. Instrumentation was modern but necessary due to the different engine.

Bracing wires, which included flying and landing wires, drift wires, and gear and tail wires, were all streamlined and purchased from MacWhyte Company in Milwaukee. The Pup and the Triplane were the first aircraft in World War I to use the RFC streamlined wires, and now there is only one firm in the United States, MacWhyte, that will take on the job, and its production is usually devoted to racing yachts. Because of the variety of wires, it required two months to get them produced, while the aggrieved cry of yachtsmen denied their mast bracing could be heard throughout the land.

Photographs of Triplanes were exhaustively examined; in some photographs an additional pair of flying wires were found that attached to the midspar in the upper panels. These additional wires did not appear in the Hawker Siddeley drawings, and apparently were added in the field when combat indicated possible torsional stress in the upper main plane. The appearance of these wires is similar to the extra set of flying wires in the SE5.

The first time I saw the Triplane, the engine had been installed and the tail surfaces were on, but the most unique Triplane features visible were the huge planks sticking up through the fuselage and lower wing, looking for all the world like diving boards pirated from a swimming pool supply house.

When I next saw the airplane, a year or two later, it was sitting in back of a hot, dusty hangar in Flabob Airport in Riverside, California, ready to roll. The metamorphosis, like the caterpillar to butterfly, was breathtaking. It was painted in original colors, with deep khaki fuselage, black cowling, and cream-colored undersurfaces. The Vickers gun was mounted with its padded windshield, and the starboard side of the fuselage was laced like a giant boot.

Because of its height, the airplane appears rather larger than it is, and it also appears quite a bit higher than it is, when in actuality it is only one foot higher than the DRI and has a three-foot greater span. The comparisons come to mind because on the day I flew the Triplane I brought over our Fokker DRI and had them side by

Three-quarters front view of our *Black Maria*.

side on the ground, as well as in the air. Mr. Earl Tavan kindly consented to let me fly the Sopwith, which, considering the research cost and more than two years of construction, was equivalent to trusting a beggar alone in the U. S. Mint.

We arrived at Flabob in a cavalcade of aircraft, including our Curtiss Junior camera plane (an antique in its own right), the bright red Fokker triplane in Richthofen markings, and my Cessna 310, with photographer and equipment.

It was a brutally hot September day, with ground temperature over 100 degrees. Getting my chute into the Triplane was a matter of wading through water that was covering the area, because Earl had with pride

taken the trouble of washing the Triplane, and hosing the upper wing is like trying to wash an upper story of the Empire State Building. Climbing through the two drift wires that go from the wings to a spot aft of the cockpit area posed real problems with my artificial leg, but I made it.

Lack of the traditional Spade grip, while not liked by the purists, still gives infinitely more throw to the controls. The standard rudder bar gave me trouble only because of a brake pedal, which had a nasty way of hooking the sole of the shoe on my bum leg, always at the wrong time.

The Warner started easily, and visability while taxiing out was pure pleasure after the truly blind DRI. The midwing on the Sopwith butts

86

against the fuselage and allows forward visibility, though narrow in scope.

I taxied out to the end of the runway, and after running up the Warner 165, turned into the wind. Runway altitude was 780 feet, and temperature was an even 100 degrees. Pouring on the coal, I left the tail on the ground for about 100 feet, then raised it instantly. I got an unexpected torque swing to the left and went off the narrow runway, clipping the growth like a McCormick reaper. Full opposite rudder and aileron brought me slowly back along with a sudden wetness in my palms, and I was airborne with no wind in about 480 feet. Obviously the triplane was heavier than the original (by more than 300 pounds), and without the slow, big, propped rotary, the performance suffers.

Climbing out, I was struck by the typical rotary torque feel that had occurred on takeoff. Rate of climb, even in the heat, was approximately

1000 feet a minute at an indicated 58 mph.

The three ailerons on each wing were pure delight and gave this flying club sandwich a crisp response equal to that of a Stearman or Tiger Moth.

I climbed to the acrobatic area in slow circles, feeling out the rudder and elevators, which have somewhat less positiveness than the ailerons. Stalling speed occurred at 44 mph, and the plane broke gently straight ahead.

In the narrow acrobatic corridor over Riverside, I wondered whether anyone was looking up and conjecturing what this weird flying machine was going to do. Wide-open throttle gave me an indicated airspeed at 3000 feet of 92 mph, and, edging the throttle back, I dropped the nose gently for a loop. With 115 mph indicated, I pulled back gently and added full power over the top, where I had 30 mph. The Tripe followed through nicely, but with a loop considerably larger in diameter than the DRI. All

The cockpit interior and instrument panel, with the stabilizer trim wheel at the lower right.

the way through, the wires sang like a demented peanut vendor and must have been easily heard on the ground, more than a half mile down.

The Tripe's structure in aerobatics felt solid and secure. Part of this no doubt was mental and engendered by the physical size of the plank struts.

In slow rolls without an inverted system, the Warner cut out at the inverted position, and it was necessary to finish dead stick.

Somehow, like most old beat-up aviators, you pick something for a horizon line, but in a roll with the Triplane, you have a feeling of three artificial horizon bars, and you are not sure which to pick. In a Cuban 8, you have to select a reference point well below the horizon, but by that time you have picked up speed, and the feeling on rollout is akin to a pilot with acute arthritis trying to maneuver a flying venetian blind.

In mock combat with an extremely fine pilot, ex-Maj. James Appleby, flying the Fokker DRI, I would have had an edge flying the Sopwith Triplane because of the stiff and slow ailerons on the DRI, but both aircraft have their limitations; the skill and experience of the pilots are more important than the actual physical differences between the two planes.

Throughout this most exciting test I was plagued by a steel, fiber glass, and wooden leg, which slipped off the rudder bar (because of a lack of rubber sole on my bad shoe).

Coming in to land, I sensibly chose the grass area and not the narrow-surfaced runway. I touched down rather faster and sooner than antici-pated at about 52 mph, at which point my bad shoe sole hooked behind the brake pedal; by vigorous jabs of both legs sufficient to move the Taj Mahal, I rolled to a stop straight ahead, wiped nineteen gallons of salty water off my forehead, and taxied back.

Reflecting on the differences between the two planes, I feel that the Sopwith Triplane is infinitely superior. It is more controllable, lovelier on the ailerons, climbs faster, and the rollout on landing is easier.

It is perhaps worth noting that these World War I aircraft, like, strangely enough, the Me 109, Spitfire, and Hurricane, were designed for grass or dirt fields, and when you start jamming them down on hard-surface runways, things can get out of hand as rapidly as Stan Laurel stepping on a roller skate.

As a lover of old aircraft and a pilot who likes to land on hay fields, I can't say enough in praise of the builders and fliers of World War I airplanes. You can physically remove more than 50 percent of your landing problems on grass or dirt strips, always keeping in mind the necessity of landing directly into the wind.

Taxiing back with the Sopwith Triplane and physically being able to see ahead and reflecting on the lovely ailerons and flight characteristics, I couldn't help wondering whether Rheinhold Platz, when he developed the German Fokker DRI almost a year later, had for some reason totally ignored the lessons that any pilot could learn simply by sitting in and later flying Mr. Sopwith's most desirable club sandwich.

Few German pilots were fortunate enough to have this in-flight view of the agile Tripe.

In flight with the correct color scheme and markings of
Von Richthofen's squadron.

Mr. Fokker's flying venetian blind in its incorrect colors and markings. A closeup view of the cantilever construction of the wings.

Fokker DRI (Triplane)

BECAUSE OF ITS step-on-step appearance, the Fokker DRI triplane at first glance has all the grace of a blacksmith lifting an anvil. But in its short span of combat tours at the front in World War I, its awkward appearance belied flight characteristics as nimble as a nervous humming-bird, and it was immortalized by the Red Baron.

The inspiration for Mr. Fokker's flying venetian blind was provided by a unique machine from Billy Sopwith's house of wonders. The Sopwith Triplane, designed early in 1916, had buried a Jack Dempsey-like surprise blow into the midriff of the German Jagdstaffels, and the inability of the Albatroses and Pfalzes to dogfight with this startling innovation forced the German High Command into a reappraisal of its own fighter aircraft.

The Flugzengmeisterei sent a letter to the German manufacturers on the 27th of July 1917 requesting that they submit bids for a triplane, and AEG, Brandenburg Pfalz, Roland, and others built prototypes. The manufacturers soon found to their chagrin that the witty Dutchman, Mr. Anthony Fokker, had made off with the triplane contract like a fox in a henhouse.

Months before the competition and bids at Adlershof, Fokker had in his usual tour of the front visited the

Richtofen squadron to find only one thing on the pilots' minds: the sparkling performance and outstanding fighting characteristics of the Sopwith Triplane. In one instance an extremely courageous and foolhardy pilot of Royal Naval No. 8 Squadron had attacked eleven Albatros DIIIs and had outmaneuvered the entire German group.

Although Tony Fokker was in many ways a brilliant pilot, he was only a so-so engineer and designer. But he had his fingers on the pulse and feelings of the German combat aviators, as firmly as a present-day George Gallup. After having been an eyewitness of the Sopwith's capabilities from a forward station at the front and after examining a crashed Triplane, Fokker returned to his factory with his usual *joi de vivre* and dumped the load of his enthusiasm on his chief designer, the brilliant Rheinhold Platz. It was to be Platz's cross to bear to translate Fokker's enthusiasm into a flying reality. When the call came from the Flugzengmeisterei, Fokker was ready.

As we have seen, because of Fokker's Dutch nationality and his enviable business success, he was resented by the German manufacterists and got little support from them. He waged a constant war of supply and demand, and from necessity developed material sources that were undesirable or unavailable to the other German aircraft firms. With the full production of the reliable Mercedes and BMW water-cooled engines swallowed up by the manufacturers Albatros, Roland, etc., like a school of sharks in a tank of minnows, Fokker had to look elsewhere for a power plant. With his usual ability to know where the body was buried, Fokker located seven hundred superb Swedish Thulin copies of the French 110-hp Le Rhone stored at Adlershof they had been written off by the Germans as out of date. Here was his engine.

With reluctance, Platz now set to work, and in a very short time came out with a triplane design that in no way resembled the Sopwith craft, except for its three wings.

All three wings were full canti-

A would-be Red Baron behind his Spandau machine guns.

lever, with the lower two bolted directly to the fuselage, while the upper stood on two vees and was wire-braced. At a time when most spars were routed sections, Platz came out with a built-up box spar joined to another box spar with a top and bottom plywood web. The double spar thus joined is light, but large enough in appearance and strength to be the ridge pole in a Jacobean manor house. The fuselage was typical Fokker, with light welded tubing, wire-braced. The gear was streamlined tubing, with ball sockets pinned for security (like the fittings on the Pfalz DXII) and with the small wing airfoil between the gear, which created enough lift in itself to carry more than the weight of gear and wheels.

Fokker flew the first triplane and promptly sent it back to Platz for balancing of tail surfaces and ailerons. After the Adlershof trials, where the test pilots rejected the safe but birdlike flexing of the wings, Fokker wisely added an outboard jury strut that attached to the wings rather than go through them as in the Sopwith Triplane.

Ordered into quantity production, the first two triplanes became the beloved pets of Werner Voss, leader of Jasta 10, and the Red Baron. In one of the most gallant and rapid-scoring series of victories in the history of World War I, Werner Voss accumulated twenty-one confirmed kills between August 30 and September 23. Voss was recognized by foe and compatriot as a human buzzsaw ready to tackle any enemy and nearly any odds, and his blue triplane, with eyes and a mustache painted on the nose cowling, put the wind up many an Allied pilot. Production of the DRI's was well along before Voss's heroic death had been digested by a saddened German flying corps.

Banking in a diving turn.

Shortly, two accidents put an instant hold on production. Heinrich Gonterwein, the "sausage buster" skipper of Jasta 15 and victor over seventeen balloons and seventeen Allied aircraft, was killed in full view of his squadron when the top wing of the triplane came off in aerobatics directly over the airport. As if this were not enough, two days later a pilot in Jasta 11 died in the same way.

Richthofen grounded his airplanes before the investigation committee arrived, and on opening the wing structure they were appalled to find workmanship on the spars so slipshod as to be almost sabotage, and other spars so badly affected by moisture as to have the strength of a wet cigarette.

Months were to go by before the modifications for structural' strength had been applied to squadron aircraft as well as to the new aircraft coming down the production line. Meanwhile, the Allies made hay while the sun shone, and Camels, SE5's and Spad XIII's were seen in increasing numbers on the Western front.

There was no complaint from Jastas operating triplanes about their agility in combat or their enormous rate of climb close to the deck or their ability to hang on the prop and hose an opponent, but their ceiling left a great deal to be desired.

The Swedish Thulin 110-hp Le Rhone was a reliable engine, but now different models—Oberursel, Siemens-Halske, and Goebel Goe engines—were tried, even along with a captured 50-hp Gnome, to see if speed and altitude performance could be improved. An interesting sidelight of the war was that the Germans put a plate on the Thulin 110 Le Rhone copies stating that the engine was captured in action so that Sweden wouldn't suffer a breach of her neutrality.

In spite of the relatively small numbers of DRI's turned out during the war, they were more widely remembered than any other type, perhaps because of their appearance and their use by the Red Baron. Slightly over three-hundred Fokker DRII's were produced, in comparison to over five-thousand Sopwith Camels, the aircraft that in the hands of Capt. Ray Brown downed the Red Baron.

Not too much information filtered to the Allies on the Fokker triplane until several were captured and used both in mock combat and checked for construction features.

No truly accurate plans have ever been found on the aircraft, as they have for such as Allied airplanes as the SE5, the Pup, the Camel, and many others. Good detail existed in the photographlike drawings of the staff artists of that great English publication *Flight*, but there was little authoritative source material available beyond this.

Following the Great War the triplanes still in existence in England went to the scrap pile, and nothing was known of any remaining until Hitler's rise to power. When the Richtofen squadron was reactivated in the middle 1930s, out of a barn or the traditional wood pile came a real triplane for the commissioning ceremonies. The experts who saw this aircraft felt that the majority of it, and another that showed up later, were real Fokker-built triplanes.

Hitler was at that time rattling his saber, and to inspire the revived Luftwaffe he had a film produced on World War I unblushingly filled with propaganda about a German squadron flying triplanes. There are some lovely flying shots of the triplanes that can be seen in this film. They are in death-defying combat, with modern Bucker Jungmans thinly disguised

The padded cockpit with a glimpse of today's instruments,
the small windscreen, and the twin Spandaus.

as Allied SE5's. Both the resurrected
triplanes were destroyed in the bombing of Germany in World War II, but
this loss did not in any way dampen
the enthusiasm of the model builders
or the dedicated aficionados preparing to build a flying copy of a DRI.
In the United States at this time there
are at least five triplane copies flying,
one with a rotary engine.

I have seen a number of the DRI
copies, but so far have flown only
ours. Reports vary considerably on
their characteristics, and at least one
owner admitted to me that he enjoyed
flying it about as much as if he had
climbed into a hive of bees in a bathing suit.

Two gentlemen with the dreams of
Richtofen and the patience and the
dedication of Christian martyrs, Tony

Bright and Dutch Durringer, were
responsible for the original construction of the DRI now in our Movie of
the Air Museum at Orange County in
Santa Ana, California. It used an awful lot of golfing and *siesta* time, for
the construction took several years.

Facing all builders of replica aircraft of this period is the inescapable
fact that original engines for World
War I aircraft are very scarce. If you
can find a modern engine that can be
squeezed into a traditional cowling
and that has the same rated power,
you still do not have the necessary
slow-turning big propeller with
horsepower developed at 1200–1400
rpm instead of 2500–3500 rpm. For
example, one Jenny in our stable had
a modern 200-hp ranger put in it in
place of the original OX5 and the

Haven't we seen this "Hun" before?

performance was only slightly improved. The Fokker DVII's that were built for the film *Blue Max* were disappointing in performance for this same reason. They were made by a Frenchman most painstakingly by borrowing an original DVII from the Musée de l'Air at the Chalais Meudon outside of Paris. Like a dedicated mole, he copied everything and turned up with DVII's that compared with the original like Siamese twins. With 180-hp Mercedes utterly unavailable, he chose 200-hp Gypsy engines out of an aging D. H. Rapide.

On our DVII, with the propeller in a vertical attitude and the DVII in a three-point position, clearance from the tip to the ground was about 18 inches. On the beautifully built DVII copies in Europe, the tip of the Gypsy metal propeller to the ground was 3½ feet. In spite of the fact that the weight of the DVII's was the same as that of the original, the performance of the European copies was so bad that they were not often flown.

Our Fokker DVII, which was used in many blood-and-thunder Hollywood air epics, suffered the substitution of a 180-hp Hispano Suiza during the making of *Men with Wings*. By this time its original Mercedes had decided to call it a day. In any case, the Hisso worked fine, and the DVII was a lovely flying airplane, with real

The colorful but treacherous Fokker DRI.

Fokker Dr1 (Triplane)

Specifications

ENGINE	165-hp Warner
	(110-hp Oberursel)
SPAN	23 ft., 7 in.–18 ft., 6 in.
LENGTH	19 ft.
HEIGHT	9 ft., 9 in.
CREW	1
EMPTY WEIGHT	893 lbs.
USEFUL LOAD	396 lbs.
GROSS WEIGHT	1289 lbs.
FUEL CAPACITY	16½ gals.
ARMAMENT	2 7.92 Spandaus

Performance

MAXIMUM SPEED	115 mph
RATE OF CLIMB	1200 fpm
STALL SPEED	47 mph
ENDURANCE	2¼ hrs.
SERVICE CEILING	19,600 ft.

SE5A

Specifications

ENGINE	180-hp Hispano-Suiza
SPAN	26 ft., 7 in.
LENGTH	20 ft., 11 in.
HEIGHT	9 ft., 6 in.
CREW	1
EMPTY WEIGHT	1400 lbs.
USEFUL LOAD	550 lbs.
GROSS WEIGHT	1950 lbs.
FUEL CAPACITY	35 gals.
ARMAMENT	2 Vickers .303; 1 Lewis .303

Performance

MAXIMUM SPEED	127 mph ind. at 3000 ft.
RATE OF CLIMB	870 fpm
STALL SPEED	52 mph ind.
ENDURANCE	Approx. 2½ hrs.
SERVICE CEILING	19,000 ft.

Plate in cockpit

Air Service Number: AS–22–296
Type: SE5A
Remanufactured by Eberhardt Steel Company, U.S.A.

The sturdy SE5A.

areas of sparkling performance by World War I standards.

Through the years we have accumulated at least one spare original engine for each of our aircraft, but with the current program of rebuilding antiques in the United States, we have no more sources of supply.

In the case of our DRI, the rebuilders early in the game decided that the squirrelly flight characteristics of the triplane and my tales of horror of riding behind a 110-hp Le Rhone in another antique airplane suggested a modern power plant. The only American engine that has rotary facial area and sufficient horsepower was the 165-hp Warner engine, and these are now getting exceedingly scarce; but they located one.

Basic construction of our DRI with the Warner engine closely paralleled the original. Fokker used a welded steel tubing fuselage, wire braced, and that type of construction was followed. The box spars are something else, and needless to say, they are as important as bones in the human frame and about as difficult to manufacture.

When Dutch and Tony finally finished the little bird and got the bugs out of it, they found that in a three-point attitude, taxiing it about was a good deal like trying to engineer a hundred-car freight train from the caboose. It's blind! Also, on taxi tests the skids were put on the wingtips for use and in expectation of ground loops. They did a good job of flying with the airplane, but took several years to work the bugs out of it.

Before I bought the DRI I had occasion to rent it from the builders for a major air show we were doing. We wanted a World War I combat act. Arriving to pick it up, I found it painted in a disappointingly dull barn red, with the wrong type of crosses for Richtofen's airplane. Otherwise, it looked every inch like the original. I was eager to fly, and I began my preflight check.

Because of the cantilever construction, the most important points to check are the center section wires, the attachments of the jury struts, the gear shock cord, and the bracing struts on the underside of the tail.

Swinging into the cockpit past the cut out in the middle plane, one wonders what happened to the world ahead, for you can only see to the sides and rear. Controls are straight forward. The stick lacks the strange top section that looked like the rear side of a toaster and includes a throttle and gun trips that must have seriously restricted control in combat.

The Warner is a lovely engine, and it started on the first pull, but taxiing was a chore and good for one stiff neck for each thousand feet of taxiway. Checking controls for freedom of movement and checking mags, I turned onto the runway. My rudder became effective in about fifty feet of takeoff roll and the elevators brought the nose onto the horizon, so that I could actually see ahead for a change. The triplane was airborne in about three hundred feet, with a eight-knot wind directly on the nose. The climb-out was at about 55 mph, and as I begin a climbing turn I felt ailerons as stiff as a boiled shirt; it felt like our old Navy Hup helicopters when we turned the hydraulic boost off. You very nearly need both hands for the ailerons.

Climbing up to altitude and settling down for an hour cross-country, I was struck again by the in-flight appearance of the upper wing so far above and so lightly hung on. It looked like the designer's afterthought. I was cruising at a pleasant 95 mph, but in looking back at my tail surfaces, I noticed a considerable flutter, at which point my eyes dropped to my chute harness to see that everything was buckled and to hope that less than forty days had elapsed since the chute's last inspection. Since the fixed-elevator surface apparently did not want to part company with the aircraft, I relaxed a bit and then remembered that the standard DRI had a camber top and bottom and was not built as this one had been, with a flat surface.

Getting used to everything except the Mack truck-like ailerons, I stalled the plane, and it fell through at about 50 mph, usually dropping the right wing. Recovery was easy and loss of altitude slight. Putting the red bird in a Lufberry circle, I could see how you could cut the circle small enough to nearly chew off your own tail. In a climbing vertical reverse, the three-wing concept worked well.

In a fit of daring equal to grabbing a live leopard by the tail, I decided to try a loop. Picking up to 120 mph, I pulled up, but because of the placement of the wings it was hard to orient with the horizon. It was a most uncomfortable feeling. Unfortunately I was a little slow and did not pull tight enough at the top, and barely got over. As the triplane fell through, I wondered whether the whole stack of wings might not collapse like a club sandwich being sat on by a fat lady. My nerves took longer than the DRI to recover from the loop, and I vowed that the air show combat act would have to be restricted to tail-chasing.

With aircraft scattering like a scarecrow in their midst, I entered traffic and had no trouble in staying with the slowest student. Choosing to land on a dirt strip (fortunately equipped with a wind sock), I glided in, and nose down had good enough

visibility so that I didn't feel I was conning a nuclear sub.

Flaring out, the DRI loses speed fast, leveling down at about 45 mph with a rather wobbly feel, and blanking out almost completely of the tail surfaces, so much so that as you are rolling along you might as well have a broomstick for company in the cockpit.

After a number of additional flights in the triplane, several years went by before I climbed into its cockpit again. But the day I did, it was with complete freedom from worry and question. But I was shortly to have the same awakening that an ice-cold shower brings in the morning. It was a rather routine flight, but what a hair-raising climax!

Coming around for my first landing, I misjudged and touched down three-point, with one wing low. There was a sharp, stiff bounce, like a mule kick. I poured throttle but had no control, with the rudder and elevators stalled out due to lower wing burble. I left the runway ninety degrees off heading, thanks to torque, and cut cross-country like Patton's tank brigade. It took nearly two hundred feet, with a total lack of control, before the tail flew enough for me to get back in the air.

From now on, like a C-47 troop carrier driver, I make all triplane landings wheels first, dropping the tail only late in the landing run, with a prayer each time to Icarus or other flying gods to keep me straight.

This triplane of ours has gone through a painstaking development process equal to the Saturn rocket, and now really looks like Richtofen's airplane, with his colors and markings. It has infinitely better aileron control than it had originally, due to control cable relocation and alteration of aileron hinges. It's now fun to fly.

SE5. There is a stirrup on the fuse-lage, and to get in you have to swing your leg over the exhaust pipe, which is all right with a cold engine, but if you carelessly brush the hot pipe on your landings it's very likely to accelerate your departure from the aircraft. Cushions are needed or a parachute, which puts one at a comfortable height. Your hand comes easily to the British circular spade stick. The rudder bar is set off the floor and has a top for your foot so that it cannot slip off when the plane is inverted. Throttle and mixture are on the right on a little shelf, and the mixture control when full open is to the rear when your throttle at the same time goes forward! Instruments are airspeed, compass, oil pressure, water temperature, altimeter, switch and booster mag, and gas shutoff.

All Hisso engines have to be loaded up with throttle back and switch off and the propeller moved back and forth until you get some fuel overflow. Check carefully to see that your gas valve is on. When "contact" is called and the prop is swung "clear," rotate the booster mag handle, and the engine will catch and start easily with a gentle rumble. It idles nicely below 500 rpm, which unfortunately is the last stop on our tachometer. After allowing the water temperature to rise and checking oil pressure mags, you are clear.

The day of this flight there was a wind of 10 to 15 knots directly on the nose. The temperature was 75 degrees; the ground elevation, 87 feet.

The heart-lifting thrill of shoving the throttle forward is never lost, at least to me, and it was there as I pushed forward the control of the SE5. The tail leveled almost instantly. Because the propeller is slow-turning (about 1500 rpm on takeoff), you have no appreciable torque and very low noise level. The SE5 was airborne in 246 feet, and could have gotten off somewhat sooner. You have nice positive feel, and you are climbing out at about 75 to 80 mph with a rate of climb approaching 900 feet a minute.

My experience in the SE5 is limited,

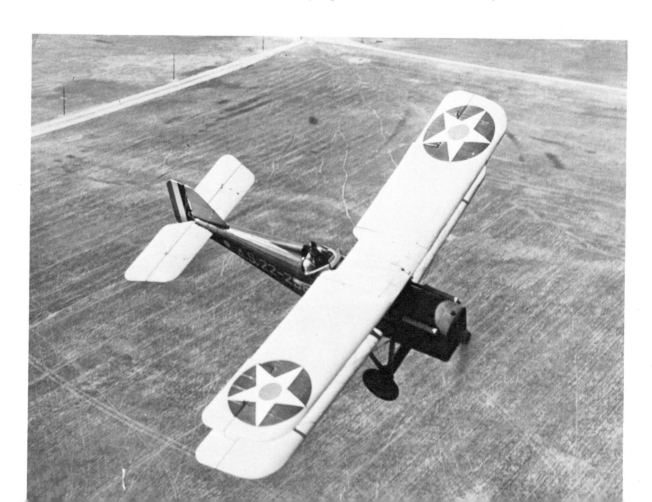

and just flying in it is a considerable thrill, I suppose *à la Battle Aces* or *War Birds*. I would be chasing the Ercoupes and Cubs out of the traffic pattern if I had the Lewis and Vickers machine guns mounted.

Straight and level at 3000 feet, I noticed slight tail heaviness, even with the trim tab wheel forward. The cockpit was comfortable, with fine visibility and very little windflow.

Wide open I was indicating 127 mph and 1650 rpm at 3000 feet. Settling back to cruise, I locked my belt and brought the stick back for a stall. It pays off gently, but with a sharp right-wing drop at an indicated 52 mph. Invariably, in a stall, the right wing dropped. I tried a spin—one turn nicely, cleanly to the right; unfortunately, it would only spiral to the left and, I believe sensibly, I did not try to force it in. With any airplane over fifty years old I eat a little raw heart with aerobatics, for no matter how carefully you check it, anything can fatigue in this length of time.

Not using a G meter, I was careful to keep heavy stick pressures out of my work with the SE5. Checking my area, I pulled up into vertical reverses in both directions, and it held on nicely and reversed well with rudder. Looping at 135 mph went well but got slightly soft at the top, where I was indicating about 60 mph, but it came through without my hanging on the belt and apparently looked good from the ground. Cuban 8's went well, but the engine spewed fuel out on my descending half roll and cut out for a period of four seconds. It slow rolls to the left nicely, with about eight seconds to complete, but you need 115 mph entry speed to carry you through for the time the engine is out. Unfortunately, in rolling to the right it resists strongly, and you get a roll that is impossible to do smoothly and that takes much time. Flick rolls or snap rolls were nice to the right at 85 mph but completely impossible to the left, for it stalls straight forward and will not snap with any combination of movements. I heaved a sigh

The forward stagger and dihedral of the wings made the SE5 too stable to be a really good fighter.

The flying British bulldog, over fifty years old and still a
flying delight.

The big tail and its bracing wires.

of relief that our temperatures and pressures were O.K. on the Hisso, and headed for home. In checking the water temperature I unconsciously checked the radiator shutter lever.

It was a lovely, sunshiny day, and as I dove back toward the field I couldn't help but reflect on the pleasure denied so many who fly today. That pleasure, of course, is the wonderful freedom of an open airplane—the sound of wires and wind, the feeling of being part of the airplane, and the sweet smell of the exhaust. Maybe today's gadget-filled airplanes are aerodynamically superior, but they are surely not as much pleasure to fly as the SE5.

The traffic pattern speeds work out nicely with today's light planes, and as I circled for a green light and got it, I started a gentle turn into my grass area, holding about 75 to 80 mph indicated. By now the strangeness of flying with my left hand and using the throttle with my right was gone. Like all early aircraft and most biplanes, they pay off rather fast, and in attempting to check my touchdown speed on the airspeed indicator I bounced but caught it with stick and a little rudder. It indicated about 53 or 54 mph. The rudder was quite positive, and the steerable tailskid was extremely helpful. Because of the steerable tailskid this airplane is one of the few World War I planes that can be landed on a concrete runway, but again only with great caution,

much room, and lots of cold sweat until you finally stop moving.

Pouring on the throttle, I went around the field again, more to prove that I could make a better landing than for any other reason. It was airborne in about fifty feet; I climbed out nicely, and on my second approach I carried a little power, flared it out, and set down like a hen on a basket of eggs. As I taxied up to the parking area I let the engine idle, then shut it off with the mixture control and switch.

The SE5 that I flew is an original British SE5, manufactured in England. After the war Eberhardt Steel Company in the United States was commissioned to rebuild the SE5's to be used as a U. S. Air Service fighter trainer, and this airplane was one of that batch. As nearly as I can determine, the major change made by the rebuilders was the plywood covering on the flat areas of the fuselage, which added to the strength.

The Wright and Hispano Suiza engine, which puts out an honest 180 hp, must be the third or fourth engine in this plane. There are no log books, but I estimate the aircraft to have had over a thousand hours, and it has been rebuilt several times.

Leaving the SE5 to climb into a sleek Douglas B-26 that we were using for electronics test bed work, I could honestly say that flying this World War I fighter is more fun.

Pfalz DXII

IN READING ANY history of the German Air Force in World War I, one of the most impressive things to the historian is the bitter rivalry among the manufacturers, who resorted to any and all means to push their respective aircraft into squadron service. Money changed hands, *frauleins* changed beds, and champagne was poured like the you know what out of the boot, often to such avail that some rather inferior aircraft sometimes scared the crease out of the well-pressed breeches of the German fighter squadrons.

The inabilities of the Germans late in the war to produce enough of the very fine Fokker D7's necessitated a production order for the Pfalz DXII, but such was the skill of the public-relations flacks at Fokker that literally no one on the German Air Force wanted anything but a Fokker product.

The Pfalz DXII was a basic outgrowth of the earlier Pfalz D3. All the designs stemmed from before World War I, when in July of 1913 the three Eversbusch brothers established a factory with the benevolent but powerful support of the Bavarian government, which wanted to be able to control the equipment going to its flying service.

Their first aircraft was the Pfalz EI, and while it looked like the Fokker Eindecker, it was a Bavarian variant of the Morane Saulnier and was built under license from the thrifty French, who were later to regret considerably their avariciousness.

Many Pfalz EI's and EII's were sent to the two-seat squadrons to ride shotgun for their less-aggressive brothers.

Demonstrating the outstanding speed of the Pfalz as it closes in fast on the Spad.

On the flight line at Orange County Airport prior to some motion-picture filming. In the background two Fokker DVII's.

Like the Eindecker, their armament was the Spandau or early Maxim, using Fokker's synchronizing device under license. Also, like the Eindecker, a twin row (shades of Pratt & Whitney) Overursel rotary was tried, but without too much success. Due perhaps to the wonderful forests of Bavaria, construction was to remain basically the same in all Pfalz airplanes. The general dependence on wood construction started with the first Morane Saulnier and lasted until the Pfalz DXII's went up in the smoke of the peace commission's fires following the Armistice.

After the phasing out of the Pfalz E series, the Eversbusch company took on the manufacturing of the Roland DI and DII, again under license, imaginative design concepts not being the brothers' long suit.

The father of the Pfalz DXII was the Pfalz DIII, an elegant-looking airplane that was certainly more graceful than its predecessor, Roland. The plywood semimonocoque fuselage, with its light spruce longerons and oval formers, was both graceful and strong. The clean lines of the Pfalz fuselage were not uncommon to the German Jastas, and manufacturers such as Pfalz, Albatros, and Roland made some of their slab-sided counterpart fighter aircraft on the Allied side look about as graceful and streamlined as a barn.

In the first model Pfalz D III the Spandaus were buried in the ply decking forward of the cockpit, making in-flight servicing about as easy as repairing a watch with boxing gloves on. This writer has had some experience with operating Spandaus, which admittedly now are nearly half a century old and only firing blanks, but the incredible number of malfunctions and misfires would make a saint cry.

The balance of the layout of the Pfalz DIII was standard: The wings were of unequal span and chord with the radiator mounted in the upper right wing. The reliable Mercedes was the power plant, and the DIII entered squadron service primarily in Bavarian Jastas, side by side with the Albatroses, where they sometimes suffered an unfavorable comparison.

The British reported a captured DIII as having excellent visibility, slow rate of roll, good maneuverability, and better all-around handling than an Albatros DV.

No model of Pfalz was truly ac-cepted by the German Air Force until the DXII. The successful birth of the Pfalz DXII was accomplished at the Adlershof fighter trials in June of 1918, and thanks to the aircraft's basic virtues and the company's "favorite son" status, it was put into quantity production for the Bavarian Jagaslaffels.

My first introduction to even the Pfalz name was when I purchased the remaining two aircraft from Colonel Jarrett's World War I collection, a Spad and the Pfalz. Due to World War II storage problems the aircraft had fallen on hard days, and the plywood of the Pfalz had taken more water punishment than some of the towels in a Turkish/bath. Because of wet and dry rot, the interior of the fuselage had been braced with two-by-fours to make it displayable. The wings were badly deteriorated, though the landing gear, the distinctive M struts, and the dual bay wing struts were fortunately in good condition.

Once the World War I airplanes were stored in a rented barn in Delaware, a period of ennui settled on yours truly as the enormity of the task of rebuilding these virtual basket cases finally penetrated my concrete dome.

Most fortunately I was able to make contact with a soft-spoken mechanical genius by the name of Robert Rust, who allowed that he would like to take on the project of rebuilding the Pfalz. He arrived with a trailer from Atlanta in the rain (I seem to have made most of my important antique aircraft acquisitions in the rain), and as he quietly walked around the Pfalz in the dimly lit hangar I edged out of his way, figuring he was going to make a dash for his car and take off like a three-time winner at Indianapolis. "Well," he said, "it's bad, but not hopeless."

Our Pfalz in its reconstruction stage in Bob Rust's workshop.

The weight of the great pyramids lifted from my back as we loaded the remains of the Spad and the Pfalz on the crowded trailer. Due to the weight of the engine, it was necessary to roll the Pfalz fuselage over and unbolt the Mercedes. Personally, the six-cylinder looked like a rusty boat anchor to me and just about as complete, and just about as valuable, but at Bob's request, amid grunts, groans, and a couple of split seams, we got the engine on the crowded trailer. With a couple of honks of the horn, Bob, his assistant, and the trailer full of two of the rattiest-looking World War I airplanes ever seen by man disappeared in the rain.

As with any of the other really fine and complicated aircraft restoration jobs, enough time was to elapse in the reconstruction to keep Rip Van Winkle happy. All through the Pfalz

reconstruction, Bob had the dedication of a Florence Nightingale, and the parts of the Pfalz traveled up and down like a window shade from Atlanta to Miami to New York and back to Atlanta again, since Bob's job required his moving.

Some of my friends have wondered in what basement I keep the printing press for the money necessary to rebuild my rare birds. Actually, in the case of the Sopwith Camel, I gave away a Nieuport 28. For the restoration of the German Pfalz, Bob received the remains of a Spad VII.

The first project with the reconstruction of the Pfalz was the Mercedes, and as rusty and battered as it looked, the inside was fine, thanks to the varnish of dried castor oil. Valve springs were replaced with American tractor springs. Rings also were American size, and the six-cylinder

110

Bosch magnetos that were missing were replaced with modern Ranger magnetos. Bob had the engine running in short order in his backyard, and like most Mercedes aircraft engines it was noisy and rough, but extremely reliable.

Of all the difficult areas of reconstruction, the Pfalz fuselage and streamlined wing fillet were the worst. The double layer of 3¼-inch-width plys that formed the fuselage were nearly 50 percent rotted away, and essentially the entire fuselage from the cockpit back was replaced. The plys were wrapped in different directions over light longerons, then covered with fabric and doped. All of this required months of work, and a complicated jig was required to hold the fuselage during the many and varied glue sets.

Enough clay and plaster went into the wing fillet to make Michelangelo happy, and because of the compound curves, each piece had to be tacked into the fillet form and glued. At this point it might be worth mentioning that Bob had gotten material from a number of sources, including the German archives and even a college in the South. For most of us in aviation, we think of aircraft construction as a precise art. Believe it or not, the German manufacturing tolerances on some of the important fittings were plus and minus one inch!

The boat builders solved Bob's next problem when they came up with acceptable spruce in lengths of 28½ feet for the one-piece upper wing, but then came more ribs than a forest of fir trees. The excessive number of ribs and their closeness to one another were to some extent dictated by the thin wing section, which for strength needed close spacing and the right wire bracing of the double bays.

The Pfalz, like the Albatros, has the fixed portion of the horizontal stabilizer and the vertical fin as truly fixed, although some British aircraft like the Sopwith 1½ strutter as early as 1911 had adjustable stabilizers to make the pilot's job a little easier.

My Pfalz DXII had a sister ship in the Smithsonian Institution; we borrowed the ship's propeller in order to copy it. As nearly as research can determine, two Pfalz DXII's were brought to the United States following World War I and were part of an enormously varied group of Allied and German aircraft that were evaluated by our military. The list of types available there would make any World War I historian drool, and included SE5's; RE8's; Bristol Fighters; Fokker DVII's; Fokker DVIII's; LVG's; Albatroses; Handley Pages; Nieuport 11's, 27's, and 28's; Spad VII's and XIII's; Avro 504K's; Sopwith Camels, Pups, and Snipes; Hanriots; and many, many more. The Pfalz DXII's apparently considered surplus following evaluation finally wound up in Hollywood and appeared in a number of films, including the classic *Dawn Patrol*.

Fortunately, most of the original German instruments still worked, but the vertical tube radiator was irreplaceable within reason, so Bob formed a modern core in the original shape, which later proved to have so much better cooling potential than the original Pfalz radiator that I flew all the time with the rear shutter closed to keep the water temperature warm enough. One departure from the original was the inclusion of hydraulic brakes and pedals to the rudder bar, and this saved the airplane on a number of occasions.

Finally one November day I was airborne on my way to Atlanta to try my shaking hands on the only German aircraft of World War I that I ever thought I would be lucky enough to fly. Bob picked me up at the airport and drove me to an outlying airfield, where the Pfalz sat gleaming in her camouflage paint. The strange colors of the Pfalz were researched as carefully as was the rest of the reconstruction, and the information came from a scholarly series published by the English magazine *Flight* during and following World War I.

Walking around the DXII in the crisp of an autumn day, not unlike the bygone days of World War I, one can reflect on the excitement of a first test flight.

Unlike the Fokker DVII or DRI, with their cantilever construction, the Pfalz is a maze of wires and includes double bays on each wing. The maintenance of this maze of wires was about as eagerly looked forward to by the German mechanics as a bath in a tub of live eels. Inspecting the wires and then the fittings; the gear and its ball sockets; the aileron elevators and rudder attach points; the glass window in the Mercedes crankcase, which tells you whether you have sufficient oil; and the radiator are all part of a somewhat unfamiliar preflight to our derring-do aviators of today.

Like most German aircraft of the period, to get in the cockpit you have to have been sired by giraffes or have a ladder. Once in the nice battleship-gray cockpit, your nose is assailed by the strong fuel smell until you find that the tank is in the floor directly under you. With incendiary ammunition aboard, what a lovely location for a sausage roast!

A little-known fact is that the German Air Force of this first global conflict actually flew instrument missions with their giant series of aircraft. They were using reliable artificial horizons as early as 1915 on night missions into Russia. The Pfalz does not

suffer from an oversupply of instruments, and there is no panel as we know them today. Instruments are stuck around as haphazardly as a modern artist's paint strokes.

Along with the inverted ram's horn on the stick, there is a radiator control shutter, a mag switch, and a fuel valve. There was no firewall in these airplanes, and it was a distinctly unpleasant feeling to see the rear of the Mercedes engine block. With six cylinders, each with the bore of a butter plate, a compression release is provided. The cockpit is not deep, and seated on my ever-present parachute, I felt like a penthouse dweller.

With my feet in the stirrup-equipped control bar, gas on, radiator shutters closed, motorcycle throttle on stick cracked, and an athlete standing on the wheel with his hand on the compression release, the Mercedes fired on the first pull and ran unevenly until the compression release was locked. The Mercedes idled slowly and a bit unevenly, with the valve springs rattling like castanets.

Taxiing to the takeoff point with runners on the wingtips, I got no real rudder response. I checked to clear myself and was on my way, with the intention of getting the feel of the aircraft on a straight high-speed taxi run. While the acceleration of the Mercedes seemed slow, the tail was up in fifty feet, and rudder response was good. The only problem was a wide-open throttle, which I couldn't close. In the space of telling I was flying. General balance and feel seemed good, so I climbed out around the field with the stuck throttle. This basic trouble was to plague me through my entire flying with the aircraft and, while in time I got rid of the motorcycle twist grip throttle, which was on one of the ram's horns, still the stand-by throttle on the left wall of

A bit gaudy perhaps, but our reconstructed Pfalz DXII is
a sturdy bird of prey.

Pfalz DXII

Specifications

ENGINE	180-hp Mercedes
SPAN	29 ft., 6 in.
LENGTH	20 ft., 11 in.
HEIGHT	8 ft., 10½ in.
CREW	1
EMPTY WEIGHT	1566 lbs.
USEFUL LOAD	596 lbs.
GROSS WEIGHT	1962 lbs.
FUEL CAPACITY	18¾ gals.
ARMAMENT	2 7.92 Spandaus

Performance

MAXIMUM SPEED	120 mph
RATE OF CLIMB	1000 fpm
STALL SPEED	53 mph
ENDURANCE	2 hrs.
SERVICE CEILING	18,500 ft.

Fokker DVII

Specifications

ENGINE	165-hp Mercedes in aircraft described in this book; 180-hp E Hispano-Suiza
SPAN	29 ft., 3½ in.
LENGTH	22 ft., 11½ in.
HEIGHT	9 ft., 2¼ in.
CREW	1
EMPTY WEIGHT	1474 lbs.
USEFUL LOAD	638 lbs.
GROSS WEIGHT	2112 lbs.
FUEL CAPACITY	20 gals.
ARMAMENT	2 7.92 Spandaus

Performance

MAXIMUM SPEED	114 mph
RATE OF CLIMB	1000 fpm
STALL SPEED	53 mph
ENDURANCE	2 hrs.
SERVICE CEILING	19,600 ft.

Another World War I flying original, the Fokker DVII,
with our Nieuport 28 in pursuit.

Completely restored—a thing of beauty in its strange but authentic Pfalz colors.

the aircraft was inadequate and was made for the hand of a Tom Thumb.

The flight was fast, and I ran away from a PT-19 as if it were moored. Wind blast was severe, for the only protection was the German tachometer mounted between the two Spandaus. Without an airspeed indicator my speed was arrived at by pacing other aircraft. Control response in the air was precise, and fast on elevators and rudders, but as in some of the spade-grip British aircraft, the aileron movement was restricted, and the inverted ram's horn kept hitting my thigh.

Visibility was excellent, and wide-open airspeed appeared to be better than 120 mph. The climb, as with many World War I planes, appeared flat, but actually was better than a thousand feet a minute, and I easily climbed away from most of the civilian aircraft. The approach was flat and fast, about 65 mph, and I moved with the alacrity of a mongoose to get the tail down as it settled. Fortunately, the first landing was in a good headwind and mild, for the tail skid bit before I realized how little control the Pfalz has because of the blanking out of tail surfaces by the

113

Close-up of the distinctive radiator of the original Mercedes six-cylinder engine. Even on a hot day the shutters must be kept closed to keep the radiator warm!

A pilot's eye-view of the twin Spandaus, and in the center of the wind-screen, the tachometer, and in front of it, the water-temperature gauge.

lower wing. Not all flights with the Pfalz were to be even half as easy as this first one.

The DXII came out to the West Coast on a trip by truck that for hardship would have equaled Peary's dash to the Pole, but it arrived in good condition. With Bob Rust's good drawings even the rerigging wasn't a problem and it was soon ready for my second flight. The flight went fairly well but was punctuated by the once again locking of the inadequate motorcycle throttle, and when I fell back to the standby throttle, it broke off. I flew fifteen minutes holding the rod of the throttle pushed forward. With this handicap the second landing had enough hair on it to satisfy an orangutan. Among the many aircraft I have been lucky enough to fly, this DXII has no peer in pure cussedness, and each landing presents enough emergencies and handling problems to make an instant trip to the local pub not only desirable but an absolute necessity.

Some years ago, the fine Air Force Museum at Wright-Patterson Air Force Base had a World War I aviation get-together, and many period aircraft were transported in for the celebration. Like many lessons learned the hard way, after assembly I did not flush and refill my fuel tanks. In a cross downwind at five hundred feet, the Mercedes decided that it didn't like its old fuel and quit. Because of the ram's horn stick and lack of ailerons, I could not make a steep enough turn to get into the area I was shooting for; consequently I wound up on an active runway at Wright Field in a ground loop that made the whip at the local amusement park look like a ride in a wheelchair.

Old engines don't fade away, they just die. The result of a balky Mercedes—on my nose at Wright-Patterson Air Force Base.

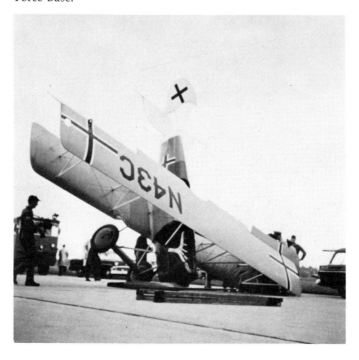

The Pfalz stood on its nose in the center of the runway, and I tied up the runway until enough bodies came out to get the ship back on an even keel. Sizable damage had been done, largely to my pride, but a stick change was made instantly; now the ram's horn is only in for show, with a straight stick used for flying.

Coming, as it did, late in the war, the Pfalz stacks up pretty well when measured against other types I have flown. Its speed above 120 mph will run away from the Spad, Fokker DVII, or SE5. Aerobatically it is clumsier and larger than any of these airplanes and with a slow roll rate, only loops seem pleasant. Diving speed must also have been great enough to run away from nearly everything.

Landing a Pfalz is harder than in any other World War I job except a DRI. In play dogfighting with our other World War I aircraft, the speed of the Pfalz seemed to be its one redeeming grace.

One mechanic propping the engine, while the second mechanic on the wheel holds the compression release on the rear case of the Mercedes.

Our DVII in the markings and colors of the famous German ace, Ernst Udet. He named his plane *Lo!* for his girlfriend, whom he later married.

Fokker DVII

"WHAT A SWEETHEART": This is my No. 1 thought as the candy-striped German Fokker DVII breaks ground. By any pilot's standards it is a delightful, exciting airplane. This particular DVII was once part of our Air Museum at Orange County. Paul Mantz during the late 1930s had instituted a search paralleling Ulysses' wanderings for the Golden Fleece. Paramount had commissioned Paul to look for aircraft to use in *Men with Wings*, and most of the World War I aircraft used in earlier movies had largely become low-rental housing

for termites. This original Fokker DVII had stayed in storage following *Hell's Angels* and was located at the same time as an original Spad 7— and both were found in nearly flyable condition! Although I often do not have a chance to fly it, there is always a brand-new excitement each time I get it airborne.

The DVII design is the work of Anthony Fokker and his brilliant cohort, Reinhold Platz—Fokker's chief aeronautical engineer in World War I. Of course the DVII is the greatest of Fokker's World War I designs, and

117

Closeup of the cockpit and, unfortunately (for the sake of authenticity), its relatively modern instruments.

for reliability, strength, and smooth, easy flight characteristics, it was probably equaled by no other aircraft in either the Imperial German Air Service or the combined Allied air forces. The DVII was one of some twenty-odd Fokker designs made in Germany and under license in Austria and Hungary in World War I. Earlier we described the flight characteristics of the Fokker EIII Eindecker, which was the granddaddy of the DVII.

Anthony Fokker, a Dutchman, was also responsible for the development of the synchronized machine gun that equipped the EIII Eindecker, and the combination of that newly developed weapon and the EIII swept the skies clean of Allied aircraft in 1915. Because of his financially large aircraft and gun contracts and his Dutch nationality, he was looked upon with ill-disguised jealousy by other German aircraft manufacturers.

Background machinations and politics as well as the growth of such firms as Roland, Pfalz, Albatros, and others had reduced Fokker by 1918 almost to the role of a subcontractor. When the Johannisthal fighter trials came up in January 1918, the DVII which was in its early stages of development, was flown to the base by Fokker, who was his own test pilot.

A Hisso-powered DVII because our Mercedes gave up the ghost.

"Du doch nicht!" Ernst Udet's insult to Allied pilots lettered on the elevators of his plane. Roughly translated, it means: "Not this time!"

The twin Spandaus, and a closeup of the fuel tank valves on the under part of the upper wing.

On the trip to Johannisthal he found directorial control poor, and against every military and trial regulation he hired outside welders and spliced in several feet more of fuselage the night before the trials opened. The DVII was an instant success. It led every flight category and was put immediately into quantity production. Now the German firms that had given Fokker such a hard time suddenly found the roles reversed, with their factories being pushed into producing the DVII instead of their own aircraft.

An interesting footnote to the history of the DVII is that many German aircraft designs of 1917 and 1918 used Mercedes engines in such amounts that there were not enough to equip the new DVII's. Anthony Fokker may have been the originator of modern "payola." If a pilot who wrecked an Albatros or Pfalz (and I can personally testify how easy it is to prang a Pfalz) did no damage to the Mercedes engine, and instantly reported this to Fokker, the engine was immediately requisitioned from the wreckage and put in a newly manufactured DVII. In thanks, the pilot was then treated to a fabulous weekend in Berlin at the best hotels —complete with *frauleins* and schnapps, all on the factory. This same treatment was accorded to many of the German aces who made their records in Fokker aircraft, and was probably more gratefully received than all the available ribbons and medals that could be given by the Imperial German Air Service!

Unfortunately, in our DVII we had an Hispano Suiza for power instead of the regulation Mercedes. The change goes back many years to *Men with Wings*, a picture Paul Mantz did using the DVII. By that year (1937) the World War I Mercedes was beginning to show definite signs of age, and

because Hissos were available, one was used with no basic structural changes in the aircraft. As soon as the new owner has a moment, he plans to replace the Hisso with a Mercedes.

As you walk out to the DVII it impresses you as being larger than it actually is. Possibly because of the coffin nose (to quote the World War I flying story pulp magazines of the thirties) and because of the thick high-lift wings. The preflight inspection is simpler by far with the DVII than with any other Allied or German aircraft of that period because of the lack of bracing wires. Both wings are fully cantilevered, and the outer N struts were added only as a sop to the German pilots, for these struts serve no structural purpose.

Apart from the engine, the gear will stand a look. Tightness of the streamlined Fokker gear fairing is important, as is the condition of the shock cord. The trailing edges of the wings, because they are wire, sometimes work through the fabric. This must be checked, as well as the integrity of tail bolts and the structure of the tail. Were this a Mercedes, you would check the radiator for leaks, and check the oil level, using the convenient transparent glass window in the crankcase.

Like all German aircraft, the first entry step is a beaut—long and britches-splitting. It seems that all German World War I fuselages are deep enough inside to bury the Hoover Dam. Once settled in the DVII with a couple of Spandaus six inches away from your mustache, you realize this is a warplane, and in case of accident and no shoulder straps, you might very easily permanently shift that Kaiser Wilhelm appearance.

Were this the original DVII, we would need two mechanics to start the Mercedes, one to twist the prop,

Lo! in flight, as pretty to fly as it looks!

the other to lock in the compression release when the engine fires. Looking for engine instrument indications in an original Fokker DVII is blindman's buff, for like all German World War I cockpits, they were renowned for poor instrument location, with every unlikely spot being used, except the underside of the pilot's seat.

In taking off, the tail comes up immediately, with complete rudder control. The temperature is 68 degrees, ground elevation is 52 feet, and we are airborne in 383 feet in a 9-knot wind. What a completely responsive airplane! The ailerons are sheer delight, and the climb out is a revelation after flying other Allied and German aircraft of World War I.

Leveling out at 3000 feet, the DVII indicates 110 mph, and trues out at 118 mph. There is no windshield, and you tend to lose your goggles if you look anywhere except straight ahead. Anyway, if you turn your head the high regulation German uniform collar will rub through your neck like sandpaper. Stalls are straight forward and hang on until 49 mph on the clock and then fall straight ahead. Loops cover about 800 feet of sky, and when started at 120 mph carry through beautifully, with no tendency to fall out at the top. I still carry a scar on my forehead where the ejected shells of a .30 Browning (replacing the Spandau) struck me during a slow roll while filming a sequence with a camera on the tail. Movie-making with a live gun can be a Purple Heart experience.

Strangely, to the vertical point, the ailerons of the DVII are all anyone could wish. Following through the inverted phase, the roll slows down. As with the P-12, the full slow roll is on the order of nine seconds.

Spins of one turn are smooth and precise in either direction. No snap rolls were attempted, unfortunately, because of time limitations.

Landings with the DVII, as with many other aircraft of that period, are much different than with their World War II counterparts. As you come in on your grass or dirt surface (it had better be one or the other, because of the tail skid), you'll find the DVII moving quite a bit faster than you anticipated and touching three points hot and skittish at about 55 mph. The only directional control is throttle, and a real blast over the rudder is necessary to stop any turning on landing. In case anyone thinks the World War I aircraft are an easy job to fly, I have watched an experienced, many-houred Stearman crop-duster pilot land the DVII and go from wingtip to wingtip, missing a ground loop by the proverbial gnat's eyelash, before grinding to a nerve-shattering halt.

As you taxi in with the DVII, you can only compare its inborn strength, reliability of power plant, and smooth, easy inflight control to its Allied World War I counterparts and realize that the Germans were as far ahead with this airplane in World War I as they were in World War II with their operational jet aircraft and V-2 rockets.

Fully dressed in Army Air Service colors and warming up
prior to takeoff.

Curtiss JN4

THE NAME "Jenny" can refer to a lady
mule, a special sail for a racing yacht,
a device used in knitting mills, P. T.
Barnum's import of the Swedish
nightingale, Miss Jenny Lind, or possibly a maiden aunt. To old-time barnstorming aviators with the smell of
castor oil in their nostrils and grease
in their fingernails, Jenny means a
large, underpowered, ungainly, stick-
and-wire biplane, beloved but occasionally damned by those who flew

her. It was designed in England by
D. Douglas Thomas and manufac-
tured in Model T-like quantities in
America by the Curtiss Aeroplane
Company between 1916 and late 1918.

The reason for the Jenny's existence must certainly be laid to the
fact that in the year 1914 only the
undertakers were happy with the
mounting casualty records of the antiquated Curtiss and Wright Pushers
that equipped the service flying

The wood-and-wire fuselage of the Jenny during reconstruction.

schools. In one class at North Island, San Diego, eight out of a total of fourteen students died in crashes before the year was out. A gallows-type humor emanated from this environment, and messages were sent from the Curtiss side of the field to the Wright side reading, "Please don't fly over our hangars because so many things fell off the aircraft that they seriously endangered people on the ground."

In less than a decade after Kitty Hawk, America's unquestioned ability to create powered flight had begun to stagnate, while Europe moved forward with giant steps, not only in aircraft design, but in training as well. It was Orville Wright who figured out that many of the nose-down crashes were happening not from structural failure but from simple stalls. His

remedy was not to hold the elevator controls back, but to actually push forward into a dive. This concept created as much furor as if he had stepped out of his Pusher in a space suit.

Curtiss, sensibly recognizing that with the public outcry as well as the military investigations, the days of the Pusher were numbered, hired as chief designer of a new tractor airplane, Mr. B. Douglas Thomas from Sopwith in England. A sizable portion of the Jenny was designed in England before Mr. Thomas' arrival at the Curtiss plant in Hammondport, New York. So much for the myth of American-designed aircraft clouding the skies in World War I.

Starting with the J series, Curtiss proceeded with the speed of a roadrunner to change the various models into what ultimately became the most widely known aircraft of its day: the JN4. Starting with comma-type rudder and no fabric on the fuselage and tandem cockpits, they went to ailerons between the wings (a sizable step backward into the past), then lengthened lower wings, then shoulder yoke ailerons, then a simplified landing gear designed for the Burgess airplane by Grover Loening. It's hard to realize that two wheels without skids forward was as much of an innovation and as patentable at this time as was Steve Whittman's later clever use of a tempered spring for a landing gear.

With the mighty conflict in Europe in full swing, Curtiss' first large customer was to be the Royal Flying Corps, who took on the JN2 with the proviso that the Dep (short for Deperdussin) Control be modified from wheel control for the ailerons to the more common stick.

In this same period of time, the Jenny received its baptism of fire and its only experiences as a warplane. Pancho Villa had foolishly allowed his troops to raid American soil, and General Blackjack Pershing (who, incidentally, received his name for his tolerant and warm regard for the black troopers in his command) was sent with an expeditionary force into Mexico, complete with Curtiss aircraft to serve as a scouting force. The high altitude, the heat, and the necessity for constant maintenance seriously cut down on the amount of available reconnaissance, but the 1st Aero Squadron came home with some accolades for its service and some wild experiences for its pilots most likely to hasten a severe coronary condition.

Major Dargue, after a forced landing while attempting to repair an asthmatic *OX* motor, was stoned by a

Art Hartman's tribute to his old flying friends at the Air Force Antique Aircraft show at Wright-Patterson Air Force Base. It was my pleasure to fly Art's replica of the old gal.

hostile Mexican crowd. He kept them at bay by repeatedly posing for an interminably slow local photographer until help arrived.

Production rights were secured by the British Government to produce the JN series in Canada and the happy outcome of this was the equally well-known Canuck. In post-World War I years, the barnstormers often chose a Canuck over a Jenny because of the better control afforded in a Canuck, with ailerons on both upper and lower wings. With Canadian production working smoothly, Curtiss moved his major manufacturing facility to Buffalo, and except for several smaller outside contractors, the main group of Jennys was built here. From the basic Jenny design were derived enough variations to keep the "old lady in the shoe" happy and over 3350 airframes were delivered by the end of this war to end all wars by Curtiss and six other firms.

Ambulance versions were built, painted white, and kept for emergencies at the different primary training bases. The rear turtle deck was lifted off and the protesting patient was put in the open area. In flight there must have been all the comfort and security of a man being lowered down an old mine shaft on a piece of clothesline.

As the war progressed there was a growing awareness that many of our pilots were going overseas without adequate advanced flying and that a better trainer was needed. Such were the exigencies of the time that Curtiss was asked to try the installation of a 150-hp Hispano-Suiza. It was a marriage made in heaven, for frankly forgetting the sometimes vastly over-promoted OX, it did not compare with the sophisticated, reliable Hispano-Suiza, designed by the brilliant Swiss designer, Mr. Mark Birkigit.

A comparison of the OX5-powered Jenny and the Hisso looks like the difference between a glider and a jet. Empty weight of the Hisso-powered model was only fifteen pounds more for nearly double the horsepower. It climbed three times as fast. Its service ceiling was nearly twice that of the OX5. Its top speed was twenty miles an hour more, and it stalled out four miles per hour slower!

Simplex Motor Company and Wright Martin had acquired rights for manufacture of the Hisso, and they were able to expand production for the United States and still fill a quota required for France. With the introduction of the Hisso, a JN4D gunnery trainer was provided, with Scarff ring and an active Lewis gun. Enough tails were shot off to make any live pigeon-shooter happy. Of course, the performance with a Hisso made the Jenny loopable and capable of aerobatics that today would barely ruffle the hair of your maiden aunt.

With a Navy sprouting wings of gold and looking for feathers for its fledglings, the natural stop was the Curtiss Plant in Buffalo and the development of another Jenny variation. Calculating the additional weight of a center pontoon, the Navy decided they needed more wingspan. But rather than change the regular span, the Curtiss engineers just added a new extended center section top and bottom, and in effect made it a three-bay airplane. As one wag put it, the new extended wings were like sausages from a grinder. With the Hisso and vertical-standing radiator, the N9's served the Navy well and weren't retired until the late 1920s.

My father, now deceased many years, often spoke of the nostalgia and pleasure of naval service flying N9's at Pensacola in 1918. It was 1942 before I was to be a naval aviator, taxiing away from the same seawall in PBN-I, the Naval Aircraft Factory's World War II answer to the World War I N9.

An enlarged radiator was required for the Hisso and, due to overheating, the cowling from radiator to firewall was left off many of the service trainers. For every aviator who got overseas in World War I there were three pilots at home who never made it and who thus flew nothing except Jennys, Tommys, and on rare occasions, a DH4.

"How you gonna keep them down on the farm after they've seen Paree?" could as easily refer to the pilots at home who, like their combat-conditioned compatriots, were now returning to the quiet of an America just barely out of the era of hitching rail and watering trough. The newness and excitement of flying spoiled many pilots for the tame pussy-cat living of America in the early 1920s. Barnstorming, an old show-business term, was rapidly applied to the activities of a whole new group of pilots who wandered from town to town and fair to fair, hopping passengers at so many cents per pound and doing plane-to-plane changes and other stunts so dangerous that nothing their equal has ever since been accomplished.

Believing they saw a pigeon in the returning pilots, Curtiss bought back quite a number of their own World War I JN4 aircraft, only to have the U. S. Government torpedo them by releasing other surplus Jennys at prices lower than the rental of equipment to haul them away! The service had standardized on the Hisso Jennys, so it was the war-surplus OX5-powered models that hit our burgeoning skies. The Hissos were also very scarce and very expensive. When the occasional Hisso Jennys, Canucks, or Standards were flown, it was usually because the pilot had won a crap game or had had too many brushes with too many treetops and decided for the safety of his pearly white skin that he'd better pay for a Hisso up front.

The breathtaking performance of an OX Jenny was such that it has never ceased to amaze me that they flew and were able to haul on occasion two people on a wing to perform everything from plane-to-plane changes to herding a live but drugged male lion around the center sections.

Early in my flying career I flew my father to a field along the Delaware River where he had gone through Navy primary flight training in Curtiss F boats and JN4D's. His Jenny flights were straight away and they flew only in a dead calm and landed in an adjoining field, then turned around like the French Penguins and returned. The area was so short I was unable to repeat the operation in a 65-hp J3 Cub, to my father's considerable amusement. My first actual Jenny ride was on my father's lap in the early 1920s, and my memory is as vague about this as it is about Einstein's famous Theory of Relativity.

My next Jenny experience was following World War II when I bought, sight unseen, a Jenny in St. Louis for the incredible bargain sum of five hundred dollars. The OX5 had been replaced by a modern Ranger, and some other alterations had been made. The day of my first test flight arrived, and it was windy and wet due to a frontal passage. To take off and return to Chicago in such weather in my old Jenny seemed to be a quest equal to Admiral Byrd's historic Antarctic flight, but I was game. Bundling up and checking the nine million wires and fittings, I climbed aboard and took off in a nasty crosswind. The wing rose wildly and with-

Airborne in about 250 feet.

out aileron enough, I booted rudder and took out cross downwind through the corn like a McCormick reaper. Getting airborne between a couple of strategically placed trees, I climbed slowly for altitude, trying to get my jangled nerves into place. Having carefully explored the forecasts at the weather bureau, I had found that because of the frontal passage I had a direct tailwind of eighty knots at eight thousand feet, which would bring me to Chicago in about the same elapsed time as if I had been flying a Beech Bonanza! Finally settling on course at eight thousand feet and looking out at the exposed elevator and flapping aileron wires, I hoped that in World War I everyone did nice wingwork, because it is amazing how much higher eight thousand feet

looks than five hundred or a thousand feet.

While these comforting thoughts were running through my mind, I chanced to look back, and a mile or more to my rear was a Constellation. Suddenly the gear dropped and the Fowler flaps followed, and this huge passenger-carrier (a famous airline not mentioned because they might not like it) slowed down and took a nice scenic circle around the Jenny. The passengers were waving from every window. With the huge Connie circling me I felt as exposed as a man taking a shower in Central Park. With a parting flirt of its three tails, the Connie departed, and I was left alone in fifteen-degree cold.

Most of the flight characteristics of my first Jenny parallel those of the

128

Curtiss JN4D

Specifications

ENGINE	90-hp Curtiss OX5
SPAN	43 ft., 7½ in.
LENGTH	27 ft., 4 in.
HEIGHT	9 ft., 10⅝ in.
CREW	2
EMPTY WEIGHT	1580 lbs.
USEFUL LOAD	550 lbs.
GROSS WEIGHT	2130 lbs.
FUEL CAPACITY	26 gals.
ARMAMENT	.3006 Lewis Gun on rear seat, on Scharff ring when used as gunnery trainer.

Performance

MAXIMUM SPEED	75 mph
RATE OF CLIMB	400 fpm
STALL SPEED	45 mph
ENDURANCE	2 hrs., 18 min.
SERVICE CEILING	11,000 ft.

Overleaf: Our Curtiss Jenny caught by the camera with a dramatic sunset backdrop.

At the controls of my Jenny.

The Jenny in her Navy colors.

OX5 model, except that I had slightly better climb. Cruise was somewhere in the area of 64 mph, and to a modern-day pilot, one of the most unusual feelings was the stretching rubber band-like quality of the control cables and the elapsed time between the feed-in of a control correction and its actual response. All Jenny landings were straight forward compared with the World War I rotary engine aircraft, and the Jenny's apparent touchdown and its flare out were like those of many of the present crop of light planes, such as J3 Cub or Taylorcraft, except that the speed was about 39 mph, and with the tail skid, the landing run was short. This particular Jenny went through many hands after mine, and when I finally got back to the West Coast and some years later joined forces with Paul Mantz, I found my Baron Munchausen-type Jenny now in his fleet of aircraft.

Following the First World War, the West Coast was a wonderful place to barnstorm; consequently many Jennys wandered around California, and both they and their pilots decided to plant roots there. From people like Paul Mantz and Art Gobel I have heard much of this glamorous era, and there is even a fair amount of motion picture film (usually newsreels) remaining of stunts such as plane-to-plane changes, pickups out of speeding boats, and fights and chases on the upper wing in flight. One such film sequence shows Art Gobel diving in a Jenny underneath the Pasadena Bridge with a girl on each top wing hanging onto the cabanes. Paul Mantz told me about the time Swede Tomick and Frank Clark for publicity hoisted a Jenny to the top of what was then the tallest hotel in Hollywood and planned to fly it off. The City Fathers, not wishing to have to pick up a Jenny out of the top of their

Model T's, refused to allow the stunt and to enforce their wishes, they sent one of Hollywood's blue-coated finest to stand guard. With blarney and a bit of the grape over several days, Swede and Frank had their friend lulled to the point that he allowed them to run the engine so as to exercise it. The following day Swede brought an ax to the hotel roof. With the OX5 bellowing its bit and a wink from Frank, Swede cut the rope holding the tail. Swede told me the Jenny bounced, wobbled, and then lunged. He ran to the edge of the building, expecting to see the tail of the Jenny stuck out of a courtyard foundation or the roof of a passing bus. But Frank's skill, with help from a divine providence that watches out over the brave, carried the Jenny out along with some telephone wires and a few toupees of various colors from those spectators who got free haircuts.

Most of my experience with OX Jennys has taken place in our work with the movies, or in historical exhibition flying. Perhaps because of the legends, there is something about a Jenny, even in walking up to it, that excites the imagination. Even by modern-day standards it is a large airplane, having a 43-foot, 7⅛-inch wingspan, but because it does not sit up high, it doesn't have the overpowering feel of a large aircraft like a DH4. To preflight the old girl you can start at breakfast, and if you are careful you can finish in time for an early dinner. It has landing and flying wires, cabane wires, outside control wires, drag wires from the engine, and brace wires from the gear. Checking the fabric, particularly the lower wing, was a wise idea, because in rough fields anything could be thrown into the lower wing, from a possum to parts of an old still. In the engine area one always checked the security of the cowling, because two fine pieces of harness leather kept the cowling from departing inflight, and use could always be found for good leather straps in the rural areas. Tire inflation and inspection of the all-wood gear to see that the termites were still just holding hands followed.

Climbing in was easier than on other vintage aircraft, and the cockpit was roomy and uncluttered, with but five instruments! A water temperature indicator, an altimeter (the size of a porthole on the *Queen Mary*), an airspeed indicator, an oil pressure gauge, and a tach.

I don't know why, but I omitted radiator inspection (looking for leaks) on my preflight, which is nearly as important as checking to see if it has both wings. Aviators in the Jenny period, if they were not radiator-conscious, often took involuntary showers (with rusty water) in a day much preceding the introduction of showers into the American home.

Choosing to taxi out with a wing-tip guide, we fired up the OX5, after having it carefully primed. The engine started and ran smoothly, but with a distinctive sort of muted whistling clatter from the valve springs. It idled nicely below 500 rph, and I taxied out after checking for pressure and rise in temperature. In taxiing, as in a float plane, you take advantage of ailerons as well as rudders. The tail skid of the Jenny swiveled within approximately 20 degrees of the centerline of the fuselage. The wood rudder bar and stick felt comfortable, but the throttle was on the right-hand side. Facing into the 10-knot wind, I was airborne in about 250 feet, apparently with a speed of about 43 mph. The climb was as slow as a man going to a funeral and didn't exceed 250 feet a minute, in spite of the fact that I was alone. The angle of climb, because of

the airfoil and the power, is always slight; the World War I planes have a feeling of being lifted to the skies in a flat altitude instead of a nose-up climb as we know it today.

With a control stick the size of a Ted Williams bat, you feel that at least you can overpower the Jenny, but the ailerons were slow; they give one the kind of slippery feeling and lack of confidence in their ability to do the job that seems to be such a part of flying the earlier 1910 Curtiss Pusher. Keeping a wary eye on the water temperature, and with a 50-to-55 mph climb, I looked for the camera plane. Gentle turns require much more coordination than in present aircraft and require leading with rudder and slight back stick as you use the ailerons. Straight and level with the throttle wide open, I rocketed at 73 mph; at the same time the water temperature began to rise and so did the tempo of my vibrating nerves.

An occasional drop of oil from the engine joined the drops of rusty radiator water to form a lovely burnt sienna mixture on the windshield and my goggles. Flying over the still, green hills of the Irvine Ranch and looking out through the forest of wires, one can't help but regret that this kind of an airplane is gone from our skies, and all of us who fly are the poorer for it. While the shadows got longer, I tried stalls, and they broke gently at 30 mph. Suddenly the camera plane showed up, and getting in formation, we shot top, bottom, side, front, and rear-quartering views.

The Stinson L-1, with slots and flaps, had no trouble staying with the Jenny at any speed. With all my attention on the formation work necessary for photography, I was shocked to realize it was getting dark and I was some distance from the airport. As it got darker, the OX5 went into

130

automatic rough, and it's probably just as well I couldn't read any gauges. I circled without lights and came gliding in like the old barnstormers, depending on the pleasant and positive elevators. Contact with the ground was occasioned by a gentle rumble from the shock cord gear, and a slight burst from the pleasantly idling OX5, with full rudder deflection, was all that was necessary to keep the course straight.

Flying the Jenny is a wonderful, exciting glimpse into the past. It doesn't begin to have the performance of other aircraft of its day, and only men with iron nerves and enormous skill could have accomplished with it what they did. Following a particularly dangerous plane-to-plane change in Jennys, years ago, a cub reporter asked the stuntman pilot what he was most afraid of. He thought for a moment and then replied, "Starvation!"

Our Standard in the Army Air Service colors of her days
of flying the mail.

Standard J1

"STANDARD" IN Webster's (the Collegiate) is a gauge, a yardstick, or a criterion of measurement. In the Roaring Twenties, when the sleeping giant that was to become aviation was just rubbing his eyes, a standard was a large, ungainly-looking biplane that moved with all the grace of a lame hippo, but like our African friend, it shared extreme stamina and the ability to shoulder a load. To the barnstorming fliers who were opening the minds and purses of rural America it was a truly magic flying carpet.

132

The Standard J1 was a product of the Standard Airplane Company of Elizabeth, New Jersey, not the most airminded city in the world in 1916. In any case, the company turned out a reconnaissance biplane that actually saw some war service in the Mexican campaign. Its major role in this early conflict was to scare more than its fair share of horseflesh in the then predominantly "saddle and saber" U. S. Army.

Two years later, by the end of World War I, the Standard Airline Company had risen like a phoenix to become the second-largest producer of airplanes in the United States. Besides this World War I trainer, a favorite of mine, which they built in quantity, they also got the seven-year itch for bigger things, and manufactured under license Mr. Caproni's flying canary cage bomber and the considerably stronger but uglier Handley Page 0/400.

Initially, the J1 suffered like the Jenny from that dread condition known in aviation as overbuilt and underpowered. The Hall Scott ex-boat engine was the designer's unhappy choice of power plant, and although it was reasonably reliable and enormously heavy, it was so rough that it was known as the dentists' delight, for only the best tooth fillings survived the vibration. The airplane is a large double bay braced biplane that looks like a Jenny that some one had put a bicycle pump on and blown up.

Unfortunately, when thinking of the Jenny and its lackluster performance, I get severe heart palpitations. It is unfair to compare a Jenny and a Standard, though, for our J1 Standard is equipped with that lovely, reliable, sweet lady of an engine, the Hispano-Suiza, whose muscular 180 hp could haul the Washington Monument if you put glider wings on it. On the other hand, the Jenny, poor girl,

The muscular but reliably sweet Hispano-Suiza, with its more-than-adequate water radiator.

sported that overavoirdupois, underpowered, parts-slinging, single-ignition OX5.

Apart from the hours of flying pleasure that I have enjoyed in the Standard, the barnstormers' delight, it was extremely difficult to find out much about the history of the airplane and its design. To my rescue, like the Jolly Green Giant helicopter to our downed pilots in Vietnam, came Otto Timm—pilot, brilliant designer, early bird, and a walking encyclopedia of knowledge stretching back to aviation's first fumbling steps. Otto's lifetime in the industry started as a teenager with a Curtiss-type Pusher he built and designed in 1910 and 1911. Unfortunately, all he had for movement was a mouse-powered, asthmatic, three-cylinder engine that wasn't powerful enough to do more than put the fear of the almighty in an

unsuspecting herd of grazing heifers.

Later in June of 1911, Otto acquired a six-cylinder Kirkham engine and made his first solo flight straight ahead when his fast-taxiing practice suddenly turned into flight. Without benefit of instructors, the hops got longer as his courage and skill mounted, and on the day that he finally described a full circle of the field and landed without mishap, he decided that he was ready for the flight exhibition business.

For the next few years he barnstormed as one of the youngest pilots on the state fair circuits, and he traveled widely. It was a rare privilege for this writer to see his meticulously kept scrapbook of this lovely, forgotten era of early aviation. One item that I copied *in toto*, because it is such a wonderful historical piece of Americana, reads:

KELLOG PICNIC
AUGUST 10, 1916
BASKET DINNER AT 12 O'CLOCK—1:30 PM
MUSIC BY MURPHY CORONET BAND
SELECTION BY HIGHLAND LASSIE QUARTET
ADDRESS—SUBJECT: LOYALTY—PATRIOTISM—BUSINESS
HONORABLE SANFORD KIRKPATRICK—3 O'CLOCK
EXHIBITION BY OTTO W. TIMM
CONSISTING OF VERTICAL DIVES, OCEAN ROLLS AND
SPARROW FLIGHT—THINGS MORE DANGEROUS THAN
LOOPING THE LOOP
AFTER AIRPLANE EXHIBITION RETURN TO TOWN
BALLGAME 5 PM—CORNER BAXTER & BARRETT
SPORTS HELD ON HIGH STREET AT 7 PM PROMPTLY
PUSH MOBILE RACES—BOYS 1st PRIZE $3.00
GIRLS RUNNING RACE—50 YDS 1st PRIZE $1.50
GIRLS EGG RACE—1st PRIZE $1.50

We have taken license in quoting the above broadside without mentioning that Otto had gone from his Pusher biplane to a tractor biplane of his design and manufacture. With

the rule of thumb that characterized aircraft designs of the time, he first built the tractor without fuselage fabric, but then decided that it would help in protecting the passengers from the elements. To his considerable surprise, it flew better and faster.

In case any of our readers think that in these dear dead quiet days one could not suffer the vandalism that seems such a part of our hippie society of the 1960s and '70s, read this clipping from Otto's scrapbook:

"THE AIRPLANE WILL NOT FLY"
THE MACHINE ARRIVED SATURDAY NIGHT IN GOOD SHAPE
AND WAS SET UP SUNDAY. DURING THE NIGHT SOMEONE MALICIOUSLY
STOLE THE WHEELS AND WRECKED THE MACHINERY
MAKING IT IMPOSSIBLE TO FLY.

$500.00 REWARD
BY CITIZENS OF KENNARD FOR APPREHENSION
AND CONVICTION OF GUILTY PARTY
BROKEN MACHINE MAY BE SEEN AT SOUTHEAST CORNER OF
THE SQUARE

The high top wing, with the plumbing for the center section gas tanks. Note the Budweiser "Victory" markings on the side of the cockpit.

Our Standard in the colors from the motion picture *Thoroughly Modern Millie.* Her maze of wing-support wires make her look like a flying antenna.

With the advent of war in Europe, Otto dropped his Marco Polo-like journeys about the country, and as a flight instructor used his very extensive flying experience to get our feathered fledgling aviators airborne.

Following the war, Otto turned out several interesting designs, one a clean monoplane with an OX5 that turned an eminently respectable 137 mph. Getting anything going this fast with an OX5 is akin to a Clydesdale beating a quarter horse in a sprint.

With his kind of background in flying and the notoriety he had received from barnstorming, a little-known firm from Lincoln called Nebraska Aircraft phoned Otto in 1919, with a frantic request to solve the world's largest jigsaw puzzle. It seems that they had bought the complete inventory of Standard Aircraft Company of Elizabeth, New Jersey. It included everything except the boss's galoshes. Unfortunately, one little detail was left out: the list of all parts

136

and construction locations! Two complete trainloads of untagged pieces of Standards had arrived and were waiting in the railroad yards!

Some months and several thousand aspirin tablets later, a line of J1 Standards was moving through the factory with the precision of Henry Ford's Model T production line. The factory was the main building in the state fair grounds. In a contemporary photograph it looked not unlike a gloomy English Victorian train station. But with the Standard production line moving, the location became a homing point for the barnstormers.

A sensible substitution of the shake, rattle, and roll Hall Scott engine was made with the Wright-built Hispano-Suiza. The latter's general reliability and extra power were to the pilots of the day like an infusion of plasma to a patient in shock.

With as many as eighteen fuselages on the production line, J1 Standards were coming out of the front door as fast as Otto could flight-test them. On one flight, a slender, tall, very youthful-appearing midwesterner rode with Otto. The name of the quiet young man would one day reach undying fame, for he was Charles Lindbergh.

A lovely red-and-black brochure describing the Lincoln Standard was also in Otto's files. In an attempt to show that the Lincoln Standard could be more than a ticket to paradise for the daring stuntmen, the company turned out a plush Standard complete with covered front cabin beautifully upholstered in mohair with two facing seats, roll-up windows, and a cut-glass bud vase for your maiden aunt, for the bargain price of $2950 FOB Lincoln. The brochure also described the kit of spare parts that went with each aircraft sold. This list in itself is indicative of the almost totally unavailable maintenance and the true measure of the mechanical skill that the pilots of this bygone day were expected to have.

Equipment furnished with every Lincoln Standard:

The Standard's big rudder and elevator surfaces.

complete kit of tools
two valve assemblies
set of complete motor gaskets
six feet ignition cable
eight pieces of radiator hose
eight hose clamps
one oil strainer
eight spark plugs
one set magneto brushes
one carburetor float

Several years of Nebraska weather had about convinced Otto to make the move to California, but before leaving he had looked at a Standard that someone had flown in. He told the owner after a careful inspection that the airplane should not be flown because it had broken wing fittings, bolts with nuts on top of wing instead of bottom, warped longerons, fuselage brace wires broken, missing drift wires, and telephone line wire replacing some of the flying wires.

The following day this same owner and a passenger flew a one-way trip to the local marble orchard, for the Standard had shed its upper wing at fifteen hundred feet. This unfortunate occurrence led Otto to suggest to the news media that it was time in this early period of 1924 for the government to step in to bring order to an aviation whose death rate was rising like that in a plague city in medieval Europe.

In the following year, the assets of Lincoln Standard were sold to a firm in Omaha—and none too soon, for the first Wacos and Travelairs were beginning to appear, with infinitely superior performance and reliability.

Two decades and some years, a war, a variety of fine aircraft designs, and a distinguished career were to pass before Otto left a pleasant, gracious retirement to help Paul Mantz build up two J1 Standards for the motion picture *Spirit of St. Louis.* Because the J1 Standards were to be used in early barnstorming sequences, which included loops and moderately high loads for these early aircraft, both Paul and Otto felt that the structural integrity should be unquestionable.

Like most of our Tallmantz restorations, the pieces of the two Standards arrived in enough baskets to keep a washwoman happy and with enough rust to put a smile on the face of King Neptune. They were purchased from owners who fortunately felt they had the value of a well-used tractor tire. Because of the forty-four foot span, you need room equivalent to a couple of tennis courts to set up the massive wings and fuselages.

In rebuilding our two Standards, each fitting was checked, and any and all wood that showed the slightest cracks, splits, or rot was replaced. Before they were through, a lot of fine spruce trees had bitten the dust, and the linen factories in Ireland had worked a night shift.

Acquiring the original engines was as easy as finding the traditional gold brick on the Brooklyn Bridge. One of the two Hissos was traded from a drag racer who was ready to mount it, but it was happily swapped for an overage Cadillac engine that Paul had in his car.

Months of work were required to get the Standards in like-new condition, but it was all worthwhile, for the early pilots and barnstormers who saw them, shed enough happy tears to float a small dory.

My first flight in a J1 came before Paul Mantz and I were associated in Tallmantz Aviation, Inc. I rented the two J1 Standards from Paul for an air show I was doing. When the old girls were pushed out of the hangar they looked as big as the *Hindenburg* and the *Graf Zeppelin,* and the props on the Hissos appeared long enough to have been carved out of the giant redwoods. They have enough wire to support the suspension span on the George Washington Bridge and sufficient linen to furnish sheets for the city of Newark, New Jersey.

We tail-wheel dollied the Standards out to the grass area, and after inspecting this riggers' nightmare and seeing that there were no tadpoles in the radiators, we climbed in.

The most noticeable item following the pants-splitting step up is the flagpole-like control stick. It is at least another foot longer than most control sticks to give the old barnstormer pilot leverage enough to control the asymmetrical weight of a stuntman out on the cabanes.

Stepping up for the first time to the massive wooden meat cleaver of a propeller on the front of the Standard would turn most any present-day mechanics' knees to jelly. Actually, once the prop has been rocked back and forth to load the Hisso, and the carburetor indicates slight overflow, it is ridiculously easy to start. The

As she might have looked flying the mail in the 1920s.

mechanic grabs the bottom of the prop and kicks it a half swing backward against compression. The pilot spins the booster mag like a whirling dervish, and with a satisfied chuf-chuf, the Hisso starts and settles down to an idle so smooth and so slow that you can nearly count the blades passing.

Taxiing a World War I aircraft minus brakes and a wingman required a rather different sort of control. You need room and the correct timing to pick the tail up using elevator and rudder, and yet bring it back down precisely without adding speed or too large a turning circle.

Taking off is quite natural, for with forward stick the tail is up almost instantly, and I was off and climbing away in 180 feet in a slightly quartering 8-knot wind. As in both the Spad VII and the SE5, the incredible silence of the long, stacked Hisso is a shock to a generation used to the ear-shattering roar of such aircraft as an AT6.

The climb-out was pleasant, at an indicated 56 mph, and only the lead of rudder in a turn was different from other vintage aircraft I've flown. The ailerons were stiff by today's comparisons.

Tucking in tight on the other Standard was easy, and formation with minor adjustments on the power and rudder produced a real feeling of the past, as though Jim Bissel, flying the other Standard, and I were a couple of itinerant barnstormers wandering across the Midwest looking for a likely spot to land and start hauling passengers. Jim gave me a wave and broke to the left in a nose-down attitude. A moment later, as gracefully as a red-tail hawk soaring in a thermal, he went over in a beautiful loop.

I followed, and the J1's wires sounded like a banshee with her tail twisted. At 105 mph (the extra 5 mph is for mother and the children), she rose like Captain Nemo's *Nautilus* and went over the top neatly. Because of the long wings and stiff ailerons, the J1 is no Bucker Jungmeister and is literally impossible to slow roll, but wing-overs and loops are delightful.

Cruising along at 70 mph indicated is a nostalgic trip into yesteryear. You glide into the pattern and then into final at 55 mph with an eye on the grass area. A forward slip at the last minute kills your float sufficiently for a touchdown on three points at about 36 mph indicated. There is a pleasant, gentle rumble from the shock cord gear, and at the last minute it is necessary for a blast with the Hisso and a large rudder deflection to hold your course straight to stop.

Looking back on my friendly years with the J1 Standard is like peering into the rarely opened flight log of a barnstormer. I have landed in plow fields so rough only a Jeep could use them. I have sweated the first turn of a spin with a wing walker trying to get back from the cabanes. I have worried through car-to-plane pickups from an open touring car, and I have flown in the sun, the rain, and the darkness.

Our company has actually flown more hours in the Standards than in any other early aircraft, and familiarity, instead of breeding contempt, has given at least this younger troop both a respect and an admitted affection for this, the nicest and most vice-less of all of the aircraft fifty years old or older that I have been privileged to fly.

Thomas-Morse S4B Scout

FAIRLY EARLY IN the Great War, it was found that admittance to the local iodine-and-bandage emporium increased in direct proportion to the number of budding eagles transferred directly from trainers such as Jennies or Avro 504 K's to first-line fighters like Camels or Spads without benefit of flight time in a transitional, intermediate training aircraft. The Thomas-Morse S4B and S4C were designed solely for this intermediate role. Ironically, some of the Scout's bad flying habits exceed those of the first-line fighters.

The history of this Sopwith-type airplane commences with the brothers Thomas, William and Oliver, eschewing careers as mechanical engineers and joining Glenn Curtiss at Hammondsport, New York, in the year 1910. Being fairly prolific designers and undoubtedly suffering from lack of appreciation for their skill, they moved to Bath, New York, and turned out a series of airplanes as varied as the fruits on an Italian pushcart. Tractor monoplanes, passenger-carrying pushers, and a metal-hulled flying boat came off their production line.

Their endeavors were blessed by a kindly providence, and Ithaca, New York, rolled out the purple carpet (well in advance of a day when communities wooed businesses) and invited their Thomas Company, their aviator school, and Thomas Aeromotor to join the Rotary Club and rest awhile. The Morse Chain Company of Ithaca, figuring that maybe aviation had more going for it than anchor chains, put up capital for merger and expansion.

Prior to their move to Ithaca, the Thomases had required the talents and services of B. Douglas Thomas

141

Woody's Thomas-Morse S4B in the Air Force Museum at Wright-Patterson Air Force Base.

(no relation) from Glenn Curtiss, who had hired him from Sopwith in England. B.D. apparently moved around with the regularity of the local bookie, but the ability to design was surely in his hands. To his credit and the chagrin of some of our American aviation historians, B.D. designed both the Curtiss Jenny and the Thomas-Morse Scout, and consequently was respon-

sible for the design of two-thirds of all American aviation production in World War I.

Seeing Sopwith in the lines of the Thomas-Morse Scout line is as easy as recognizing a sunrise. The lines of the Scout closely approximate the lovely prewar Sopwith Tabloid that set so many records in its day. Unfortunately, there is an awkwardness and clumsiness in the Scout's flight handling, which makes it anything but a Sopwith product, but more about this later.

When the Archduke Franz Ferdinand was assassinated at Sarajevo and Europe was plunged into war, America had allowed its initial lead in this new sphere of flight to lapse, due primarily to congressional and military lethargy. Cavalry saber charges and wooden ships and ironmen thinking had hamstrung both design and philosophy of flight, and America was satisfied with 60-mph weak and untrustworthy pusher biplanes. Europe, on the other hand, was showing the world monoplane air speeds of 126 mph, altitude records of over twenty thousand feet, and endurance flights of over five hundred miles of ocean.

The first Thomas-Morse Scout went through acceptance and teething troubles in the summer of 1917, and some of the changes incorporated in the later-produced S4B included shortening the fuselage two feet, nine inches, putting clips on the rudder bar; and perhaps strangest of all, taking the dep or wheel control out of the Scout and replacing it with a stick. It wasn't until twenty years later and the advent of the P-38 that a single-seat fighter was conceived with a wheel control.

October of 1917 saw the first production contract for the S4B, and Thomas was off, unshackled by the chain part of the business, to a production that by war's end totaled over six hundred Scouts and enough spares to build over two hundred more.

An interesting variation of the Scout was the float model delivered to the Navy. The floats apparently had all the watertight integrity of a tissue-paper bikini and required a pumpout after every flight, but the snappy performance of the Scout in comparison to the N9 made the former popular to the pilots, if not to the bail-out detail.

The first model S4B came out with a 90-hp Gnome, which from all reports was about as reliable as a leopard with a thorn in its foot. The Gnome required a pressure fuel system that even with the engine shut off with the coupé button, still shot raw fuel into the engine and through the valves into the cowling. As the ignition was fired again, as in a final approach, a lovely fire more than sufficient to toast a platoon of weiners and marshmallows would start. This spectacular firework-making Gnome was unlikely to make too many friends among the pilots.

The S4B also had been built with the upper ailerons considerably extended at the tip, somewhat in the shape of the Taube. Also, the elevators were large for the size of the aircraft.

General construction of the Tommy was par for the time. It included four main longerons of ash, which, viewed from the side of an uncovered fuselage, have somewhat the appearance of a ski jump due to their sharp rise from the tail. The wings were wood, with an RAF 15 air foil used for lift.

No basic changes were made from the S4B to the S4C except a most desirable reduction in elevator and aileron area, and a change from cable-controlled ailerons to the push-pull bell-crank system used most successfully on the Nieuports up to the 28-meter. I can speak from limited experience that the Nieuport 11 Bebe and the Spads VII's and XIII's had wonderfully light ailerons, due in some measure to push-pull rods.

Another happy change (practically greeted with street parades at training bases where Tommies were flown) was the change to the reliable 80-hp

Landing the Scout during the filming of *Lafayette Esca-*
drille.

Le Rhone engine, built by Union
Switch and Signal Company in Swiss-
vale, Pennsylvania.

An interesting commentary on the
testing of the 80-hp Le Rhone in the
United States was that because of a
scarcity of castor beans for producing
castor oil, Union Switch was forced to
go to a heavyweight machine oil for
its engine. Contrary to the prophets
of doom, the engines seemed to thrive
on this. As our readers probably

know, the rotaries use a caster oil
forced into the whirling engine along
with the fuel, and in theory because
the castor oil was vegetable-based, its
lubricating qualities did not suffer
from contact with the mineral-based
gasoline. Following the war, many
rotaries were flown with heavy oil in
place of castor oil, without apparent
harm. (Without much to go on except
legend, my own operation of World
War I rotary types has always been

144

Closeup in flight of the Thomas-Morse Scout.

Thomas-Morse S4B Scout

Specifications

ENGINE	80-hp Le Rhone
SPAN	27 ft.
LENGTH	20 ft., 3 in.
HEIGHT	8 ft., 6 in.
CREW	1
EMPTY WEIGHT	890 lbs.
USEFUL LOAD	435 lbs.
GROSS WEIGHT	1325 lbs.
FUEL CAPACITY	27 gals.
ARMAMENT	1 or 2 .30-caliber Marlins

Performance

MAXIMUM SPEED	95 mph
RATE OF CLIMB	450 fpm
STALL SPEED	53 mph
ENDURANCE	2 hrs., 15 min.
SERVICE CEILING	15,000 ft.

Standard J1

Specifications

ENGINE	180-hp E (Wright) Hispano-Suiza
SPAN	44 ft., 7 in.
HEIGHT	10 ft., 7 in.
CREW	2
EMPTY WEIGHT	1700 lbs.
USEFUL LOAD	1100 lbs.
GROSS WEIGHT	2800 lbs.
FUEL CAPACITY	42 gals.

Performance

MAXIMUM SPEED	89 mph
RATE OF CLIMB	600 fpm
STALL SPEED	34 mph
ENDURANCE	3 hrs.
SERVICE CEILING	15,500 ft.

The Standard J1 as she might have looked flying the mail.

Skylarking in Ernie Freeman's S4B over Southern California.

with castor oil, which, apart from its most obvious properties, is the very devil to clean off an airplane and is soluble only with alcohol.)

My first touch with a Tommy-Morse was while looking for World War I aircraft for the picture *Lafayette Escadrille.* I contacted the late D. B. (Woody) Woodward, who had just spent the better part of several years of chain-gang-like labor in rebuilding the only surviving Thomas-Morse S4B. Sensibly, he had substituted an 80-hp Le Rhone for the cranky and treacherous Gnome and had accumulated a sizable number of hours in the Scout.

Along with my Camel, a Bleriot, and several other types, we went to location in Santa Maria, California.

As nearly always the case, the location was picturesque and the World War I hangars really looked the part. The field was a magnanimous twelve hundred feet long, bordered by bogus trees created out of telephone poles and the branches from prolific eucalyptus trees.

Operating the Camel out of this was no problem because of the Camel's jump takeoff capabilities and its short landing roll, but the Garland Lincoln Nieuport with the 220 Continental and its 85-mph approach speed and the Thomas-Morse's squirrelly characteristics were quite other buckets of fish.

An incipient ground loop was part of the Scout's characteristics, primarily because of the landing gear's loca-

145

tion almost under the engine. And because of this lack of balance it required a very strong man to lift the tail skid high enough to get it into a wheeled dolly.

With Woody conducting a checkout prior to my first flight, we walked around the S4B checking security of aileron hinges and flying and landing wires, looking at the exposed tail control wires so reminiscent of the Jenny, and then at the tail skid, which included a spring leaf on the leading edge of the wooden skid. Woody had replaced the wire wheels with 30 by 5 disc wheels, which I felt also tended to increase the ground loop problem due to the raising of the three-point attitude even higher. The engine was nicely cowled, with no opening except a cut-out on the bottom.

Climbing into a cockpit with room to swing a cat was a pleasant change from the Camel, and instrumentation of airspeed indicator, altimeter, compass, fuel level gauge, and pulsometer were adequate for their day.

The afternoon was lovely in smog-free Santa Maria, with a field elevation of 350 feet and a 12-knot quartering wind. Loaded beside my avoirdupois were 2 Marlin .30-caliber machine guns with welded blocks, 26 gallons of gasoline, and approximately 5 gallons of castor oil.

Some difficulty was experienced with starting the blameless 80-hp Le Rhone, and I suggested opening the intake valve of each cylinder and squirting a charge of fuel in as the engine was rotated by hand. Woody had only been priming every other cylinder and felt that priming them all would flood the engine, but with the wheeled mixing lever in the rear position, the engine fired, started, and idled nicely. Taxiing out, visibility was better than in the Camel, but the nose was considerably farther away

from the cockpit than in the humped-back bird.

After checking over my shoulder for traffic, I pushed everything forward. For a surprising beat or two the Scout barely moved, and then with a ponderous sort of shuffle and the 80-hp Le Rhone singing a merry tune, I began to move down the field.

Well past the point where the Camel would have been airborne, the tail was still on the ground, and I was beginning to worry. But I broke ground at about an airspeed of 50 mph and with no more than 420 feet of field used up. On breaking ground, the aileron controls felt like they had been welded, and the climb could not have been more than 450 feet a minute, less than half that of the Camel.

In my first gentle climbing turn out of the field, I felt that oft-remembered but never pleasant feeling of total insecurity when an airplane feels like it will suddenly leave you controlless. The Bleriot and the Curtiss Pushers both have the feeling, and you are never sure when flying them who is really conning the ship.

Throughout the hours that I flew the S4B, I never felt secure, and the adequate rudder over large elevators and rock-stiff ailerons felt as far apart as a racehorse and a mule.

Slowly climbing to altitude, I cleared myself and stalled the Scout. Stalls varied, with the airspeed from 47 to 53 mph, and were usually accompanied by a sizeable wing drop, which was not correctable without a strained arm muscle and an altitude loss of about 100 feet.

Although told that the Tommy had never come apart in the air, enough gallant lads had spun in with Tommys in World War I to boost the coffin-makers' stock tremendously. I never felt like rolling or looping the Tommy, and I didn't care who knew it.

The distinctive stars of the Scout from a bird's-eye view.

The prop caught in a seemingly bent attitude at about 500 rph.

Tail heaviness in flight was such that Woody had installed a World War I auto-pilot (a heavy shock cord from under the tank area to the stick). He used this on any flight of longer than ten minutes. Cruising speed was a blistering 88 mph indicated, and I was quite content to stay in the vicinity of our bogus World War I airfield. Apart from the unbalanced feel, the cockpit was comfortable, and the small windshield deflected enough air for you to leave your goggles up.

Circling the field, I glided in blipping the cut-out and leaving sky-writing puffs of smoke behind me. Coming in at 65 mph, I was leery of forward slipping it as I would the Camel. Over the fence and with the tail settling out with the stick slightly forward of neutral, I touched surprisingly fast, at over 53 mph indicated. In comparison it felt twice the landing speed of the Camel. There is a slight burble over the tail surface and a sense of no apparent control, but thanks to the responsive 80-hp Le Rhone, a burst of power over the rudder kept me straight every time I started to drift because of a crosswind.

Lifting my helmet to let the sudden perspiration run out, I taxied back with the tail skid, digging a trough like the Panama Canal in the soft ground.

I have flown only one other American-built fighter trainer of World War I, and that is the Standard E1. Its characteristics were as pleasant as the Tommy's were bad.

Following the war, the Thomas Company designed a variety of aircraft, but lost the production contract on the MB3A, their own design, to Boeing. Most of the surplus Tommys wound up in every conceivable conversion, with OX5's, other rotaries, shortened and lengthened wings, side-by-side seating, and tandem. Several have seen movie service, notably a squadron in *Hell's Angels*, with wing cut-outs and Sopwith-type vertical fins.

If I had been Sopwith, I think I would have sued for defamation of character, for the Tommy is to a wingless kiwi bird as the Sopwith is to hawks and falcons.

149

In the left-hand seat of our old reliable. Note the broad
wing and the exposed control cables.

Ford Trimotor

HERE IS A wonderful old airplane, beloved by nearly all who fly, and known far and wide by the rather pale and wishy-washy name of "Tin Goose." It is most ineptly named, in the writer's opinion, for it should be labeled with an honest-to-gosh muscle-in-the-shoulders kind of name like "Tin Ox" or "Tin Elephant," for it is most assuredly as slow as an ox, but just as strong and as long-lasting as an elephant.

All Ford Trimotors turned out numbered only 198, plus several experimental versions. These were manufactured in less than one generation, between the years 1926 and 1933, yet these gentle, reliable, safe, all-metal aircraft were to have a revolutionary significance. But to the awkward, ailing, spruce-and-bedsheet aviation industry, the durability and strength of the new metal-corrugated Ford arrived with all the impact of a Little Leaguer trying to catch a Ted Williams line drive.

The Ford Trimotor saga must start with the story of Bill Stout, an aircraft designer of merit and a promoter *extraordinaire*, whose career began in World War I. Bill Stout's first design was a cantilever monoplane constructed in 1918 and 1919, called the "Vampire Bat." It was a clean, neat aircraft in its day and was followed by a twin-engined Navy torpedo bomber built of metal and containing not only all of Stout's original designs but his entire bankroll. The Navy had commissioned him to construct the twin bomber, but on one of the aircraft's first flights, the Navy test pilot managed to torpedo the plane into a total wreck. Bill Stout wound up losing an airplane, his shirt tail and his nest egg as well.

Parts of Stout's career reads like that of P. T. Barnum, especially so at this slight twilight period in his fortunes following the bomber crash. Taking pen to paper and burning the midnight oil, Stout wrote a letter to many of the United States' greatest industrialists, seeking new financial backing. One paragraph of his letter read, "I should like a thousand dollars and I can only promise you one thing, you'll never see the money again." Believe it or not, he raised $125,000 this way from people like Ford, Kettering, Chrysler, Firestone, Scripps, Dodge, Fisher, and Wrigley.

Henry Ford's interest in Stout and his aircraft caught fire like a bucket of gas in a barn full of straw, and he hired the engineer. Ford authorized use of a plot of Ford property, and Stout began construction on the very successful Ford 2-AT Air Pullman. It employed the traditional trimotor construction technique, but for power used a single Liberty engine.

These 2-AT's pioneered a reliable airline schedule in 1924 and 1925 on a Chicago, Detroit, and Cleveland routing. Thanks to Ford's farsightedness, pilots were required to wear a blue-and-gold uniform, and included in the crew was a flight escort, a uniformed attendant who went along on each flight to make the passengers more comfortable.

Ford, the hard-headed realist and businessman, and Stout, the promoter and engineer, often mixed with about the same facility as oil and water. Stout had attempted to improve the 2-AT design by converting it into a trimotor configuration. Unfortunately the 3-AT was unsuccessful. This setback along with other problems led to the break between the industrialist and the designer. In 1925, Ford bought out all the stock of Stout and opened the airplane division under William Mayo, who from this time forward was to control the destinies of one of the world's greatest aircraft.

Following a disastrous and destructive fire, the factory reopened with a new design, the first trimotor, the 4-AT. Its brilliant draftsmen were Otto Koppen, John Lee, and James McDonnell, (chairman of McDonnell, aircraft designer of the F4H, the world's fastest carrier fighter.)

This first Trimotor had an open cockpit and all of the protection and comfort of the roller coaster at the local amusement park, but the cockpit was soon closed in, and the cabin had an interior design and comfort never previously conceived of in aviation. The long fuselage, which appeared to drag on the ground and apparently gave the plane its wobbly gait, doomed the Ford forever to the name "Tin Goose." But the public took to the flying washboard like migrant sharecroppers to a deluxe penthouse. The relative comfort of the Ford's twelve seats and sixteen-foot cabin with six-foot headroom came as both a surprise and a pleasure. Cabin attendants on some of the Ford-equipped airlines served such exciting and enticing menus as cold sandwiches and water from a Thermos.

Even on the fords used on the airlines by 1930, there were still only thirteen gauges on the panel. For those who don't remember or haven't seen them, the early Speery Artificial Horizon used on the Fords and other aircraft of the day had the rear horizon face tinted a delicate sky color, and the pivot point was not an illuminated marker but a real monoplane, gear tail surfaces, wings, and all. Say what you will about the ever-present desire to simplify, few pilots ever misunderstood how to read this earlier-designed horizon. Another lovely feature was the wooden control wheels, taken from the deluxe model T's. They were as necessary as a Charles Atlas muscle-building course because of the heavy control forces on the Ford in certain flight attitudes.

Fords had the lasting qualities of the great apes, because while they served the airlines well for a period of approximately five years, they were dropped like a hot rivet when the Boeing 247 came in in 1933, to be followed in 1934 by the Douglas DC-1, DC-2, and then the immortal DC-3. As nearly as can be determined, there are now twelve Trimotors still actively flying in the United States, plus an undetermined number in Mexico and South America, as they fluctuate between private owners and museums.

In this modern age of supersonic speeds, there is one airline still using the snaillike slowness and short take-off and landing capabilities of the Ford. Island Airways in Lake Erie might be called the airline into yester-day, or the airline into nostalgia. Among its other claims to fame, it is the shortest airline in the world: Its route system (when we measure route systems today in thousands of miles) is seventeen miles one way; and when other airlines of today trumpet mini-skirted stewardesses, champagne, and *cordon bleu* food on all flights, Island Airways is proud of the fact that it carries hunting dogs, sacks of fish, children with schoolbooks, and every type of passenger and cargo all in the same compartment, minus heating, cabin pressurization, and air conditioning.

The home of Island Airways is the island of Puttin Bay in Lake Erie, and Island Airways covers the areas of Port Clinton, Puttin Bay, Middlebath Island, North Bath Island, and Rattlesnake Island in its major route system. The entire round trip with all stops is completed in less than forty-five minutes, and in an age when we have runway lengths now on the order of ten thousand feet and up, at least one stop

Taxiing out with a full load of passengers. Each passenger has his own large window from which to view the changing terrain below.

The "flying washboard" with sightseers, circling over the Pacific coastline.

on Island Airways' route has a field length of less than fifteen hundred feet.

Milton (Red) Hirschberger who began this operation in 1929 using Monocopues, Wacos, and a 5-place Standard. The smaller aircraft were retired in 1935. Hirschberger got a fleet of five Ford Trimotors and flew the route until 1953, when the line was bought by Ralph Dietrich, an ex-Air Transport Command pilot. Probably no communities in the world have ever been more dependent on aerial transportation than the people served by Island Airways, and perhaps the only close parallel would have been the magnificent effort of

our Air Force to supply Berlin during the blockade. There is probably no other airline in the world where children depend on aerial transportation to go back and forth to school, where anything from pets, reels of barbed wire, champagne corks, or diesel fuel may be joining you in the cabin on any trip.

In a day when it appears that at least in controlled areas at our major airports we may see VFR aircraft relegated to operating with at least five miles visibility and at twenty-five-hundred-feet ceiling. Ford Trimotors are operating safely and well and have flown nearly forty years on this airline without a fatality, and yet are operating with FAA approval in five hundred feet ceiling, and one-mile visibility.

Among other rather remarkable characteristics of the Ford is its ability to be an acrobatic airplane. Prior to World War II, Harold Johnson awed the pilots and the thousands of spectators at the Cleveland Air Show with a brilliant display of aerobatic virtuosity. He demonstrated slow rolls, loops, and Immelmans, and finished his act by leveling out just off the ground and looping in a Ford Trimotor. So far as this writer knows, no other large airplane ever built has so ably demonstrated its strength or controllability.

In this unpleasant and unhappy age of brush wars and insurrections, in remote and backward countries, an aircraft's ability to operate in and out of rough areas and short fields has taken on the luster of a diamond in a box of lead washers, and whatever one may say of the Ford's blinding cruising speed of 85 to 95 mph, there are few flying machines ever built that can beat a Ford off the ground, unless they be hot-air balloons or helicopters.

Apart from the Ford's ability to survive and return like the proverbial bad penny, there are those who see in the original design a possibility of redevelopment. Hydro Aircraft, Hydro Forming Corporation of Gardena, California, has built an airplane called Bushmaster, which in many respects resembles the Ford Trimotor, and with good reason, because many of the original drawings of the Ford were acquired from Mr. Stout.

The Bushmaster was designed with the enduring qualities of the Trimotor, but using modern engines and modern construction techniques. This Bushmaster flies with three 450-hp Pratt & Whitney Juniors instead of

the wide variety of Wrights and Wasps that powered the original Ford. It also uses constant-speed propellers and an extended dorsal fin to give it better single-engine performance.

Our introduction to the Tin Goose commenced one fall day when Mr. Dale Glen, of Idlewild, Kansas, dropped in to talk to us about a flying project that he was interested in. In the course of our hangar flying, which is as natural to us as breathing, we found out that Mr. Glen had a flying 4ATE Ford Trimotor. There seemed to be a strong possibility the Ford would have the same ability to attract at an air show or in barnstorming as the late Marilyn Monroe. Over a period of some time we negotiated with Mr. Glen to operate the Ford Trimotor. On one sunshiny California day, the Ford floated over the northern end of the airport and settled on our modern concrete runway as gently as a mother hen on a nest of fresh eggs.

To inspect and check out the intricacies and techniques of the Ford were novel and new experiences to me, but to my partner, Paul Mantz, it was nothing but an excursion into a memory bank of wild escapades acquired over his decades of motion-picture work. Studio technicians to whom Paul was always a hero told me these two hair-raisers.

For the picture *Only Angels Have Wings*, Paul Mantz was supposed to spin a Ford—and not just one turn, but between ten and fifteen turns. On two occasions, after laboriously climbing to twelve thousand feet, no amount of wrestling rudder, elevators, and ailerons could force the Ford into a spin, so Paul landed and aft-loaded the baggage area with pigs of lead. This time, after climbing to altitude, the Ford spun lazily and beautifully downward. Paul completed his fifteen turns of a spin and effected a beautiful and perfect recovery. This is on film and is still seen occasionally on TV. I don't know how anyone else feels about spins or aerobatics in a Ford, but they are not only spectacular to the onlookers, but heart-stimulating to the pilot.

The other story concerns a time when Paul had to execute a night landing for a motion picture and was flying as copilot in the Ford. The pilot became blinded by the motion-picture arc lights, misjudged, and smashed into a telephone pole on the final approach, knocking one of the outboard engines out of its mount and starting a first-rate fire. Still airborne, the pilot panicked, but Paul took over and flew the flaming Ford around the field on two engines, and landed it. Everyone got out, but the incident became a legend.

As the Ford Trimotor taxis up, say what you will about C-5A's and the Boeing 747's, the old Ford is still an impressive-size airplane, and despite its unstreamlined appearance, still a graceful one. In making a walk-around inspection of the airplane, you can put away your standard screwdriver and your Philips head, for all control cables are out in the pure sunshine to be inspected at will.

Corrugated aluminum has over the years proved to be a pretty trouble-free covering for the old girl. Lovers of instrumentation inside an aircraft might be a little disconcerted to find the engine instruments for each outboard engine lodged in the engine egg, where only a pilot with twenty-twenty vision can assess them.

The more than sixty feet length of a Ford Trimotor, from propeller to tail, causes about the same amount of problem as an extension put on a dog's tail. Because of the design of the tail wheel and rudder post, one must be very careful never to make too abrupt a turn, for it's quite possible to twist off the tail wheel. In an earlier day, when most airports were small and many surfaces were rough Ford's had many tail wheel problems. The Pilots had to be careful not to make any stalled-tail-first landings, as in some U. S. Navy carrier landings that type of overload could put great stress on the fuselage as well as on the tail wheel.

In at least one instance, in South America, a Ford Trimotor carrying an overload of drilling machinery was mistakenly landed tail wheel first, and it promptly broke in half, trailing the tail behind the airplane and shredding drill pipe all over a muddy airfield. Incidentally, in this particular instance, the structural integrity of the Ford to some extent had been destroyed by opening up a large section on the roof of the fuselage to get these overlong lengths of pipe aboard. This airplane was actually repaired on location with hand tools and flew again.

Walking further around the Ford, one finds a relatively small engine egg behind each Pratt & Whitney engine. The streamlined cell covers the wing-attached structure gear fittings, engine mount, and the triangular oil tank.

Our version of the Ford had three 450-hp Pratt & Whitney engines and three Hamilton ground-adjustable propellers. In a day when one of Barnum's midgets could prop many airplanes, the height of the engines and propellers on a Ford must come as something of a shock and certainly require not only starters but engine stands for maintenance.

The relatively simple landing gear and the wide tread and softness of the gear made landing and taxiing on the Ford a positive delight.

157

A portrait of the "grand old lady of aviation" that I like to remember.

My old friends Jim O'Reilly and Joe Tymczyszn of the Experimental Test Pilots Association. Again, note the exposed control cable. The Pratt & Whitney engines each delivered 450 hp.

As we walk around to the starboard side of the aircraft, open the door, and climb into the cabin, we are struck with the notion that here is another easy-access aircraft, like a Lockheed Lode-Star, in which a woman in a miniskirt can climb into without exciting any more attention than the passage of a funeral. One also notices that every passenger sits by a window. It is a big window, big enough to take in all the heat of the day and the cold of the night, and transmit every noise. With the roar of the engines and the slap of the cables on the side of the fuselage, it is no wonder that the protesting ears of passengers considered this airplane the archetype for a boiler factory.

The headroom is good except for the inside dormers of the wing-attached fittings, and as you walk between the twelve lovely wicker seats, the door to the pilot's cabin looked to be about the size of the entry to a doghouse containing a thin Chihauhua. Inside the pilot's compartment you find that the Trimotor has more room than a Twin Beech. Actually,

cockpit space requirements have not altered much in all of these years of flying, except that now the space has been much more carefully utilized.

For reasons known to economists and perhaps because of the Depression, only one set of flight instruments was included in the air transport aircraft of that day. Consequently, all of your flight instruments are in the center of the panel and are supposedly available to either pilot or copilot. In the dead center of the control pedestal are the trottle and mixtures. The three throttles are about the size of golf balls and on very short arms, and this takes a little bit of getting used to, because the actual throw and movement of the throttle are not as long as the throttle movements of today.

All of the early Trimotors use what was called the Johnson Bar Brake System. Briefly, it was similar in response to the Spitfires and Hurricanes of World War II in Britain. You actually pulled back on the lever, and whatever rudder pedal was deflected at the time caused the selection of that brake.

The lever system had some limitations, and one of them was that it stood directly in the center of the floor between the pilot's and the copilot's seats, making hurried egress from or access to a cockpit nearly impossible; it was also great for hooking and tearing pockets. Our Ford Trimotor, unlike the Johnson Bar-equipped Trimotors, had toe brakes, which were quite positive, but we rarely used them, and depended instead on the differential throttle.

My experience in Ford Trimotors spans some seventy hours of flying time, and like so many pilots of another day, I grew to love the old girl, but I could never get over the fact that the old sweetheart was so slow

The Tin Goose—the venerable Ford Trimotor.

Ford Trimotor

Specifications

ENGINE	3 450-hp Pratt & Whitney Wasp Juniors
SPAN	77 ft., 10 in.
LENGTH	49 ft., 10 in.
HEIGHT	12 ft.
CREW	2 pilots, 1 steward
EMPTY WEIGHT	7500 lbs.
USEFUL LOAD	3743 lbs.
GROSS WEIGHT	11,243 lbs.
FUEL CAPACITY	277 gals.

Performance

MAXIMUM SPEED	135 mph
RATE OF CLIMB	1100 fpm
STALL SPEED	64 mph
ENDURANCE	510 mi. or 4 hrs.
SERVICE CEILING	17,300 ft.

she couldn't get out of her own way. On my first flight from Orange County Airport to Van Nuys, we averaged somewhat less time than we would have had if we had driven. Unlike most modern-day aircraft, Ford flies best with the load aft. This has something to do with the characteristics of the tail of the Ford, and on occasion when flying with other pilots in a lightly loaded Trimotor I have had to go to the rear of the cabin and put my back flush up against the rear-cabin bulkhead to get enough aft load to get the tail down on landing.

Sometimes, if the loads are light, for safety and easy landing the Ford begins to look like a chauffeur-driven vehicle, with all the passengers placed in the rear. Except for the noise level and the stark cockpit surroundings, seating is quite comfortable but noisy, and the manifold smells of the forward engine are with you every moment. If you haven't been in something this big for a while, you sit high enough to give you oxygen starvation.

Before takeoff, the checklist is, of course, very simple. Fuel, mixtures forward, look out to see that your engine gauges on your nacelles are working properly and reading properly, check your mags, and you're ready to go. As you push the three throttles forward, the tail of the Ford comes up almost instantaneously, very much as it does in the Spad. In an incredibly short time, not much more than four plane lengths, you're off the ground and climbing steeply. Control forces are heavy by today's standards, but there is a fine, solid, positive feel about the controls that gives the pilot a most secure feeling. Cruising around in the warmth of the California sunshine and with the engines throttled back, we had an indicated pleasant 88 mph. Speed was

never the Ford's strong point, and in spite of various experimental models that had wheel pants and Townsend rings and even in one case NACA cowling, very little speed was ever added to the Ford.

Stalls in the Ford were straight forward, with little tendency to drop a wing. The stall broke in the early 50s, but if a wing did drop it took muscular structure to get it back up again. The Trimotor has a sort of a neutral stability, and because of the long hours taken on cross-country flights, I often let relatively inexperienced people fly the Trimotor and found them usually quite capable of keeping it on an even keel in a good attitude, usually to their great and pleased surprise and amazement.

Due to ground-adjustable propellers and three engines, one of your most interesting and immediate attention-getters is your inability at first to synchronize your engines. This takes a bit of doing and is a real tip-off to how well a pilot knows a Ford Trimotor.

Personally, I never did anything aerobatic in the Ford, and I have the greatest respect in the world for anyone with the nerve to stunt it; but in a day of lower and lower structural minimums for aircraft, it is still a most heartning and happy thought to know that there is nothing that you can do with the airplane to tear it apart. I wish this were so of all aircraft.

One of the few hazards left in flying the Ford is the enormous eye appeal of this airplane, and the fact that every pilot for miles around who spots you in the air wants to fly formation with you. The great big wing just behind your left shoulder creates blind spots and can give you some uncomfortable formation moments.

Most of California was lucky

enough to see the Trimotor over the years, but one of the great problems in barnstorming the Ford at any air show was that very few people ever arrived much before ten or eleven o'clock in the morning, and, of course, during any air show, all charter flying ceases. So while we found that many people wanted to fly in the Ford, the setup of most air events made it nearly impossible financially impossible to earn enough to pay for the old girl's board and lodging.

Certainly the thrill of flying a Trimotor never leaves one, and following the footsteps of people like Admiral Byrd, who surveyed the South Pole first from a Ford, and sitting in a seat most of the airline pioneers sat in, helps to make the trip a pleasant one.

I landed the Ford on many different types of terrain, from hard-surface military runways to grass strips, and its good landing characteristics are legendary. I doubt very much whether with the size of the control wheel and the necessity to get it back in one's lap on a three-point landing that there were ever many fat Ford captains. On final approach, one of the very unusual characteristics is that one approaches a landing with power on the center engine and with both outboards cut back and idling. Also, on a final approach if you get a wing down making a steep turn into landing, you'll find that unless you have the muscles of a Hercules, you may have to use both arms to straighten the Ford out. You can come in at any airspeed from 80 to 55 mph, power on or power off, but because of the thick wing section and the drag on the airplane, it slows down a great deal faster than any of our other aircraft, so your float is much less than it is in an airplane such as the DC-3.

You can make perfectly safe wheel landings and then bring your tail down, but as I mentioned earlier in this chapter, you never make a stalled landing where the tail wheel touches first. In any kind of a breeze the performance of the Trimotor is fantastic, and it takes not much more than one to two plane lengths' difference whether you're going out empty or carrying a load. A trophy that I keep rather happily is one that I won for short-takeoff performance in a Ford Trimotor against antique airplanes of the same vintage as the Ford, and most of them biplanes. In its day the Ford was quite capable of beating everything else off the ground in any kind of wind, and the climb or angle of climb is really breathtaking.

Having had the pleasure of flying a number of the STOL aircraft, I have yet to fly any of them that will pack a load like a Ford and still perform with a Ford. We had the pleasure of operating our Ford for a period of almost two years, but because of the limitation of air shows and the fact that you are flying a big airplane with three engines and two pilots, we found it difficult to make it pay in spite of its enormous appeal. This airplane appeared in the motion picture *The Family Jewels* with Jerry Lewis, and of course his antics stretched one's imagination. Unfortunately, it was the last major motion picture the Ford Trimotor starred in.

Because of the Ford Trimotor's dizzy speed, most of my returns to Orange County were at dusk or early evening after a show, but I never left the flight line without glancing back at that so-recognizable silhouette of the Ford against the setting sun and thinking that as long as there are airplanes flying in anybody's sky, the sun will never completely set on the Ford Trimotor, grand old lady of aviation.

Spirit of St. Louis

"DANS L'ESPRIT DE Lindbergh" was the United States theme at the 27th Paris Air Show in May 1967. No better bridge of friendship could have been found than the celebration of this greatest of all flights. Even after the passage of forty years, the man Lindbergh and his Ryan monoplane had not lost their luster to the French.

Spirit of St. Louis No. 2 came into existence because of a phone call from the Department of Commerce asking if we at Tallmantz Aviation could or would furnish a flying replica of the *Spirit of St. Louis* for the Paris Air Show. Promptly forgetting lessons learned the hard way in sixteen years of military service, I volunteered myself and my company. In between the acceptance of the challenge and the completion of the plane there was enough action to satisfy James Bond and enough dedication to compare favorably to Sir Galahad in his quest for the Holy Grail.

Chalk, a black floor, welding torch, and chrome molly tubing were the maternity instruments of our *Spirit*. It grew slowly but steadily, thanks to the plans furnished by the project "We" group in San Diego and the many original photos furnished by the Ryan Company. As the fuselage took shape, many problems arose, not the least of which was the search for authentic components. The engines, propellers, instruments, wheels, and tires of the period are almost as extinct as the pterodactyl and tyrannosaurus. Most of the help in locating these rarities came from within our own organization and was due primarily to our company's ability to hang on to material like the proverbial pack rat and our men's encyclopedic memory of our own stored

163

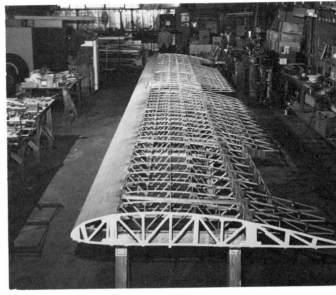

Don, a Tallmantz mechanic, truing one of the ribs of the wing of the replica of the *Spirit of St. Louis* being built for the Paris Air Show of 1967.

Hand-constructed forty-six-foot wing of the *Spirit* replica rests on jig prior to being covered. It's minus the balsa wingtips.

The high uncovered wing gets its final touches prior to covering, while in the back the covered fuselage is being painted.

The wing being set on the fuselage to check rigging. Supervising is T. Claude Ryan, chairman of the Board of Ryan Aeronautical Company and founder of Ryan Airlines, Inc., and H. J. Van Der Linde (center), former chief mechanic of Ryan Airlines and a member of the original crew that built the original *Spirit*.

equipment and the location of other aviation treasure troves.

I must have made the Man of the Year award with the Shoe Manufacturers Association, for in checking construction progress I was not unlike Lindbergh, and the fifty trips or more a day to check in the hangar wore out many shoes and put a permanent out-of-round on the knee bearing in my wooden leg.

During construction, all of us at Tallmantz lived in an insulated cocoon whose walls, ceiling, and floor were *Spirit of St. Louis*, and each problem in manufacturing became everyone else's problem. To capsule all of the months of work, planning,

research, and hunting for materials and components in a few pages is like trying to stuff a struggling genie back into the bottle, but certain moments do stand out.

Our construction crew was simply superb and would have been as difficult to replace and as rare to find as free lunch in a saloon. Each left his particular mark in my memory: To keep the sparks out of his hair, Harvey wore a welding cap on which was riveted a large red button and a typical military quarter-panel sign stating, "In an emergency press here."

Jim Appleby, ex-Air Force major and first-rate aviator and builder, prayerfully watching his *Spirit* wing

The entire Tallmantz crew, including girls in the office, ribstitched the forty-six-foot wing over an eighteen-hour period in order to have it ready on schedule.

Steel tube structure of the cockpit area of the fuselage showing the wicker pilot's seat.

spars as they were loaded with weight to test their strength, keeping his fingers crossed that they wouldn't crack under the overload.

Pat, our A-1, coming in with a happy smile and word that a beautiful polished Hamilton ground-adjustable propeller for the *Spirit* had been found wrapped in protective paper, as well as a spinner that would fit it, all locked in the gloom of our parts archives.

Mama Cat, a beautiful half-wild Persian kitty who sat in the hangar and watched each stage of construction as welding sparks flew, wings were sewn, and the aircraft plumbing was installed.

Our other cat, Ball Bearing, coal black, who turned out to our surprise to be Mrs. Ball Bearing and had six lovely kittens in the baggage compartment of Al Williams' Gulf Hawk. It took many hours out of production to locate the kittens that Mrs. B. did not want us to find.

Don, doing the time-consuming and difficult job of constructing wing ribs that had sixty-three individual wooden pieces in each rib, becoming so turned on that we wound up with more ribs than we needed. He now has a living room full of spare *Spirit* ribs.

The photographers, Dick from Ryan and Don Dornan (free lance),

166

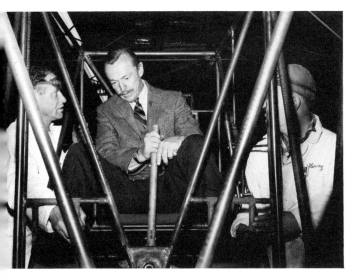 

The author getting the feel of the control column.

Jim Appleby, in charge of building the dead-ringer replica, watching the overhauled Wright J5 run up for the first time.

who did such marvelous work and asked our people so often to resaw or refit something that one of our crew in a rare fit of pique commented, "We are building one *Spirit* to fly and one to photograph."

As a change, the groans from our crew were directed to the construction drawings, which had never been corrected in the originals. This happened as often as it did in *Spirit* No. 1, so technically we had Lindbergh's and Ryan's original problems.

For laughs, the wag who put a large Budweiser Beer knob on the cabin door of the *Spirit* knowing I would have a fit when I came out on my regular rounds. The jigs used to build the *Spirit* had tic-tac-toe games scrawled on them when the guys got too punchy to work or the tension got too strong.

Construction techniques came from the past, with our people heating and bending the axles across an R2600 engine stand and Harvey standing on

an oil drum and pouring sand into an odd-size tube so it could be bent without cracking the wall.

As the monstrous wing of forty-six feet length and seven feet of chord took shape, someone asked where the lifting rings were. As though pretrained, a chorus of our mechanics said, "You're looking at them!"

Don Dornan, one of our photographers, had his No. 3 son born the night that the entire Tallmantz crew stitched the wing of the *Spirit of St. Louis*. With time running out, a stitching job on the wing fabric estimated to take a week and one half by the FAA was finished in fourteen hours.

Every single person at Tallmantz worked, including girls in the office, clean-up people, and yours truly, who sewed the rudder, one elevator, and one aileron. Weird sounds were heard like "Move the needle over a bit," "O.K., down just a hair," "Push through," for in sewing wings you

167

need a pusher and a receiver. The fabric is sewn to every one of the nearly fifty ribs, with dual stitches every 1⅝ inch of length along the rib.

Test flight time arrived, and we ran up to the wire like a bronc trying to get out of a bucking pen. The wing, which looks equal in size to a Boeing B-52's was carried on the mechanics' shoulders an eighth of a mile to be mated to the fuselage. The night before the first flight we had planned on a cherry picker to handle the huge wing, but human power was so good we never again used anything mechanical to put the *Spirit* together or take it apart.

By a stroke of good luck the Wright J5 engine turned out to run beautifully. It was in good shape when we bought it, and we also used parts from four other spare engines that we

had spent months looking for. The final night of assembly the mechanics, who had been working a steady thirty-six hours, looked down to see Harvey, with a live spray gun in his hand, sound asleep bolt upright. He had painted not only the *Spirit's* wheel but the posterior of his partner, who was standing close by and was also asleep.

The final day dawned with slight moisture in the air and such comments from the rapidly growing press group as "I wonder when he really flew it?" None of them knew that it hadn't even been taxied. But several thousand people were there to see the *Spirit* take off.

On run-up one cylinder was dead on both mags and cold to the touch. Chances of having two bad plugs in the same cylinder is one in ten thou-

Finally assembled and ready for its test flight at Orange County Airport.

sand. Thanks to a kindly providence, this really was no problem.

After the preflight and the laborious effort of climbing into the cockpit, the Wright J5 started easily with a never-to-be-forgotten chatter. With warmup complete, I lined up on the field, poured full coal, and was off. The *Spirit* was as blind as a nuclear sub under a polar icepack, but I could keep some semblance of heading by watching out the side windows. As it broke ground, I checked all the controls, and they all were within tolerances and satisfactory.

Climbing gently toward the Pacific, I found the accompanying helicopter and throttled back for picture-taking. After a stall or two and some familiarization, I headed back to the airport. At 180 degrees downwind I initiated a long forward slip so as to clear my path ahead and then had an easy landing, three points, on the wet grass.

It was a thrill to meet the excited crowd, but there is a deeper and unseen pride in my small corporation's real accomplishment—for with six months and forty five thousand dollars of Tallmantz Aviation money, a weary but proud crew saw a slender silver monoplane take off on its maiden flight, fly out toward the Pacific, and return some eighteen minutes later and land without incident. In the vast spectrum of the U. S. aviation industry, only Ryan, Curtiss-Wright, and Hamilton Standard contributed to this re-creation of the *Spirit* legend, and they have our eternal gratitude.

Following the celebration flight to San Diego our thanks go to the wonderful people of that lovely city who successfully concluded a public subscription drive for the purpose of buying and housing *Spirit* No. 2 in the San Diego Aerospace Museum.

Being towed for its test flight.

My trip to France and the Paris Air Show in May 1967 was in the cargo hold of an Air Force Lockheed C-141 jet, so this *Spirit* No. 2 can truly say it too has flown the Atlantic—but in six hours and some minutes instead of the original thirty-three hours, twenty-nine minutes, and thirty seconds. Nursing a cold that would have given a polar bear the sniffles, I slept on a mattress underneath the *Spirit* most of the way over.

Coming into France, the lovely countryside west of Paris was wet but green and showed through the occasional holes in the cloud deck. We landed at Le Bourget for record purposes and later went to Evereux, which is outside of Paris, to unload and assemble the *Spirit*.

At that time an incident happened that also occurred in the original assembly. Only four men seemed prepared to take on the task of lifting the huge wing out of the 141, while thirty Charles Atlases pulled mightily on the free-wheeling fuselage, which two anemic ten-year-olds could have handled with considerable ease.

The first flight test, with the author at the controls over the ocean south of Newport, California.

In the two weeks in Paris, my few years of schoolboy French returned, and I came to feel a warmth for this lovely city of parks, boulevards, and twinkling lights.

General De Gaulle reluctantly gave the U. S. Government his special permission to fly over Paris only as long as the *Spirit* followed each bend in the Seine. In case of engine failure or carburetor ice (which had been plaguing me for some time) I was instructed to put the *Spirit* in the river. I leave to the readers' imagination the sleepless nights resulting from the tension. With my overactive imagination I could picture the dire consequences of such a splash in the Seine. The rep-

Carroll Wright, Tallmantz mechanic, and an Air Force mechanic fueling the *Spirit* in France prior to the flight at Le Bourget.

Carroll Wright pulling the J5 through after assembly at
Evereaux prior to the flight to Le Bourget.

utation of my firm, which had built
the *Spirit*, and of myself as its pilot,
and the prestige of the U. S. Government would suffer greatly from such
a debacle. Fortunately, the heavy
wobble pump and some last-minute
asbestos on the primitive heat jacket
kept the engine running. Looking out
from the small, side cockpit window
on a sunny Paris and the lovely châ-
teaus and finally passing the Eiffel
Tower made all the effort and worry
worthwhile.

Landing at Le Bourget and climbing on the reviewing stand and having it collapse, due as some say to my
heavy teddy bear flying suit, was only
an anticlimax.

"Spirit" in Webster's Dictionary
has some fourteen definitions, but to
myself and the people of Tallmantz
Aviation it will always remain a
warm, vital piece of history that we
made come alive in six unforgettable
months.

The pressures of reconstructing a
one-of-a-kind, enormously complicated historical aircraft, and doing all
the things right for the U. S. Government, had to some extent pushed out
of mind the interesting flight characteristics of this famous airplane.

Following the Paris Air Show, I
rather reluctantly saw the *Spirit* into
its new home at the San Diego Aerospace Museum, never expecting to do
much more than admire it from afar.
Two years passed and John Secondari
of ABC called us concerning a television project called "From Kitty
Hawk to Paris." With suitable ar-
rangements and an insurance policy
on the order of the treasure of Gen-
ghis Khan, I was permitted to send

171

my mechanics to San Diego to once again assemble *Spirit* No. 2.

Going to San Diego the night before the filming, I arrived at Lindbergh Field in the rainy dark. I guess I had forgotten the real grace and beauty of the *Spirit*. In a wet-reflected night-lit hangar, full of modern Beech and Cessna aircraft, it shone like a prima ballerina in a group of grade-school ballet dancers.

Most TV shows operate on a stricter budget than motion pictures, so you are naturally aware that every minute of filming time is vitally important. Next morning I arrived at Lindbergh Field to find magnificent, towering cumulus clouds covering all quadrants of the sky. In our area of the West Coast, these cumulus clouds follow a frontal passage, but they dissipate fast, leaving a bold blue sky

The first test flight in France. Flints in the field cut the tires to cords.

and a crystal-clear atmosphere.

With the *Spirit* gleaming in the early-morning sun and the clouds breaking fast, I tried to get airborne as soon as possible. Camera mounting takes time, but finally I climbed aboard the *Spirit*. As always, with my wooden leg and the long reach and the abbreviated door of the *Spirit*, getting in is a chore, and I manage it with all the grace of a hippo attempting a high jump. Once inside, the cockpit is roomy and the wicker seat comfortable, at least for several hours.

With its restricted visibility, for taxiing you need a neck as long as the Loch Ness monster or a couple of wingmen with track shoes and a good turn of wind.

The instrument panel is oval in shape and for its period carries a plethora of instruments. Certainly a sizable part of Lindbergh's success can be laid to his skill and experience in instrument flight, largely accumulated in his years of flying the U. S. air mail. For IFR flight, Lindbergh had a bank and turn, a bubble type inclinometer, standard air speed, altimeter, clock, tack, oil pressure, temperature gauges and the little-understood (by present-day pilots) earth indicator compass. With the instrument panel starting at cockpit roof line and dropping below your knees, you cannot see forward except for a periscope, with about the same miniature screen area as the earliest television sets.

You start the J5 by rocking the propeller, then a few shots of prime, and it usually takes off on the first swing. It does not have high compression by modern standards, and with the weight of the Hamilton ground-adjustable steel prop it is rather easy to hand-prop (otherwise known in aviation as the Armstrong starter using both arms)! It has a distinctive bark

The author in front of the *Spirit* talking to the press after the successful test flight.

and sound well remembered by those lucky enough to ride behind a J5.

We lined up on Lindbergh Field's main runway, and on signal I took off holding a three-quarter back formation position with our Stinson L1 camera plane. The tail came up in the lightly loaded *Spirit* in about forty feet, though full power and forward stick can lift the tail skid off the ground at any time. Holding position required fancy rudder work and relaxation of the throttle, for I overhauled the L1 very quickly at about fifty knots. Climbing out, I found again that it takes Charles Atlas-like strength to handle the ailerons. This type of aileron was installed at Lindbergh's request when he felt that larger, more positive ones might exceed the structural load on the heavily loaded *Spirit* in rough air. Rudder and elevators are adequate but must be used constantly, and they were en-

173

larged considerably on the later Ryan B5's.

I was climbing at 65 mph with full carburetor heat, which at least on this J5 is about as valuable as an ice retardant as an Antarctic blizzard. Formed up on the camera ship and off the airways, we deliberately drove into the edges of building cumulus for a mood shot on the *Spirit*.

The moment the mist formed around the *Spirit*, I stayed glued on the bank and turn, and when I popped into the sun again the camera ship was still out ahead, where I had left it drumming along like a Coast Guard ice breaker.

Flying the *Spirit* is unlike any other plane, not only because of the limited visibility but because even our beautiful copy of the original has an aura about it. In all the hours that I flew this lovely plane I could never completely divorce myself from its rich history and the feeling of having a small hand in re-creating a moment of greatness.

The camera plane wanted to shoot the *Spirit* against difficult backgrounds, so over the period of several hours I flew over the water and along the beach, over plowed and green fields, and against the background of beautiful skies. Every so often I would get a pop on the J5 that sounded like ice, and for a while I would have to pump with the wobble pump like a demented organ grinder.

If you want to clear yourself ahead you can skid the *Spirit* rather easily with its small fin and absolutely flat wing. Strangely enough, the lack of adequate forward visibility doesn't bother me too much.

Stalling the *Spirit* is difficult, because as lightly loaded as it is, the slightest nose down or power will keep it flying, for it breaks gently with the air speed reading 32 knots and slight power, and 35 knots, power off.

Cruising air speed is 82 knots and, because its design is quite clean for its day, it is quite capable of the advertised 120 mph.

Oil pressure indicated 70 and oil temperature 150 as I turned into traffic at Brown Field outside of San Diego. Previous scouting had indicated that at Brown Field we would have landing backgrounds approximating those when the original *Spirit* was built and test-flown.

Turning from the base leg leading with rudder and aileron and indicating 55 mph, I went into a nose-high forward slip that I carried almost to touchdown, only straightening out at the last moment. The entire trip down was punctuated with backfires from the J5 that would scare hell out of the range officer at a police pistol range. I wore goggles down, because there was a whirlwind draft going through the old girl. On touchdown it rumbled along like a grumpy bear, and until it stops you are hoping nothing animal, vegetable, or mineral gets in your path because you sure as hell can't see it until you hit it.

I am often asked why Lindbergh chose this design, with the seat aft of the gas tank, and as I have heard it said, it was to expedite the manufacture by keeping all gas load under the center of gravity and center of pressure, and because he didn't want the tanks behind him in case of a crash.

Throughout my life I will always carry the memory of the pleasure of flying this airplane and for a brief moment re-creating one of aviation's greatest milestones.

The *Spirit* being swung up into position in front of the
American pavilion at Paris.

Spirit of St. Louis

Specifications

ENGINE	Wright Whirlwind J5-G
SPAN	46 ft.
LENGTH	27 ft., 6 in.
HEIGHT	6 ft., 9 in.
CREW	1
EMPTY WEIGHT	2150 lbs.
USEFUL LOAD	3100 lbs.
GROSS WEIGHT	5250 lbs.
FUEL CAPACITY	420 gals.

Performance

MAXIMUM SPEED	120 mph
RATE OF CLIMB	100 fpm loaded
STALL SPEED	45 mph empty
ENDURANCE	36 hrs.
SERVICE CEILING	18,000 ft. lightly loaded

An exact replica of Lindbergh's *Spirit of St. Louis.*

Three-quarter forward view of our Boeing in its Navy
colors as an F4B1.

Boeing P-12

Specifications

ENGINE	450-hp Pratt & Whitney Wasp Junior
SPAN	30 ft.
LENGTH	20 ft., 1⅜ in.
HEIGHT	9 ft., 4½ in.
CREW	1
EMPTY WEIGHT	1916 lbs.
USEFUL LOAD	620 lbs.
GROSS WEIGHT	2536 lbs.
FUEL CAPACITY	57 gals.
ARMAMENT	1 .50 Browning; 1 .30 Browning; or 2 .30 Brownings

Performance

MAXIMUM SPEED	166.3 mph
RATE OF CLIMB	2500 fpm
STALL SPEED	58 mph
ENDURANCE	4 hrs., 15 min.
SERVICE CEILING	26,400 ft.

A special favorite of mine, the Boeing P-12.

Boeing P-12

THERE ARE CHAMPIONS in every field of endeavor, and they are always sought after by the rank-and-file of us ordinary humans. Such a champion and such a sought-after plane is the justly famous and exciting Boeing biplane of the P-12 series. It is an airplane that has always held an irresistible fascination for me since my airplane model-making days in the 1930s.

The P-12 series almost spans the period from World War I to World War II. Its basic design draws much from World War I biplane aircraft, being small and compact, with two synchronized machine guns of .30 caliber, and differing mainly in its construction and reliability of powerplant. Many of our present crop of Air Force generals and flying admirals somewhere in their training had the pleasure of flying either the Boeing P-12 or the F4B series.

The delightful performance of the later P-12s and F4Bs was contrasted markedly with a general weakening in the knees and the shattered nerves that characterized the landings of the inexperienced pilots in the early models. Those planes had a nasty habit of porpoising and galloping on landing if not set down smoothly. Usually the only remedy was instant power and another circuit, but if the pilot's pride forbade this, a split second later he would have to extricate himself from an upside-down airplane and at the same time figure out some sort of excuse for his commanding officer.

One thing that all the Boeing biplane fighter series had in common was that they were all built like a certain brick edifice, and the pilots took advantage of the planes' near-indestructibility in flight and their

177

The F4B1 was a pretty open airplane!

outstanding performance to practice maneuvers unknown to an earlier generation of pilots.

The early P-12 had a bolted square aluminum tubing fuselage, fabric-covered from just forward of the cockpit. It also had a metal turtleback extending to the tail, which could be removed with quick-attach fittings for almost instant maintenance. The wings were wood spars, wood ribs, and fabric-covered, with the rib stitching very close for strength. There certainly must have been some sore fingers and weak eyes in the Boeing plant, for this exceptionally close stitching carried flight loads in excess of nine Gs!

The 450-hp Pratt & Whitney Junior engine, with a non-regulated constant-speed propeller.

The first Boeing P-12 was a factory-funded project, Model 83, which came out early in 1928 and quickly attracted the attention of the military services. Its only basic change was in 1930, when the square tube fabric fuselage was replaced by dural semi-monocoque design. In its entire history, 586 aircraft were built, and the last of the series were still being flown in 1942, after World War II had broken out!

As we walked out to the flight line to commence our test hop in an early fabric covered 100 Series model, we missed the riding boots and spurs that were part of the uniform of the U. S. Army Air Service pilot of 1928. The brilliant yellow wings and olive fuselage with red, white, and blue striped tail made a much more exciting color scheme than anything we have today, and the short, coupled fuselage, narrow-tracked gear and big, un-cowled Pratt & Whitney would make any pilot's mouth water.

A walk-around inspection of the aircraft included the streamlined flying and landing wires; the main gear fittings; the covers over the fuel and oil tanks with quick-locks; and the tail wires and fittings. As you climb on the wing of the P-12 you find it's a big advantage to have long legs to reach the cockpit. They must have had to lower the short pilot in by windlass, as they did for the gallant knights of old. The cockpit is quite roomy, but with the top of the fuselage narrower than the center, it gives the cockpit rim a most typical lengthwise Boeing appearance.

This Boeing starts up, as all 450-hp Pratt & Whitney 985's do, with manual prime, wobble pump, and a couple of pumps of the throttle. It runs sweetly and nicely. I belted myself in with the regular belt as well as a standby. As I taxied out, the directly

connected tail wheel was sharply positive, and I was aware of what could happen if I were to use rudder suddenly in a three-pointed attitude. As I turned into the wind and waited for a light from the tower, I bent slightly forward behind the high, nonregulation windshield, with my shoulder well out of the cockpit. Having flown this bird to Phoenix for a show when the temperature at altitude was 45 degrees, I can only shudder and sympathize with those Army Air Service pilots during the time our government forced them to carry mail in the Boeing P-12h in the winter of 1934 with temperatures on the order of zero. They were still expected to duplicate airline reliability under night and instrument conditions with a bank-and-turn indicator. Thank heaven for parachutes and heated cabins.

With a green light from the tower, I push 37" on the throttle, and with one quick stiff-legged bounce it was off and flying. The temperature was 61 degrees, with a wind of 8 knots; ground elevation, 52 feet; roll for takeoff, 94 feet.

Talk about your STOL aircraft instantly after breaking ground; with the P-12 you can pull the nose up to about 40 degrees above the horizon with an airspeed of 65 mph under full power and climb out at an indicated 2900 feet a minute! It's really a breathtaking performance. I leveled out at 5000 feet with full power and true out at 154 mph, which is somewhat slow and is probably due to instrument error. It was a beautiful, clear day with a few white puffball clouds at 3000 feet, and I was several miles out over the blue Pacific, paralleling the coast (and, incidentally, wearing a Mae West). My first stalls broke cleanly at an indicated 58 mph with power off. The Boeing will fly with any sort of power, and you are down to about 48 mph before it quits flying in a power-on stall.

The next maneuver was a loop, a bit too slow at 120 mph but about right at 130. Because of the drag, it doesn't gain much altitude, and you can pull the first half of the loop quite tight. You can go over the top with about 1100 feet altitude gain and an indicated 60 mph at the top.

Hammerheads are pulled fully vertical, and the P-12 will come down with full reversal in the same slot if started just before you hit 65 mph on the clock. The plane will not spin to the right; it will just enter a diving spiral to the left. The first turn is sloppy, and after this the nose drops instantly to a fully vertical position and really whips, taking a turn and a half to recover. Cuban 8s are delightful when started at 130 mph, and

as long as one doesn't spend too much time on the rollout, they are fine. We have an inverted fuel system, but you lose oil pressure in about five seconds inverted.

Perhaps the most disappointing thing in this airplane is its rate of roll. Going back to the construction of the Boeing P-12, the civilian Boeing 100, and the F4B1, the ailerons were roughly triangular in shape, with a very narrow width on the inboard end. This was changed markedly in the later models by increasing both chord and span of the ailerons. In our airplane, a slow roll in either direction with full deflection takes between seven and eight full seconds to complete.

With some minor constrictions of the heart muscles, I rolled the little girl on her back, dove, and at 200 mph

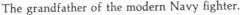

The grandfather of the modern Navy fighter.

The delicacy of line of this responsive airplane.

pushed up to try an outside loop. As everyone knows, this is most uncomfortable, and at about the time I hit the straight-up position without ailerons or rudder, it went into a fast snap roll to the left—so fast in fact, that for a second or two I had trouble orienting myself. Pulling the muscles a bit tighter I again tried an outside loop, this time starting at the top. I slowed down to 60 mph and pushed forward, being extremely careful to neutralize controls and only using elevators; as I went past the vertical I poured the coal to it, hoping the air flow over the tail would bring it around. Again, it went into a fast snap to the left. This ended my attempts at an outside loop, for the ocean far below was getting to look colder by the second.

After considerable sloppy patterns in the sky trying to get a snap roll out of the P-12, I finally arrived at the solution, which is to stall it at about 60 mph, and as it starts over on its back, pour full power. In this way you can get a fair snap roll.

Finalizing my flying in the P-12, I try full aileron deflections with the nose slightly above the horizon in a stall at 50 mph indicated. It just mushed down without dropping a wing, and with a rate of descent of 1800 feet a minute. Trying the same thing with rudder in full deflection, it suddenly snapped over on its back and entered the first quarter turn of an inverted spin. I got it out with immediate power and opposite controls. (Paul Mantz, who flew this Boeing for many years, had said in no uncertain terms that if it ever really got in an inverted spin, your only recourse was to bail out and let it go, for like the small-tail Fleet biplane, the tail surfaces blanked out and you could not recover.)

Diving toward home is a pleasure, for there are no restrictions speedwise

The Tallmantz Boeing in its original markings as an Army
Air Service P-12.

and you can dive the P-12 vertically 10,000 feet if you wish. As I entered base leg, I put it into a forward slip, but with the small rudder, you cannot hold direction, and it drifts 90 degrees in about five seconds, which is sufficient to flare out for a landing. It touches on 3 points at 56 mph and rolls about 800 feet. As I taxied in I contrasted the landing in the grass to those on concrete, which are hairy! Because the tail wheel is directly connected with the rudder, unless you set the plane down with the rudder straight ahead, it will stand up on a

wheel and ground loop, then shortly thereafter roll up in a ball (which it has done on two previous occasions, but fortunately not with me).

As I swung a leg out of the P-12 I checked my G indicator, and it showed 4 positive Gs and 2 negative. Although the P-12 has certain control limitations, it is still one of the most exciting airplanes to fly that it has ever been my pleasure to climb into and the knowledge that you can't tear it apart in any attitude really makes you a tiger!

Lockheed Vega

EVEN IN THE 1970s the Lockheed Vega, built nearly half a century ago, is still the lovely, graceful, efficient airplane that set a new pattern in the sky in the 1920s and 1930s.

The history of the Lockheed Vega airplane starts fittingly enough with Allan and Malcolm Loughead, the brilliant California brother team whose early Model G seaplane and the F-1 multi-engine flying boat pointed the way for their later designs. In June of 1918, the twin engine F-1, remodeled with wheels, started its flight across the United States, but cracked up taking off from Gila Bend, Arizona. In spite of the unfortunate crash, the attempt to fly across the country was a sign of things to come.

Following the war, in spite of the S-1 single seat biplane, beautifully designed by Jack Northrop, and pas-senger hopping and charter work in the old F-1 flying boat, the Loughead brothers were forced to close their doors. Malcolm went into the manu-facture of the highly successful hy-draulic brakes for automobiles, while Allan sold real estate. A new Lock-heed Company was formed by the brothers some years later to build the fastest commercial airplane. It used Northrop's original monocoque ply-wood fuselage design pioneered in the tiny single-seat biplane.

The first Vega, named *The Golden Eagle*, was finished just in time to be ready for the 1927 Dole Race to Hawaii. Sponsored by the powerful Hearst Newspapers, *The Golden Eagle* was the best-equipped aircraft in the race; still, it disappeared in the Pacific, never to be seen again. The wonder-ful lines, the speed, and the efficiency so impressed aviation in general that

183

Taxiing out to the runway at the beginning of our flight commemorating the thirtieth anniversary of Continental Airlines.

in spite of Lockheed losing its first aircraft in the ocean, bona fide orders began to pour into the little plant in Burbank, California. While the Depression deepened and a shocked America attempted to rise from this crippling blow, airplanes—Vegas, Air Expresses, Siruses, Altairs, and Orions—poured from the Burbank plant and later the Detroit factory. In all, only 197 single-engined Lockheed aircraft of all models were built, but they held more national and interna-tional records than any other types of airplanes in all aviation history. Just a very few of the great pilots who flew Vegas included Wiley Post, Ben Eielson, Art Goebel, Roscoe Turner, Frank Hawks, Billy Brock, Jimmy Mattern, Paul Mantz, Amelia Earhart, and Ruth Nichols.

Our beautiful white-and-red Vega came out of the Detroit factory on January 20, 1929, was sent to the Montana Development Company, and then went on to its time of Glory

184

when it served as the *Viking* in the Macmillan Arctic expedition. The *Viking* surveyed much unchartered land in Labrador and Greenland in 1931. After a succession of three owners and a passage of many years, the plane now resides in the Ford museum in Detroit.

Anytime anyone thinks the wooden Vegas are flophouses for termites or are antiquated playtoys, note this: the level flight speed of a Lockheed Vega has exceeded 340 mph (at altitude), and a Vega has reached an altitude of over 55,000 feet!

The real pleasure and the extensive flying in our Vega has come only since its complete renovation and rebuilding in our own shop. The people at Continental Airlines, who have been wonderful friends to our museum, besides bringing us a Douglas DC-7, also agreed to help in the reconstruction of our Vega, which through the years had gradually deteriorated. The reason, of course, for Continental's deep interest was that the airline started thirty years ago flying Vegas from El Paso to Pueblo, Colorado.

Robert Six, the dynamic, brilliantly successful president of Continental, gave his blessings and the go-ahead, and the complete rebuilding of the Vega commenced. In my opinion there have been few tougher projects than the Vega. Here are some of the things we found when we stripped the fabric from the airframe and components: The window area was rotted out to the center of the fuselage; the horizontal tail and tail wheel mounts were almost floating free in the rear of the fuselage; much of the bottom skin of the fuselage was soggy; the major bulkhead separating the pilot's compartment and the cabin as well as the bulkhead that holds the gear were riddled; the ailerons were wet

sponges; all glass had to be replaced; the 300-hp Wasp Junior badly needed overhaul. There were many other items, but these will serve to show you the scope of our project.

Five months of back-breaking labor saw the Vega in the air once more, but not without a flash doping fire that burned the top two-thirds of the freshly covered wing. We had been planning to give the new overhead automatic sprinklers in the hangar a try, but this was surely the hard way to check if they worked. We replaced the wing fabric, and the Vega was ready for her new life. The tremendous skill and dedication that went into rebuilding N965Y are plain to see, and any pilot can only experience a real thrill when he walks up to her.

It's not a small airplane, with its forty-one-foot cantilever, high-lift wing and absolutely clean fuselage and empennage. It is impressive! To climb into the pilot's seat of the Vega can be done in two ways: either through the cabin and a miniature pilot's door the size of the keyhole in *Alice's Adventures in Wonderland* or,

The tail of our Vega with the markings of Varney Airlines, one of the pioneer lines in the West, and a foundation stone of the Continental Airlines system.

Our Lockheed in Amelia Earhart's colors and plane numbers.

if one does not suffer from fear of heights, up the front left-hand side of the fuselage by using two handholds that would scare a high-wire artist. Once seated on the upper wing, you slide back the hatch and drop into the well.

Although the fuselage is rather wide, the pilot sits dead center in the cockpit. I am told on good authority that in the good old days, on occasion when a cabin passenger was feminine, the pilot's compartment was somehow wide enough to suddenly accom-modate a pilot and copilot. The battleship-gray enamel sealing the wood inside the cockpit is enough to make one stand up and sing three choruses of "Anchors Away." The passenger cabin is original in appearance, with cut-glass ceiling lamp. The folding seat, rear seat, walls, and ceiling are all covered in red leather. (An upholstery story likely to make any Vega owner wince: Some many years ago a friend short on cash hired an immigrant upholsterer to redo his shabby Vega interior. The friend ar-

186

A proud moment with the man who made the Vega a reality, Allan Loughead.

The big 300-hp Wasp Junior with a Hamilton ground-adjustable propeller.

Note semi-airwheels and Venturi horn.

rived the next morning to find that the upholsterer had used nice long nails and had happily hammered clear through the fuselage, so the outside of the Vega looked like a porcupine.)

Back in the pilot's compartment, we notice standard and gyro instruments. A three-foot long Johnson bar, which controls the trim tab and something under the panel that looks like a hatbox, this contains the starter solenoid. On the right side is a fuse box, with exposed fuses that looks like something out of a Victorian hotel. Like all Pratt & Whitneys, the 300-hp Wasp Junior starts nicely, and as you taxi away from the line you realize that in spite of being 6 foot one, if it weren't for about 8 inches of cushions, you couldn't see anything out of the high windshield. As it is, you still don't see closer than 150 feet. The cable brakes are actuated by a second set of larger pedals directly above the rudder pedals, and they require a double-jointed foot. I remember once, after breaking a leg in a parachute jump and while it was still in a walking cast, landing the Vega by alternately punching the two pedals with the cast. Fortunately I had no crosswind, or the Vega might have been reduced to matchsticks.

Before departure from the line, always pull your gas tank caps, and sight-check the tanks. Don't depend on the glass toothpaste tubes, which are laughingly supposed to indicate fuel quantity. On takeoff the acceleration is not fast, due to the Hamilton ground-adjustable propeller, but on one particular flight the tail was up in about 100 feet, and the plane was airborne smoothly at 62 mph with a ground roll of about 750 feet. The temperature was 55 degrees; wind, 5 knots; and there was light rain. The climbout was at about 800 feet a minute indicated. The Vega's controls are

a little stiff by today's standards, and the plane has a certain solid sort of multi-engine feel. Settling down at Altitude and cruise power, one is conscious of wind noise and we were aware of the perpetual shower bath on this rainy day due to the hopelessly unsealable windshield panels.

At 2000 feet, the Vega indicates 136 mph, carrying 23½ inches manifold pressure, and at 1875 rpm. At about 90 percent power it indicated a most respectable 154 mph. With the bigger engine, thin wheels, wheel pants, and a constant-speed propeller, the Vega could top 200 mph true. Pretty good for an old lady!

Stalls produce a slight right-wing drop and plenty of notice, but if one perversely holds the stick back, the plane will whip rather sharply to the left and into a spin. The power-off stall occurred at 53 mph, and the power-on stall was beyond the lowest reading on the dial, or at about 49 mph.

Chandelles were pleasant, starting at 120 mph and winding up on top at 70 mph. As in all early aircraft, one must lead with rudder and make a genuine effort to coordinate controls; otherwise you can skid around like a hog on ice.

Sitting this close to the engine, you need Aunt Fanny's earmuffs, or earphones, for over a period of time the engine can really deafen one. In the first steep turn, my necktie hung up on the bare aileron cable, which runs through the cockpit, and for a moment I thought I was the No. 1 victim at a western hanging party. Flight visibility is good back under the wings, forward, and through the top sliding hatch. By turning your head, your eye level is just right to look in the open wing root. The dark inside-exposed area of ribs and cobwebs reminds one of the attic in Dracula's castle. The Vega is a study in contrasts: older construction methods; fast; slightly stiff on the controls; no room for radios; plenty of room for passengers and baggage.

As a entered downwind for landing, I was at 1000 feet, and I put the nose in a high forward slip at 95 mph, which I continued for 180 degrees of turn, losing the thousand feet and landing easily in the very first part of the runway. The nose-high forward slip is a wonderful way to kill a lot of altitude but is impossible in most of our modern airplanes, with their interconnected control systems and inadequate control throw.

It is necessary to use ballast in the baggage compartment, or to have passengers, for the Vega is tail light. Our touchdown was on 3 points and smooth at 65 mph, with very positive rudder control down to about 30 mph. The tail wheel is full swivel. If you are a bit fast on landing, the Vega has a tendency to settle in increments because of the long strut travel, so that it feels to the pilot as though he had made 3 or 4 landings—yet you are solidly on the ground all the time.

During our 6000-mile commemoration flight of Continental Airlines' thirtieth anniversary, at one time I carried nearly 2000 pounds of useful load out of a mile-high field, with temperatures touching 90 degrees. In nearly every way the Vega would be a superior airplane today, with fantastic load carrying capacity, speed, strength, and good instrumentation.

As I taxied up to park, I could only be happy that I had had a chance to fly this airplane, which has written such a great page in aviation history.

In Amelia Earhart's markings out over the Pacific.

Al Williams' Curtiss Gulf Hawk

ORNITHOLOGISTS AND LOVERS of our feathered friends tell us that there are some 290 recognized members of the hawk species. The research to locate and catalog this extensive bird family required centuries.

The hawks that I speak of here inhabited the shimmering blue of our skies for less than twenty short years, in the twenties and thirties. They were known by such exciting and heart-stirring names as Falcon, Sparrow Hawk, Condor, Sea Hawk, and Kitty Hawk.

Princes and kings in ancient times kept hawks and falcons because they were noble birds of prey. The hawks ranged in size from the small sparrow hawk, to the much larger gyr falcon, but all were characterized by strength, swift flight, and the ability to dive at

high speed. In aviation the name "Hawk" is synonymous with Curtiss.

The United States had bred a few monoplane racers in the early thirties, but by far the most successful racing planes were the Curtiss racing biplanes. One doesn't have to know much about genes and heredity to see the father-son succession in the successful Curtiss racer series and the military biplanes that followed.

While Al Williams' lovely Gulf Hawk was actually a Curtiss Navy F6C-4, only a few basic differences existed between the P-1 army Hawk Biplane and the Navy version. The most important was the substitution of the air-cooled radial engine for the liquid Curtiss Conqueror, and the addition of a tail hook. The added strength in the rear part of the fuse-

We replaced the early 1820-hp Wright that came with the Hawk with this Pratt & Whitney R-1340 and a Hamilton Standard constant-speed propeller.

lage of the Navy version usually kept our intrepid aviators from suddenly winding up on the carrier deck sitting on the teak with the front of the hawk sailing forward, and the rear of the now-empty fuselage snapping backward on the arrester cable.

There is no doubt that with the F6C-4 the Navy had decided finally that radiators belonged in a Victorian home rather than on an aircraft whose pilot was dependent not only on the mechanical integrity of the engine, but on a temperamental radiator with enough pipe and fittings to keep any plumber's apprentice happy.

Following the introduction of the Curtiss F6C-4, no liquid-cooled aircraft ever flew again off carriers in quantity, with perhaps the sole excep-

tion of the British Seafire, a seagoing Spitfire.

For the people who fly, and primarily for those who make a living at it, the name Al Williams is a legend; in this writer's opinion he was one of the greatest aviators who ever wore a helmet and goggles.

Al was a man of many parts. Among them, he was an able writer, with very considerable knowledge of politics, history, social science, and economics. Al was a pianist of almost concert caliber, as well as a boxer nearly good enough to fight for a living in the ring.

With a mind and a body that could encompass a scholar's dreams and an athlete's prowess, Al was also something of a rebel and a believer in self-created destiny. The military is happy to use talents but not always dreams, as was once again demonstrated in the service career of Lieutenant Alford Williams. As a Navy pilot he set many records, but as the rugged individualist, he was perhaps better fitted for civilian life.

When our story first touches Al, he has just taken delivery at Curtiss in Buffalo of a Navy F6C-4 fighter, sporting, of all things, for power, a British Bristol Jupiter sleeve valve engine.

Al gave many flight exhibitions and demonstrated aerobatics and dive-bombing with the Gulf Hawk. In the years that followed, Al's name was to become a legend to pilots everywhere, and perhaps most of all, to the youth of my generation, for Al never forgot that the pilots of tomorrow come from the sky-lifted eyes of today. In the 1930s he helped create a club and a group of junior aviators. They had wings and certificates and programs leading toward flying. Many thousands of them later served their country gallantly in World War II.

Gulf Oil sponsored Al and furnished the wherewithal, not only to keep the original Gulf Hawk flying, but also enough for him to buy both a single-seat Grumman F3F and a two-seat version. It is almost impossible in our day of the tight dollar to realize that in the late 1930s Gulf Oil paid the gas and oil bills of any aircraft owner who flew to the Miami Air Races. I was one of the many who flew to Florida, thanks to the far-sightedness of the company.

World War II had come and gone, and like many other pilots, I had put away my naval aviator's greens, except for weekend Naval Reserve flying. Through circumstances too time-consuming to relate here, I had become interested in collecting and restoring antique aircraft and had started with a Messerschmitt Bf 109, a Sopwith F1 Camel, a Nieuport 28, a German Pfalz DXII, and a Spad VII. When acquired, these aircraft were all almost basket cases. In spite of facing a project in rebuilding about as easy as constructing the pyramids with a couple of wheelchair patients, I was still vitally interested in any different antique aircraft.

On a dull market day, my cousin, who is a broker on Wall Street and a yachtsman of international fame, was discussing the unusual interests of his family with another broker. Inevitably, my aviation interests came up, and my cousin's business associate mentioned that he knew of a couple of old aircraft stored in a New York aviation trade school soon to be closed. To find a really rare or unusual antique through this kind of a lead is about as likely as the old prospector literally falling into the mine shaft of the Lost Dutchman mine.

The broker's tenuous lead reached me in several months, and I called him when I was in New York City, expecting to hear about an early home-built airplane. When he mentioned that he thought one of the "wrecks" was Al Williams' old Curtiss Gulf Hawk, I nearly exploded. The shattered door hinges on the telephone booth were testimony to my speed in reaching the school. The midtown Manhattan building looked old enough to have been built by Peter Stuyvesant's stonemasons, but on the fifth floor rested a real Hawk; forlorn, broken feathers clipped, but nonetheless, a Hawk. Not only did it show its proud heritage, but it was still in the colors and markings of Al's Gulf Hawk.

Months were to go by, with correspondence with the school all favorable to my acquiring the Hawk.

Al Williams' famous Gulf Hawk, fully reconstructed and
a gem to fly.

Al Williams' Curtiss Gulf Hawk

Specifications

ENGINE	650-hp Pratt & Whitney 1340
SPAN	31 ft., 6 in.
LENGTH	22 ft., 10 in.
HEIGHT	8 ft., 11 in.
CREW	1
EMPTY WEIGHT	2161 lbs.
USEFUL LOAD	802 lbs.
GROSS WEIGHT	2963 lbs.
FUEL CAPACITY	50 gals.
ARMAMENT	2 .30 Brownings

Performance

MAXIMUM SPEED	155 mph
RATE OF CLIMB	2000 fpm
STALL SPEED	57 mph
ENDURANCE	3 hrs.
SERVICE CEILING	22,900 ft.

Lockheed Vega

Specifications

ENGINES	300-hp Pratt & Whitney Wasp Junior; Hamilton ground-adjustable propeller
SPAN	41 ft.
LENGTH	28 ft., 6 in.
HEIGHT	9 ft., 2 in.
PASSENGER AND CREW CAPACITY	5
EMPTY WEIGHT	2050 lbs.
USEFUL LOAD	1000 lbs.
GROSS WEIGHT	3050 lbs.
FUEL CAPACITY	135 gals.

Performance

MAXIMUM SPEED	168 mph
RATE OF CLIMB	800 fpm
STALL SPEED	53 mph
ENDURANCE	7.5 hours (slow cruise)
SERVICE CEILING	17,800 ft.

The Lockheed Vega, a versatile aircraft of the Thirties, under Varney Airlines colors.

I was engaged in a motion picture in California when I got a hurried call from the school saying that due to circumstances beyond their control, they had to have the school building cleared the following day of all equipment, including the Curtiss Hawk. Lockheed Constellations being the fastest aerial transportation coast-to-coast in those days, I boarded the first one available.

My brother, who had a farm in New Jersey, met me with his truck and a few farmworkers, and we raced to the school. Unfortunately, no disassembly had been done, and we had to take the aircraft apart with Stilson wrenches and tools hurriedly purchased at a nearby hardware store. It was a dark, rainy, dismal day, and the steelriggers we had hired to lower the plane to the street had apparently had a bit of the grape to ward off the chill, and the sounds coming from the court six floors down and the roof above sounded like an Irish wake. I expected to see bodies falling like raindrops while they were rigging the "I" beam on the roof to lower the Hawk.

My most vivid memory is standing precariously on the railing of the wet, windswept fire escape six floors above Manhattan's unyielding concrete streets with one puny leg trying to ward off the pendulumlike movement of the descending Hawk fuselage as it threatened to smash against the building's side.

Five hours of labor worthy of the French penal colonies saw the Hawk and its components stowed on the straw in the truckbed, and standing before a desperately unhappy and perplexed toll collector at the Holland Tunnel. It is only fair to mention that this was New York's rush hour, and traffic, as always, was backed on

The Gulf Hawk refurbished and as A1 had known it.

every approach street for more than a mile. Living safely in California now, I can honestly say that this exact timing was planned. With a last horrified look and the honks of thousands of enraged motorists behind me, the toll collector despairingly waved me through. If this rather unfair problem had not been created I believe we would still be trying to get one large fighter airplane off Manhattan Island.

Brother's New Jersey barn kept the Hawk dry for months while I tried to find some way of getting it to the West Coast without coming up with the equivalent in gold bullion of the San Francisco Mint. I might well have looked to the bronzed doors of the Mint, for the Gulf Hawk was to become the most costly and long-lived project I have ever attempted in the antique aircraft restoration field.

The quoted rates for trucking an airplane as heavy as the Hawk from New Jersey to California closely approximated the national debt. Consequently, we solved the problem by buying a used furniture van at auction, and following a trip as fraught with as much travail and perils as Lewis and Clark's famous expedition, the Hawk arrived in California at my hangar in Riverside.

Literally years were to elapse before Al Williams' Curtiss Hawk was in flying condition, but in spite of the many problems, the Hawk's reconstruction required less specialized skills than, for example, the Pfalz D12.

An inventory of missing items, or items to replace on the Hawk, read as follows: The wheel brakes and backing plates were gone; all movable tail surfaces were missing; the cockpit was gutted with an ax, the panel and pedals were gone, and the throttle quadrant was missing; the metal-skinned fuselage, which Al had added

in the thirties, was beaten in by hammers as though by demented tinsmiths; the lower-wing ribs hung down fore and aft of the spar like a windsock on a hangar in a dead calm, and all were broken. One has only to look at the blueprints on the Curtiss Hawk and realize that every rib top and bottom is different in both taper, depth, and chord, to realize the enormity of the woodwork repair.

The engine remaining in the airplane was an early 1820-hp Wright with a fixed-pitch propeller, and the engine was in deplorable condition, with accessories missing as well. We replaced it later with a Pratt & Whitney R1340.

During the first year, most of the woodwork and ribs were completed on the lower wing. In the second year, the woodwork on the upper and lower wings was finished, and the movable tail surfaces were finished. During the third year, we bought a Navy SNJ, and turning my Navy gold wings to the wall and getting a good grip on my nostalgia, we tore it completely apart and used a great many of its components in the Hawk.

Engine prop, wheels, brakes, instruments, throttle quadrant, pedals, and many other items came out of the supply bin of this now badly stripped ex-Navy advanced trainer. I must admit to some moments of uncertainty in destroying one aircraft to build another, for the memory of night formations in SNJ's in the warm summer evening around Corpus Christi with the moon brightly lighting the cumulus clouds, and the twinkling lights of the city and the moonlit water below, remain some of the loveliest moments of a lifetime of flying. The SNJ will always be a favorite airplane to me.

In the fourth year, the components began to go together. The massive

The colorful, fan-shaped tail section.

steel tube wire braced fuselage was sand-blasted and painted, and the original fuel tanks were pressure-checked and reinstalled. Interestingly enough, the tanks were contoured for both sides of the fuselage and were actually part of the original outer skin of the aircraft. Imagine their vulnerability for any weapon larger than a BB gun!

The single-span upper wing had been covered with two layers of Irish linen when it was picked up in the school and was still quite capable of denting anything except a diamond-tipped fabric punch. When stripped, the upper wing had much of the complexity and strength of the Eiffel Tower and looked to be about the same length.

We recovered the wing surfaces in a heavy ceconite, and because of the speed of the aircraft, the stitching had to be close, adding many a callus to some already sore hands. The potato-bag weave of the heavy ceconite covering posed some finishing problems, and heads were scratched bald before a genius came up with using an automobile body filler on top of the dope,

Taxiing out for the test flight—the moment I had waited
for throughout all those long months of reconstruction.

which created a lasting finish at least the equal of the best thirty- and forty-coat pre-World War II dope finishes.

Reskinning the Hawk's fuselage meant removing every piece of metal skin and painstakingly flattening them out on the hangar floor, then, jigsaw-like, cutting new pieces and arduously reassembling them like the most complicated puzzle. With no photos to guide us, the routing of wires, controls, and instruments required a great deal of the old "cut and try."

The most stirring of all times in a pilot's career is certainly his first solo, and yet any flight in a strange airplane, representing years of concentrated work, research, and pork barrels full of money can, believe me, represent the same quickening of the pulse and weakness in the knee area.

It was a lovely spring day in Riverside, and the newly painted orange-and-blue Hawk was a sight to behold. The Pratt & Whitney R1340 engine, in spite of its massive appearance, is like its smaller brother, the R985, a relatively easy engine to prop, and because of the weight of the Hamilton constant-speed propeller, you can swing it through comfortably. The engine started with its pleasant characteristic—chunk-a-chunk—and with oil pressure up and everything reading O.K., I started out from the line. I tried the typically weak SNJ-At6 brakes, and memory of dragging one's feet or throwing out an anchor to stop came to mind. A full-swivel tail wheel on the Hawk did not add to my comfort.

Visibility on the ground was never good on the military Hawks, and with the beer-barrel metalized fuselage, it is even worse. In spite of my six-foot-one frame and a thick seat-pack chute, I could safely clear the area ahead only by employing our old primary flight training tactics of seesawing down the taxiway. Running the propeller through, checking fuel, oil pressure, temperature, head temperature, carburetor heat, and freedom of controls pretty much completed my takeoff check.

The full-throated bellow of the Pratt & Whitney lets anyone not stone deaf know that a real airplane is on the way, and the large square

With power, climbing at 1800 fpm.

rudder has almost instant response. Getting the tail up in level altitude so I could see the narrow runway area required about 150 feet in the 8-knot wind. As the Hawk broke ground, as always I checked all axes, and the controls were smooth and positive, with only the ailerons giving less response than I might have wished. Rigging was first-rate, and I climbed out with an indicated 100 mph and 1200 fpm on the rate of the climb.

In spite of the tapered wings, power-on and power-off stalls are straight forward, and the Hawk doesn't leave you, as some tapered-wing aircraft do, by suddenly finding to your surprise that the earth is now where the sky had been a micro-second ago. The power-on stall was uncomfortably nose-high and broke at about 46 mph, while the power-off stall broke easily at about 55 mph.

Due undoubtedly to the big engine and its closeness to the cockpit, as well as the small cockpit opening, the Hawk is just plain *hot*, and you could probably fly around in your undies in wintertime without undue discomfort.

Leveling out at 1850 rpm and 28 inches of manifold pressure and pushing the throttle wide open for about a minute gave me almost 155 mph indicated at 3500 feet of altitude.

197

Leaving aerobatics to another day, I let down, proud as a peacock, into the crowded gnat-like swarm of light aircraft hovering around Riverside. From the 180 point, the narrow runway began to take on the fearsome aspects of an aircraft carrier deck, but by a forward slip I was able to keep the runway clear until just the second before touchdown. I varied from 75 to 80 mph in the forward slip and required several seconds of straight-ahead 3-point attitude before the speed killed to the late fifties and it landed gently, with considerable spongy travel on the gear struts not unlike the Lockheed Vega.

The rudder kept the Hawk on course, but for the uninitiated, there is an uncomfortable and completely unjustified feeling of its getting away from you directionally.

Later, many pleasant hours were spent in the Curtiss Hawk, exploring its aerobatic characteristics and its air show possibilities. If one could add a small portable coolant unit, *à la* the astronauts' survival suit, aerobatics in the Hawk could be great fun. But without it the additional power required for starting adds an entire new heat factor to the already hot cockpit.

Like the Boeing P-12, F100, and F4B1, all the Hawk series "were Hell for Stout," and no maneuvers that my delicate carcass could survive could tear these airplanes apart. It is a comforting thought when standing on the rudder in a vertical dive with the altimeter wildly unwinding and the wires howling, that this bird is not built from the same grade of tissue paper as our current crop of airplanes.

Many but *not all* aerobatics are pleasant in the Hawk. Loops can start at any speed from 120 mph up, and because of the horsepower and the high-lift wing, you can climb with them and play with them all the way around. Cuban 8s or Immelmans require a little more speed because the carburetor on the 1340 cuts out when inverted. Snap rolls at 85 mph are wallowy and not crisp, as in a Stearman, partially due to the fact that the ailerons are inadequate and that the wing wants to keep on flying. Slow rolls are disappointing and must be entered nose high at a speed sufficiently great to finish the entire roll from the vertical, because the engine quits cold and the limited ailerons make the roll quite slow.

It is perhaps worth mentioning that the Boeing F4B2 and the Hawk were great air show airplanes in their day and made beautiful loops in the sky and a great deal of noise that thrilled the crowds, but they are in no way comparable to the modern international class of aerobatic aircraft, such as the Zlinn, Yak, Chipmunk, Jungmeister, Pitts, or others whose sole purpose for existence is precise, delicately controlled aerobatics.

Taxiing in the Gulf Hawk after a show, one sees the unvarnished admiration for this most beautiful of birds in the eyes of all pilots. It is doubtful to this aviator that a lovelier-looking biplane ever flew.

Curtiss P-40E

THERE CERTAINLY WAS never a more exciting and pugnacious nose and spinner on an aircraft than the painted tiger shark front of the Curtiss P-40 fighter. The immortal P-40 of the Fying Tigers was an outgrowth of the Hawk series of the 1920's, and its rugged construction and general reliability drew much from the earlier biplane.

Like its Navy counterpart, the Grumman Wildcat, the Curtiss P-40 was the only Army Air Corps aircraft to be in squadron service prior to World War II and still operational in one squadron at the end of the global conflict. Unfortunately, when World War II broke out, the performance of the P-40 was already inferior to that of the majority of its antagonists, and in spite of the many changes, from Allison to Merlin and back to Allison engines, as well as its gradual increase

in maximum load-carrying capacity, from 8000 pounds to over 11,000 pounds, it still remained just a sturdy, reliable fighter that really shined only in the hands of the skilled pilot and the careful tactician.

Although it served in every theater of World War II—North Africa, the Soviet Union, the Far East, and Europe —its most gallant hour was its service in China, when between December 1941 and July 1942 the American Volunteer Group, flying P-40B's and -E's, destroyed 286 Japanese aircraft against the loss of eight pilots killed and four missing in action. In China, the newer P40E was gratefully received and was vitally necessary to combat the superior performance of the Mitsubishi A6M Zero Sen fighter. The armor, the bulletproof glass, the self-sealing tanks, and the mounting of additional .50-caliber guns instead

Buckling in and running through a cockpit check in the P-40E.

of .30's, plus its ability to dive away from a Zero, made the Tiger P-40E an extremely formidable antagonist for the fast but structurally weak Japanese fighters.

Our's is about the last remaining short-fuselage E Model P-40 still flying regularly anywhere in the world. Several times while flying this P-40 I have been boiled in coolant, covered with hydraulic oil, immersed in engine oil, and I have considered making peace with my Maker if He would only listen, but somehow, after each episode, I come down a little more enthusiastic about its ruggedness and good flying qualities.

Early aircraft, as you now know, are really my deepest and most personal interest, but for the motion-picture industry and for our Movie-

land of the Air Museum we still fly and collect the famous aircraft of both wars. The opinions of the flight characteristics and handling qualities of the P-40 are, in my case at least, not based on combat experience and consequently may be somewhat disputed by a veteran fighter pilot.

On my first flight in this particular P-40 I spent an overly long time taxiing and the engine boiled on takeoff, fogging the windshield and leaving me partially blind. I made my first landing in the shortest circle of the field ever managed, with my nerves playing like the string section of the local symphony. On my second flight, the canopy blew off due to a broken release spring in the emergency exit system. The noise was like an exploding cannon and the damage was

A beautiful in-flight view from below showing the wheels
in their rotated flat position retracted in the wings.

nearly as great, for the canopy went at about 240 mph, tumbling and tearing holes in the wing root, fuselage, and stabilizer. When my stomach settled down, I found the flight characteristics and handling qualities unimpaired, so I flew 350 miles to my destination, and except for about a week with an ear trumpet (due to the short stacks of the 1250-hp Allison and a cold from the super air conditioning), everything turned out all right.

Unlike my flights in World War I and other early aircraft, I never walk out to the P-40 or any military aircraft or World War II without first getting the *Pilot's Aircraft Handbook*. It rests, when in flight, between the parachute and the seat. It's a comforting research library, if ever my brain becomes as hard and unyielding as the aluminum seat does on a long flight. A walk-around inspection of the P-40 is like a night stroll in some of our tougher cities. You'd better keep your eyes open for unsecured cowling; hydraulic, coolant, oil, or fuel leaks; loose trim tabs; rust or corrosion; and improper tire pressure, which are all "sight" items and grounds for downing the aircraft. Finally, when you climb up the root of the wing and settle in the cockpit, you find it rather strangely shallow, yet the instrument board seems far enough away to need 7 × 50 binoculars to read the gauges. After buckling in, the starting procedure is simple, requiring fuel, boost pump, battery switch, ignition, and energizing; then you must keep it running with primer until the forward movement of the mixture control takes over.

My naval career will probably be scuttled for this opinion, but there is no sweeter engine sound than that of a lovely-running Allison, and as the engine settles down, one should be most careful to see that the coolant doors are manually opened. As you taxi out to the takeoff position, you feel like the rear man on the fire department ladder truck trying to see around the long front end, yet "S" turning clears the way ahead, and the wonderful steering of the Curtiss tail wheel makes it easy. Prior to takeoff, you go through a standard checkoff list, with particular attention paid to the Curtiss electric prop and its idiosyncrasies. Due to the relatively short fuselage of the E model (later lengthened 3 feet in the N version), each inch of manifold pressure on takeoff can be felt, and considerable opposite rudder must be used to counteract torque. At 46 inches and 3000 rpm on the 1710–99 Allison, we are airborne in about 800 feet. Comfortable climbout is at 140 mph, 35 inches, 2600 rpm, and almost 2000 fpm rate of climb.

Lifting the gear on the P-40 means moving the gear handle up, then pushing the electric hydraulic power button on the stick that actuates the pump; unless the button is held for approximately thirty seconds, the gear will sometimes trail. The electric power drain is considerable, on the order of 35 to 38 amps. At 5000 feet without a proper canopy (in this case, one that does not close completely), we can get almost 290 mph indicated.

Unlike most other fighter aircraft, the P-40 requires a rudder trim for any airspeed change of 5 mph or over; consequently, unless you want to look like someone born on the side of a hill, you have to perpetually retrim rudder for every difference in attitude or speed. The ailerons are pure delight, and in my opinion far pleasanter, faster, and lighter than those of the much-vaunted P-51.

During the filming for this pilot report, I had the all-too-rare oppor-

Pulling away after a run on a bogus Zero.

tunity to chase a bogus Zero around (a structurally much-altered AT-6, which we use for motion pictures) and had no trouble staying with it at its low speed. Stalls develop rapidly with the P-40 and generally roll to the left, with a sharp drop of the nose. With flaps and gear up, it stalled at 88 mph indicated, with buffet warning enough so you would have to be solid lead not to get the message. In aerobatics, due to the lovely ailerons, rolls and inverted flight are delightful as long as you keep the cockpit free of old box lunches, dead cats, and other loose items. After twenty seconds in-

verted, the pressure starts to drop and it's time to go right side up again. Rolls can be made from 130 to 250 mph. A loop commenced at 240 mph at 5000 feet hit 7600 on top, with a speed over the top of 120 mph, and required either a heavy foot or rudder trim most of the way around.

If the reader wonders about the stunt altitudes, recognize the writer's backbone color, for if you ever really lose a fighter and don't have plenty of recovery altitude, your relatives will soon be looking in the classified section of the telephone directory under the "Mortuary" column. Through the

The colorful, typical Flying Tiger nose.

The climax of our air show as I finally caught up with my "bogey," the bogus Zero.

years I have made it a practice to stay more than *high enough* when checking out a fighter in stunt maneuvers, and on occasion the precaution has paid off.

I generally do only speed maneuvers with fighter types and never spin them for a show or rarely ever do snap maneuvers. In our combat sequence for air pageants, I use mainly fly-by maneuvers, for the FAA can take on all the menace of a summer Texas thunderhead when you turn into a crowd. This turning away and the fly-bys are most proper safety precautions. In practice the Zero and the P-40 dive from opposite ends of the field, looping in front of the crowd, and because the loop is so much larger in the P-40, I throttle back and widen my pullout, letting the bad guy get on my tail.

With two passes and the kids in the audience howling for the sheriff, the Zero loses me and I pick him up and chase him through climbing figure 8s. On cue the Zero cuts loose the smoke and dives to his well-cheered destruction behind some carefully selected natural screen.

Currently in my shows I am flying a P-40N, which is a later two-place model of the P-40E and is one of the very few P-40's ever built with a full operating set of controls and gyro instruments in both cockpits. This P-40N is slightly less prone to veer for the jackrabbits on takeoff than the E, but otherwise the stunt capabilities are the same, and my two-place N model actually has gun mounts and ammunition boxes in the wings.

Returning to the field after my check flight, and trying to insinuate the Hawk between the lagging local traffic, makes me wish he still had loaded .50's. The gear should be dropped at 175 mph or below, with flaps below 140 mph. The gear requires the reverse of the takeoff sequence, and after approximately thirty seconds of the electric pump, one should crosscheck by attempting to move the large emergency hand pump located by your right hand. It's as large as a Louisville slugger, and if you can activate it, you can be sure that you and the P-40 are due for a base slide on your respective posterior with the gear as yet unlocked and ready to fold. If it checks out hard and unmovable, you're O.K. The approach is at about 105 mph with 90 to 95 safe over the fence. Your visibility is as good as any liquid-cooled aircraft and your all-out stall speed with flaps and gear down is about 78 mph. Wheel landings seem to be easiest and directional control is good, though the tail is light and requires full backstick. Cowl flaps are manually opened. As you taxi back be careful to reach for the top handle for the flaps, for the handle below it is for the gear.

As the P-40 spins around to a stop and the wonderful sound of the Allison dies, I wonder how many of the more than seventeen thousand Curtiss Hawks built in World War II still fly and give pilots as much pleasure and thrill as this one does for me.

Boeing B-17 Flying Fortress

FEW OF THE air crews that so successfully spearheaded the American bombing offensive in Europe in World War II were ever aware of the Army Air Corps Project A in 1934 as being the father of the most successful and well-remembered heavy bomber of all time: Boeing's immortal B-17.

Unfortunately, but in keeping with a surprising number of experimental aircraft that ultimately become fine operational military aircraft, the original Boeing 299 crashed at Wright Field, Dayton, Ohio, in 1935 after having exceeded all requirements for speed, load-carrying, and altitude. But checkoff lists, which are a part of every housewife's day and are life-saving factors in today's complicated aircraft, were relative unknowns in 1935. Model 299, with both the

A giant in its time, our B-17 is dwarfed by the tail of a younger brother, the B-47 Stratojet, at March Air Force Base, California.

Closeup in flight with a good view of the broad wing and
the 17's armament.

Boeing crew and the Wright Field
Air Corps evaluation team aboard,
crashed shortly after takeoff solely
because the mechanical gust locks had
not been released in the cockpit.

For a lesser aircraft this would have
spelled its end, but a few far-seeing
advocates of American air power were
able to save the contract, and it was

let for thirteen YIB-17's instead of the
original sixty-five. The balance of the
purchase was made up of the fine,
steady, reliable Douglas B-18, already
obsolescent before purchase. The sad-
dle-and-saber-oriented Army officers
still controlled the Air Corps purse
strings, and the concept of a lot instead of few of quality appealed to the

The ubiquitous B-17 of World War II.

Boeing B-17G Flying Fortress

Specifications

ENGINES	4 Wright Cyclones, 1820–97's, 1200-hp each
SPAN	103 ft., 9 in.
LENGTH	74 ft., 9 in.
HEIGHT	19 ft., 1 in.
CREW	10
EMPTY WEIGHT	32,720 lbs.
USEFUL LOAD	22,280 lbs.
GROSS WEIGHT	55,000 lbs.
MAXIMUM OVERLOAD	72,000 lbs.
FUEL CAPACITY	2520 gals.
ARMAMENT	13 .50 Brownings: chin, nose, dorsal, center fuselage, ventral, waist, and tail

Performance

MAXIMUM SPEED	300 mph at 30,000 ft.
RATE OF CLIMB	900 fpm
STALL SPEED	85 mph
ENDURANCE	8½ hrs.
SERVICE CEILING	35,000 ft.

Curtiss P-40E

Specifications

ENGINE	1250-hp Allison 1710-99
SPAN	37 ft., 3½ in.
LENGTH	31 ft., 8½ in.
HEIGHT	10 ft., 7 in.
CREW	1
EMPTY WEIGHT	5590 lbs.
USEFUL LOAD	1959 lbs.
GROSS WEIGHT	7549 lbs.
FUEL CAPACITY	148 gals. internal tankage
ARMAMENT	6 .50-cal. Brownings

Performance

MAXIMUM SPEED	352 mph
RATE OF CLIMB	2860 fpm
STALL SPEED	78 mph
ENDURANCE	3½ hrs.
SERVICE CEILING	32,400 ft.

The distinctive tiger shark nose of the famous *Flying Tigers* P-40s.

Chiefs of Staff. No one as yet outside the Air Corps had any concept of strategic use of aircraft.

The year 1938 was a banner one for the supporters of the B-17. With great foresight, the Air Corps committed the major part of its B-17 force on a long-range navigational flight to South America, and it was successful beyond hope, both from a training point of view and as a showing of the flag, à la Teddy Roosevelt. This great feat very deservedly won the Mackay Trophy.

Even prior to this great flight, the Air Corps had ordered more B-17's—thirty-nine, to be exact—but they weren't delivered until July 1939.

With the Panzer hobgoblins of Hitler running across Europe like demonic imps and with the British lion backed in a corner, we gave Britain our ace in the hole, the Flying Fortress. Unfortunately, in combat the Fortress was found to have walls of clay and about as many teething troubles as a puppy on a new shag rug.

The Fortress burned with all the alacrity of a college celebration bonfire. It had enough systems failures to give the plumbers' guild a permanent nightmare. The .30-caliber guns were, even at this stage in the war, not much more lethal than Daisy's best air rifle. The crews suffered from oxygen fatigue and the ever-present drafts. Allowing for the B-17's many faults, Edward Wells, Boeing's brilliant engineer, and his staff undertook the general redesign of the Fortress and transformed it into what was to become a truly offensive airplane, though it never would be the untouchable Fortress that its lyrical publicity claimed.

The E model had basic structural changes. It was six feet longer than the earlier models, with ten feet greater span on the horizontal tail surface. The armament was increased to .50 caliber, with twin-power turrets added to the top of the fuselage and the bottom of the waist position and twin .50's in the tail position.

No fanfare was made of the changes with this model and subsequent models and changes came with the regularity of sunrise and sunset. On later airplanes literally hundreds of modifications were made, including ball-and-chin turrets, different engines, different and expanded tank capabilities, and different propellers. The alterations in the 17's that only battle experience could determine were essentially fed into the models with no break in production.

Only the flight crews that hit the silk or never returned were aware what a Barnum-type publicity campaign had been waged for the Fortress and how great a disservice it was to claim utter invincibility for the B-17's. So heavy was this loss in men and machines that it was quite possible that the losses of the big bombers on their massive raids over Germany might have been staggering if the raids had been continued without fighter escort, and all future daylight raids would have been canceled.

The advent of the P-47 jugs was as gratefully received by the bomber crews as a cold keg of beer in the Sahara. Because of their range, the great Republic P-47's were able to fly all the way into target and still escort the 17's back to England. Just prior to this happy appearance the losses of B-17's damaged and destroyed exceeded more than two hundred a week, and neither America's Model T-like production lines nor all the Air Corps cannon-fodder flight training schools could begin to make up for this kind of mayhem and destruction.

To the glorious battle flags of the

Eighth Air Force and other units flying B-17's must go a star of honor, for even with heavy losses approaching the debacle of the Light Brigade at Balaklava, the B-17's were never daunted nor turned back from a raid.

A possible surprise to some of our air historians is the fact that nearly twice as many B-24 Liberators were built as B-17's, and that the Liberator was not only faster but carried a heavier bombload than the B-17. But the B-24 never received the popular acclaim given to the so-called Flying Fortress. Such is the power of advertising.

The vulnerability of the B-17 never really improved, for unfortunately it burned easily and was readily deep-sixed by frontal attacks, not, as widely supposed, because of lack of forward firing guns, but due mainly to the absence of heavy armor plate which no one thought to add for protection on head-on runs.

Construction of a B-17 might well have originated with the engineers of the Brooklyn Bridge, for the truss-type main spar was braced between sections with girders, and an interior corrugated skin made extraordinarily stout structure. The wing section also gave the B-17 high lift. The fuselage was made up of assemblies, each of semimonocouque structure riveted skins to stringers and bulkheads.

Engines were different models of the 1820 Wright series, and although they were sometimes prone to use oil as though each aircraft had its own Texas gusher, they were still liked and trusted.

Early in the design (as for the DC-3 and the C-47), the wheels were left protruding from the nacelles far enough in the retracted position to be used to actually land on and still have differential braking. On many an occasion this one design feature made

literally weeks of difference in returning a battle-damaged B-17 to full operational status.

The battle damage of B-17's transcended all expectations of what any aircraft could take and still fly. B-17's returned to England with the whole nose blown away, almost to the pilot's instrument panel. They crashed on the coast of England on a descending path starting almost at target zone, with only one red-hot engine still operative. They got home with only ailerons and elevators and the tiniest stub of the vertical tail remaining.

The structure was sound enough to absorb a gash clear through the fuselage from the wing of an angry Messerschmitt, and only on landing did the fuselage buckle, without harm to the crew.

On the dreadful daylight raids not to lose an engine or sustain damage in one of the major structural parts was akin to a rodeo star sitting out his stint in the grandstands.

It has always seemed to me from my own experience that flying a fighter required less raw courage than that required by the bomber crews, who had to constantly walk through flak corridors and incredible Luftwaffe fighter interception. Every job in war is tough, but to sit like a lobster in a trap waiting to be speared by German 20-mm cannon shells is the highest type of devotion to duty. A flak vest or armor on such a plane seems to have all the protective ability of a Wrigley's gum wrapper.

In spite of the fact that I am qualified to pilot many types of aircraft and flew some years before World War II, as an ex-Navy pilot, I was in some awe of the magnificent size and rugged appearance of the B-17. The only large airplanes that I had been lucky enough to fly before World War II were a Boeing 247, a DC-3, and the

The B-17 tail as it might have looked in formation.

venerable pleasant Tin Goose, the Ford Trimotor. It was to be many years after the war before I was to get my chance to fly a B-17.

Following my purchase of Paul Mantz's great fleet of historical aircraft and the merging of our firms under the name Tallmantz, both he and I undertook the task of looking for a flyable B-17 to answer the many calls from the motion-picture industry.

I must digress from my story for a moment to tell a tale about Paul that he loved to tell on himself. Shortly after the war he was in Florida doing the flying for the great movie *Twelve O'Clock High*. One of the scenes required was a crash landing in a B-17 with the wheels up. As mentioned earlier, like the DC-3 and C-47, the wheels protrude so that on touchdown you can actually use the brakes even with the wheels fully retracted.

The scene required Paul to come in with two engines feathered and slide through a command tent and other assorted objects. Like all movie shots it had its own high pucker factor, and Paul was earnestly convincing both himself and the studio production manager of the hazard to life and limb and the necessity of getting a rather large handful of cabbage for all this risk.

An ex-Eighth Air Force man came along and claimed he had made three wheels-up landings in England and that it was such a piece of cake he would do it for the sheer sport. Paul vainly tried to push him back, like the old pitchman at the carnival who is badgered by annoying kids.

Finally, the necessary coin of the realm was agreed to by all, and Paul took the B-17 *alone*. He had rigged everything in fours, the throttles, mixtures, props, cowl flaps, and had everything fitted so he could reach them from the pilot's seat.

The crash was one of the high points in *Twelve O'Clock High*, but it did not go off without an additional set of heart murmurs for Paul. The command tent was rigged with a balsa pole to break away when Paul slid into it. During the night an unpredictable wind arrived and flattened the tent; without consulting anyone, the grips set it up again, but this time with a piece of drill pipe in place of the original balsa.

The morning dawned clear, and Paul took off alone. Lining up perfectly, he slid the B-17 in on its belly and steered for the tent. At the last moment something told him to miss the direct, head-on approach. Instead of the canvas and balsa he expected, the drill pipe mashed the fuselage like a giant guillotine. Luckily Paul was unhurt.

When we built our nonprofit International Flight and Space Museum, we received Air Force permission for a long-term lease on a B-17. Unfortunately, the original aircraft consigned to us was stripped, so the Air Force let us have a B-17 in storage at Davis Monthan Air Force Base. Our Fortress is B-17 G-85-DL S/N 4483525. Like most large aircraft it was a white elephant, and what few people realize is that repairs on any aircraft like this are the responsibility of its new custodians and not the Air Force.

We started by replacing the glass and all the fabric and the tires, and then two 1820 Wright engines, and then a propeller, and—and—and. It took a crew of six a month and a half, and our costs were nudging fifteen thousand dollars when Jim Appleby, our ex-Air Force general manager, flew it home.

He was afraid of the superchargers, so he had them locked off and consequently could only draw thirty-one inches for takeoff, which is barely cruising power. The enormous run-

212

ways at Davis Monthan were none too long, and his breathtaking rate of climb approximated that of some of the new Volkswagen-powered planes. The first order of business when the ship got home was to set the turbos.

We were now able to support a number of Air Force shows and projects. Our restoration kept going, and we stripped and painted the B-17 (Wow!). We should have owned Sherwin-Williams. We located, bought, and mounted dummy turrets and guns.

As massive as the old girl is, she is rather restricted inside and is no great jungle gym for a guy like myself with one leg. Unable to enter from the front hatch under the pilot's compartment like some of my more Tarzan-like contemporaries, I go in the *Alice in Wonderland*-like rear door. If I took a left at the pass, I would be going to the tail gunner's compartment and be forced to thin out some to get over the tail wheel to the rear guns. Incidentally, these rear guns were the Fort's most valuable protection, and their lack was the initial reason why so many of the first Forts were lost in combat. If we turn right on entry we come to Hurricane Alley, where the waist gunners, more polar bears than men, endured the unbelievable cold of the open windows in the winter skies over Europe.

Farther up the companionway is the ball turret, with its rack and its limited ability to be raised and lowered. It was well known that ball-turret gunners were chosen from Singer's midgets, but small-in-stature was no measure of the long-on-guts necessary to operate in this lonely and exposed position.

Through the radio compartment (whose door to the bomb bay always reminds me of the water-tight ones on a submarine) and across the inches-wide catwalk between the

bomb racks is only a few feet, but it was not unusual during the war for a crewman to stand in the cyclone blast and cold to dislodge a live bomb, with his only safety a couple of ropes that a junior usher at Grauman's Chinese Theater would sneeze at.

The pilot's compartment would be spacious enough to stable a quarter horse if it weren't for the forward turret and other mechanisms filling the area. Between the pilot's and co-pilot's seats is a hatch that drops down to the crawlway to the bombadier's and navigator's positions. This front section is also relatively large, but on the later 17's it was somewhat cluttered with .50-caliber Brownings as well as assorted items like bomb sights, navigator's paraphernalia, etc.

As a pilot the most noticeable thing to me is that when you sit down in the left seat you look directly in front of you at an instrument panel about as bare of instruments as an 1898 Chanute hang glider. Like the early transport types, the gyros and flight instruments are in the center of the panel above the engine control pedestal. The pilot on IFR was forced to look to the right to scan, and the co-pilot to the left. It undoubtedly was a great maintenance and money-saving feature, but by even the standards of 1942 it was primitive.

With my wooden leg, the thick control column is noticeably short, and no matter what the seat adjustment, the big half wheel hits the peg leg a good part of the time. With many World War II bomber pilots of my size, any movement in winter furs must have been not only difficult but extremely uncomfortable.

Prior to my pilot-seat entry, the walk-around inspection of the B-17 is large-airplane routine, with the exception of seeing that the ball turret is stowed and its door locked (otherwise one might find the turret ripped off on

213

takeoff and the B-17 straddling a rolling ball like a sea lion in the circus). Perhaps the only other thing that really differs in a walk-around inspection is checking the four exposed turbo wheels for freedom of movement and no apparent cracks or damage. Without operating turbos, your B-17 has about the power of an anemic J3 Cub.

Back again in the left seat, the appearance of the control pedestal is cluttered, but primarily because the turbos add another set of four levers to your throttle's propeller control and mixture controls.

With our crew chief having pulled our propellers through, the checklist is in order, and essentially includes intercoolers cold, generators off, cowl, flaps open, hydraulic brake pressure and locked brakes with chucks, turbos off, boost pumps on, and fuel check. As on most large aircraft, you should use an APU or outside battery cart.

Using the start for about twelve seconds, you hit the primer and the mesh, and with a cloud of white smoke big enough to hide a small outhouse, the Wright cyclone starts with a satisfying bark. All engines follow starting procedure, from one to four.

At one time as copilot on the B-17 I managed to leave one of the subminiature switches in mesh (it is only a fraction of an inch down) and managed to burn out an expensive starter during an hour's flight.

Taxiing out requires room, and with the 103-foot wing you are continuously aware that civilian taxi strips were never built with a B-17 in mind.

Our crew chief is standing by the electric hydraulic pump switch, for the brakes can lose pressure, and as happened often in World War II, the old B-17 with nothing to stop it drifts off into the boondocks wreaking havoc on property and aircraft like a herd of enraged pachyderms.

Taxiing is slow, for to stop fifty thousand pounds requires room, and forward visibility isn't equal to that of a new Cessna 310. Like many Navy aircraft you taxi at all times with a locked tail wheel, which is the twin of another lever under the control pedestal, which locks elevators and rudder.

Having threaded our way between envious Beech, Piper, and Cessna drivers, we are ready for the runup. Apart from the pre-takeoff checklist, it is a good idea to look to the rear before the runup. Small aircraft seem to have a bewildering need to taxi behind when you have full power on, and they can be promptly scattered like maple leaves in a hurricane.

Adjusting your turbos with your throttles is the main difference from a normal checklist, and with all other items it takes several minutes to run through everything.

Lined up for the takeoff with your tail wheel locked, you walk the throttles forward with your right-hand palm upward. Possibly because I am not an experienced B-17 pilot this has always seemed awkward to me, and having the handful of throttles seems like trying to manipulate four spades with one hand while you dig a hole in your garden.

The tail comes up in about 1000 feet of roll, and shortly thereafter you are off slightly tail low and indicating 105 mph and accelerating. With gear up, a manifold pressure of 32 to 35 inches and a recommended climb at 140 mph, you have a chance to look around.

The ailerons are heavy, as is the rudder; and looking out to the left as I turn, the enormous wing has all the rounded, broad-backed look of a sperm whale. The rudder for my

214

wooden leg is perhaps the heaviest of any airplane I have flown since I lost the leg, and it requires real effort to use.

Cruising is faster than the handbook says, and is an indicated 170 mph at 5000 feet, with 25 inches and 2000 rpm. Starting turns with aileron are standard, and fortunately not much rudder is needed. Banks are kept shallow, because if flown with a warload a steep bank can sometimes exceed structural load limits for a B-17. Stalls with flap and gear down pay off at 80 mph or below, with not much wing drop; real care on recovery is needed so that you don't get fighter-type secondary stalls. Engine-out for the B-17 varies enormously, depending on the engine or engines, and requires fairly immediate rudder trim and heavy rudder forces. It will fly nicely unloaded on two and will go a helluva way on one.

Traffic pattern speeds were about par for current business aircraft. We began the landing checkoff list. One strange item is the miniature switch that controls the massive landing gear on the B-17; there is also another miniature switch for the flaps. Good visibility was available on the turn-in, and airspeed was about 105 mph. The float was appreciable; feeling for the ground a couple of apartment house stories away is always difficult in a strange, large airplane. It sat down at about 85 mph, and I had to be extremely careful of the brakes, for they were touchy (at one time I had burned a good chunk off a tire by touching the pedal too hard). The tail comes down an awfully long way back, and you feel a little like the engineer of a Rocky Mountain freight train. Unlocking the tail wheel and taxiing back to the line is the matter of a few minutes. Exiting through the nose bombadier's hatch is a great way to lose the seat of your trousers, because they always seems to be snagged on something sharp there.

As I look back at the bulk size and shape of our war-painted B-17 I muse that for me at least the majesty of flying any four-engine airplane far exceeds in pleasure the freedom of single-seater flight. Being lucky enough to handle the "Queen of the Heavies" is a never-to-be-forgotten experience even if it is more than a quarter of a century after the Fortress's bright day of glory.

Flying the left-hand seat of this "Queen of the Heavies" is a never-to-be-forgotten experience.

North American B-25 Mitchell

BEAUTY, THEY SAY, is in the eye of the beholder, and while the angular lines of a B-25 Mitchell bomber are more in keeping with Zasu Pitts than Rita Hayworth, still the reliability and exquisite handling qualities of this best of all medium bombers made it a pilot's pinup in World War II. Before the international holocaust was over, nearly ten thousand B-25s were to put their bent shoulders to the wings of war.

The idea for the B-25 germinated in a U. S. Army request in February 1938 for a fast medium bomber, and along with other manufacturers who sought the contract, North American entered the NA-40, a rather lumpish-looking shoulder-wing aircraft sporting Wright cyclones of 1300 hp, and a greenhouse-like area that looked like the aviary in the local zoo. Fortunately, or unfortunately, on the ferry flight to Wright Field it crashed and burned, though its crew got out all right.

In spite of the disappointment for North American Aviation, akin to having all of your money in stocks during the stock market crash in 1929, the NA-40 was completely redesigned and reengined under the able leadership of I. L. Atwood and R. H. Rice, and emerged from its cocoon as a B-25. It was so impressive and beautiful that the Air Corps ordered it sight unseen. It became one of the few aircraft ever purchased in quantity that had no X model or prototype.

There was little resemblance between the first *vingt-cinq* and the NA-40, for the horsepower had been

In the control tower at Guaymas, Mexico, sending out a flight for the filming of *Catch 22*.

increased by more than a third, the speed upped forty miles per hour, and the crew increased from three to five. The bombload had doubled, and the armament had gone from three hand-held .30-caliber Brownings and one .50, to two power turrets with twin .50 calibers, plus single .50's in the nose and tail.

Throughout the war the B-25 was to wear as many different hats as the top banana at Minsky's burlesque house. Among jobs and models, the B-25 served as high-level bomber, low-level bomber, torpedo plane, gunship carrying a .75-mm cannon, multigun strafer mounting as many as eighteen .50-caliber guns, reconnaissance-photographic aircraft, VIP transport, and trainer. A highlight in its career was its use as the immortal carrier-born Tokyo Raiders, which were to strike the first sparks of fear in the heart of Japan.

This bold judo punch was conceived early in the war, and both the B-26 Marauder (the Widowmaker) and the B-25 were considered, but the enormously superior takeoff performance of the B-25 made it the only choice for the carrier-borne attack.

The raid requirements are interesting, for the B-25 had to carry a 2000-pound bombload, have a range of 2400 miles (almost the distance from Los Angeles to New York nonstop), and be able to take off in 700 to 750 feet. Modifications for the raid included removing the bottom turret, replacing the tail guns with broomstick dummies, and adding nearly 400 gallons of gas to make a total fuel capacity of 1141 gallons. The Norden bombsight, being at that time a secret and rare as the alchemists' formula for turning baser metals into gold, was left home, and a simple substitute sight of cross hairs and body English were added to this mission, whose altitude was never to be over 1500 feet.

Members of the 17th Bombardment

In the left-hand seat of the *Vestal Virgin* over the Gulf of Cortez, and in tight formation.

group and the 89th Reconnaissance Squadron made up the crews who became more sailors than aviators. Having had the pleasure of flying a lot of hours in the left-hand seat of a B-25, I marvel that these relatively young and inexperienced volunteer Air Corps pilots were able to coax out of the B-25 that almost unbelievable takeoff performance. Needless to say, on breaking ground they were as far from V-2 speed as we are now from the outer galaxies.

Aircraft carriers of the day had deck elevators more in keeping with Navy Curtiss Sea Hawk biplanes than B-25s. Consequently, the B-25s spent the entire voyage lashed down on the open deck. Due to a most unlucky and chance meeting with a Japanese patrol boat, the raid was launched many hundreds of miles farther out than

anticipated, and in a violent storm with heavy seas. Lt. Col. Jimmie Doolittle, stunt pilot, race pilot, recordholder, and scientist, led the flight off the pitching deck.

Tokyo, Nagoya, Yokohama, and Kobe were struck by the swift, low raiders. The actual damage in no way matched the incredible psychological shock that the Japanese received. Till this time, the Japanese homeland had been inviolate, and the bombing was as unexpected as having a Martian land at the gates of the Imperial Palace in a flying saucer.

With only the most primitive weather reporting from China, all aircraft on the raid were lost. No radio facilities, bad weather, darkness, poor maps, and shortage of fuel caused the loss of every plane and a few lives. Fortunately, only a few crew members

218

were captured by the Japanese, and most made it back to friendly hands. As a result of this gallant raid, Japan kept four first-line fighter groups stationed in the homeland to protect against other raids instead of reinforcing urgently needed Japanese fighter squadrons in the Solomons.

Another figure as legendary as the great General Doolittle was also to have enormous influence on the design and abilities of the B-25. Lt. Col. Pappy Gunn, U. S. Army Air Corps, ex-naval aviator and manager of Philippine Air Lines, became a fearsome thorn in the side of Japan. He was anything but the comic-strip character that his name resembles. His one-man crusade against the Japanese began following the fall of the Philippines and the internment of his wife and children in a Japanese prison camp.

Colonel Gunn's activities sometimes took on the color and aura of the pirate, Captain Kidd. His love affair with the B-25 started when he and his crew chief made a midnight requisition of a Netherlands East Indies B-25 and flew it to Port Moresby in New Guinea. Later they flew with the Third Attack Group from a secret base in the Philippines and operated ten B-25s and three B-17s.

Due to a disappointing dearth of bomb targets in the South Pacific and a lack of aircraft with more than mosquito-bite strafing capability, Gunn decided, with the imaginative and capable help of Jack Fox, North American's dispossessed Royal Netherlands technical adviser, to build a B-25 that had enough firepower to sink everything but a battlewagon or cruiser. Four forward-firing .50-caliber guns were added where the bombardier and navigator's positions had been, and these were followed later by other homemade mounts for packages of two .50's on each side of the nose of the fuselage. Later, these were followed by the tentpole-like length of a 20-mm cannon buried in the bombardier's crawlway.

The ultimate proof of the effectiveness of Pappy's gunship concept was

Lining up for inspection of pilots and crews at Base *Guaymas*.

the lopsided Japanese defeat in the Battle of the Bismarck Sea. Coming in at a height where the sharks and porpoises had to duck, the A-20s and B-25s were purported to have put three Japanese cruisers, seven destroyers, twelve merchant ships, and fifteen thousand troops in the deep six! An additional one hundred Japanese aircraft were claimed by the multigun 20s and 25s.

In a later incident, a Japanese destroyer was sunk by a single 75-mm shell from a B-25. The same aircraft managed later to down a four-engine reconnaissance aircraft with his second round.

Before we leave armament, it is perhaps well to mention the ill-conceived remote twin .50 turret that faired into the bottom of the fuselage of the early-model B-25s. It was necessary for the gunner to adopt a graceful position akin to milking a cow, but because of the optical arrangement of the sighting periscope he not only looked down but faced backward to the path of flight. The gunner's effectiveness was rapidly reduced because of the strange optics, and many suffered from severe cases of airsickness. Because the lower turret gunner with this installation was about as useful as a pickpocket in handcuffs, the installation was removed on all subsequent models.

Some four hundred G model B-25s were turned out beginning in 1943, and as a model group they were to carry the heaviest bored airborne cannon of the war. It was probably an old cavalryman singing two choruses of "The Caissons Go Rolling Along" who mounted a French 75 mm in the B-25. Potent weapon that it was, the rate of fire was limited, with rarely more than two rounds expended in a run, and because it required a steady platform for proper air, the B-25 be-

came very vulnerable to ground fire. The gunner-navigator had to hand-feed the heavy shells, stay out of the way of the 21-inch recoil and hope that he didn't blow his eardrums with each shell. With each 75-mm shot, the B-25G hesitated like a Missouri mule at the edge of a crevasse. As the war progressed and few targets of value were available, most G models were converted to multi-.50-caliber gun installations.

Following the war, Paul Mantz, my late partner, was to be one of the first people to buy and operate a surplus B-25. Paul recognized the superiority of the B-25 plan form and its future uses as an infinitely versatile flying camera platform. Our company has now operated B-25s two years shy of a quarter of a century—far and away longer than anyone else in the world.

The optically corrected Cinerama camera nose that is such a trademark of our company came about with a series of steps, both varied and protracted. As some students of the motion-picture business may know, the industry's interest in aviation dates back to as early as 1913. In one of the early film melodramas, a death-defying aviator named Glenn Martin (later to become president of one of the great aviation firms in the world) rescued a fair damsel by air from the greasy clutches of a villain with enough hair to make him a dead ringer of King Kong. In this early day and later, some kind of aerial camera platform had to be provided, and up until World War II a wide variety of aircraft were used for such filming, ranging from Jennies and C3B Stearmans to Lockheed Altairs and Ford Trimotors. The cameraman rode anywhere from the upper wing and the gear spreader to hanging out the door securely anchored with a piece of frayed clothesline.

With the ending of the filming of *Catch 22*, this may indeed be one of the last times a squadron of authentic World War II bombers will be ever assembled for a formation flight so reminiscent of those days.

Most of the aerial cameramen were a hardy breed who graduated from hand-cranked cameras that looked like the phone on the pool hall wall, to considerably more modern power-driven models.

It actually took a war and the ability to buy postwar surplus material cheaply before the perfect aerial camera platform came into existence. It was the B-25, an airplane with strength, speed, stamina, range, and adequate room inside to mount the cameras. Sophisticated aerial filming really began with Paul's conversion of the B-25. Unfortunately, with the standard "Crystal Palace" greenhouse nose, no unobstructed panning shots could be made, so Paul started the conversion with large flat panes of safety glass. Unfortunately, under stress and high speed several panes of glass blew out, reducing the camera and flight crews to a state of nerves that no amount of Miltown could calm. But soon a solution to this was found.

When the new three-camera Cinerama process came into existence, the Cinerama Corporation approached Paul with the possibility of doing something in a flying vein that would give the audience the idea that they were sitting in the pilot's seat. With Paul's experience in over two hundred motion pictures, the ideas began flowing like a summer rain. Paul came up with a real cliff-hanger: Why not fly through the Grand Canyon?

The filming, which was a wild ride, stole the show and was seen by millions of people all over the world. Due to the excellent illusion of racing through the canyon, a sizable part of each audience headed for the rear of the theater on the dead run, hoping to make an exit before the green waves of airsickness overtook them.

Apart from Paul's skill and enormous knowledge, the only camera airplane in the world capable of carrying the great weight of the three huge Cinerama cameras was the B-25. At a cost of fifty thousand dollars and six months' work, Paul completely re-engineered the nose. The wrap-around unbraced glass was so well conceived and installed that after many years we are still using the same airplane.

This most successful first Cinerama picture was followed by Lowell Thomas's *Seven Wonders of the World.* Again, the same airplane with Paul as a pilot flew all over the globe. More than one hundred countries were visited, and the Pyramids, wildlife in Africa, and the Iguaçuand Angel Falls in South America were just a few of their targets. The high point of that trip was reached when in diving at speed into a live volcano for one cushion-swallowing second of film, both engines quit cold, apparently due to rising hot gases from the lava. Paul's skill and the stamina of the B-25 and its Wright R2600 engines saved the day.

In between other motion pictures and new Cinerama productions, our versatile B-25 managed test programs for the U. S. Government and private industry. Diversification was the order of the day, and we dropped borate on forest fires; made tests on drouge parachutes; flew inertial guidance systems; performed drop tests on missiles; acted as a target tow vehicle; and pioneered terrain-avoidance radar.

Being an old ex-Navy pilot type, my knowledge and experience of B-25s was confined to enjoying their angular lines from afar. When Paul and I became business partners, one of my first orders-of-the-day was to get a good checkout in the B-25. Before this could happen, one of Paul's most experienced B-25 drivers unex-

In the cockpit of our camera plane with its special optical nose.

pectedly became ill, and because of important commitments, it became my task to bring the B-25 home without ever having even ridden in one.

Through the years I have believed in two books; the Bible and the *Pilot's Aircraft Handbook*. They both have enormous value, and both are often treated with about the same lack of interest. Armed with these two volumes, I climbed the ladder to the pilot's compartment with all the alacrity of Louis XVI going to the guillotine. Unless you have been accustomed to flying heavy military types, jumping from civilian light twins to a B-25 is akin to a small-boat sailor stepping from a star-class boat to an America's Cup racer.

In this first flight I left the walk-around inspection to perhaps the most capable crew chief in the world, ex-Marine Master Sergeant Robert Siemieniewicz, a wonderful, completely unflappable type, who is better than the best copilot.

Getting settled in the two-way seat and sliding open the window

were matters of a minute, and with brake pressure up, I turned on master switches, fuel boosts, and kicked in primer, energizer, and starter. About four blades went through, and the big R2600 Wright coughed out a Cadillac-sized belch of white smoke and caught as I came in with mixture control. Several minutes later, with oil pressure and all engine instruments reading O.K., I released the brakes to taxi.

Precisely one second later I came upon the green-eyed monster that haunts all new B-25 pilots: brakes set so delicately that a mayfly lighting upon the pedal can send the pilot right through the windshield like catapult ejection. My taxi to takeoff position was a sight to behold: It looked like Bojangles Robinson doing a shuffle off to Buffalo.

Finally, at takeoff position, I collected what nerves I had left and proceeded over the foreign (to me) but lengthy checkoff list. Finishing the runup and dropping quarter flaps, I turned on for the takeoff roll using a

223

A beautiful closeup nose view of *Luscious Lulu* in flight.

Bringing in a B-25 on one wheel, a sequence from the film
Catch-22.

North American B-25 Mitchell

Specifications

ENGINES	1700-hp Wright R2600
SPAN	67 ft., 7 in.
LENGTH	52 ft., 10 in.
HEIGHT	15 ft., 9 in.
CREW	5
EMPTY WEIGHT	20,300 lbs.
USEFUL LOAD	13,200 lbs.
GROSS WEIGHT	33,500 lbs.
FUEL CAPACITY	974 gals.
ARMAMENT	Varied: 1 Power Turret Twin .50 plus 5 other .50's; other armament as many as 18 .50's or 75-mm cannon

Performance

MAXIMUM SPEED	284 mph
RATE OF CLIMB	1325 fpm
STALL SPEED	85 mph
ENDURANCE	5½ hrs.
SERVICE CEILING	25,000 ft.

running start and engines to control heading, but still being as shy of excess brakes as a high school girl on her first date. With 44 inches of manifold pressure, and Bob following on the throttles, I raised the nose wheel at about 70 mph, and at about 90 it flew off heavily but solidly. Instantly raising the gear, I accelerated through lift-off at 135 mph and raised my flaps.

Even with the strangeness of this new airplane and the rush of events, I could not help but feel the truly heart-lifting thrill of flying a big, powerful, heavy military bomber. At least for me this is an experience completely unduplicatable by flying any plush tweed-and-leather present-day light twin.

With 140 knots and a 500-foot-a-minute cruising climb, I settled back. The ailerons were heavy but positive. The rudders were about equal to moving the anchor of the *Queen Mary* with one foot. The elevators also felt stiff, with the wheel yoke position more forward than seemed natural.

Paralleling the lovely sun-swept coast of California, I tried steep and shallow turns. If one is admiring the scenery instead of paying attention to the nose, one can lose altitude in steep turns like a safe being pushed out of a window. Another unusual feature alien to small twins, and more in keeping with jets, is the ability of the heavy B-25 to zoom for altitude like the elevator in the Empire State Building and to seemingly coast up 2000 or more feet without much apparent effort.

With the normal fuel load not too much shy of 1000 gallons, I did not worry about fuel, and my true airspeed at easy cruise was 230 mph at 8000 feet, with a 26-inch and 1850 rpm. Easing over the yacht-laden harbor of jewellike Newport, I turned

on the downwind leg for Orange County Airport. Looking at the 3500-foot runway, I felt like the driver of a diesel long-haul rig getting ready to park in a Volkswagen space.

Slowing down to 150 mph, I dropped the gear and added power to hold the safe single-engine speed of 145 mph. Turning on base, I allowed myself the luxury of a split second of personal back-patting. This Walter Mitty-type reverie did not prevent me from holding up one finger for one-quarter flap and dropping my speed another 10 mph.

Calling, in somewhat less than the accepted tones of a nerveless B-25 plane commander, for full flaps, I rocketed across the tumbleweed and dirt toward the end of the runway. Chopping everything, I eased back and touched as lightly as thistle-down at about 90, with the ever-to-be-remembered squeak of heavy-laden tires well landed. Somehow, whether it be Sopwith Camel or B-25, my first landing in a new airplane always seems to be the best I ever make. I don't know why, but it's true.

With big Bob heaving a well-deserved sigh of relief, the old Lead Sled boiled down the runway with nose wheel still off the ground. It seems on landing to accelerate rather than slow down, but like a safe-cracker laying down a vial of nitroglycerine, I gently let the nose wheel down and started applying the sharp brakes. The runway was fast disappearing, and I turned off the end of the runway with a matadorlike flourish compounded of speed, hot brakes and a fortunately located high-speed exit lane.

It was to be hundreds of hours and many years later before this first experience with my favorite multi-engine airplane returned to mind. The best-selling book, *Catch 22*, the brilliant and exciting satire of a B-25 bomber base in the European Theatre, was to be made into a movie. We were lucky enough to be chosen to do the aviation sequences of this major picture for Paramount and Mr. John Calley, the film's talented producer.

Our task was apple-pie easy! We had only to locate an entire squadron of eighteen B-25s. We had to get them ready for ferry, fly them as far as three thousand miles to our base in Santa Ana, and reconvert them to wartime configuration. We had to locate fifty thousand dollars' worth of spare parts, plus turrets, guns, bomb shackles, releases, doors, etc., for an airplane now a quarter of a century old. We had to locate many old B-25 pilots and get them off the shelf and retrained. Our mechanics force was expanded to ten times its normal size.

Even with the time-consuming task of choosing the best-available B-25 aircraft from as widely located and unlikely spots as Long Island; Grey Bull, Wyoming; Buckeye, Arizona; Champaign, Illinois; and Houston, Texas, we were able to ferry our first flight of B-25s to location a scant few months after the first go-ahead. It would take Baron Munchausen to do proper honors to this unbelievable renovation of the B-25s, for with en-

gine changes, hydraulic problems, completely rebuilding bomb bays, recovering surfaces, locating glass, and a million other unforgettable incidents, we were becoming as nutty as the squirrels in the Black Forest.

Parallel with the herculean job of rebuilding B-25s was the most ably managed job of training flight crews. Under the leadership of Jim Appleby, general manager, and Frank Pine, vice president for operations, we instituted a school for B-25 drivers that would have turned an airline green with envy.

I am ashamed to admit that in spite of the almost permanent indentation on my stern from sitting on the 185 pages of the B-25 handbook, I still was surprised at the things I learned from attending our ground school classes.

Because of the sensitive brake system of the B-25, I had been finding all sorts of reasons not to fly it after I lost my leg. But with the urgent necessity of leading the squadron and doing the stunts, and with Jim and Frank's sensitive assistance, I got back in the left seat of the B-25 and got my puppetlike wooden leg and foot adjusted again to the response of the hair-trigger brakes. Like my first taxi experience, the B-25 spent consider-

Bombardier's view.

A bevy of beauties in right echelon. In the lead ship, *Laden
Maiden*, I'm about to peel off.

able rubber and brake discs trying to
prove who was boss.

The weeks flew by like Aurora's
Golden Chariot, and like it, we were
finally one day off in formation for
Hermosillo, Mexico. In joining up
over the ocean south of Newport
Beach, for five minutes we had all the
elements of a Chinese fire drill, but
ultimately everyone got into position.
Three and a half hours later we landed
at our newly built airstrip and checked
through customs all intact.

As the months passed on location

I again became familiar and at complete flight ease with the B-25. I developed a fondness for the airplane and its characteristics that I am sure will last a lifetime: the indescribable excitement of a gang takeoff with 17 other B-25s only 100 feet apart; the massive, ponderous beauty of five 3-plane V's of B-25s turning against a background of building cumulus clouds; the excitement of seeing the bomb bay doors open and 150 bombs drop as one toward the green, white-capped Sea of Cortez; the pleasure in getting back one's ability to stay in tight formation with 15 other planes; the heart-stopping night-flying sequences where 0-level passes are made at the base, turning inside the unseen mountain barriers that ringed three sides of the area. These and many other incidents were all part of *Catch 22.*

While this is probably the last time a squadron of authentic World War II bombers will be assembled for a picture, I expect that the B-25 will outlast the venerable DC-3, and I hope and expect to still be flying this best of all medium bombers for many years in the future.

Corsair

THE WHISTLING DEATH was as real to the Japanese on the bloody beaches of the Pacific in World War II as the devastating Black Death was to the peasants of medieval Europe. This scourge of the *samurai* was the Chance Vought Corsair, also known as the U bird, a cranked-wing razor of an airplane that initially frightened some of its pilots nearly as much as it later did the Japanese.

When this pirate of the air first flew in March of 1940, it had the most powerful engine ever installed in a piston-engine fighter and one of the largest propellers ever put on a plane. To give the propeller clearance, the wings were given the inverted gull shape, which also helped the pilot in combat due to the immeasurably increased visibility. An added feature, which not even the designer had planned on, was the emergency water landings planing capabilities of the Corsair, due also to the inverted gull.

Initial carrier trials with the Corsair proved disappointing, and positively dangerous to any but the most experienced Navy test pilots. The extraordinary speed of the Corsair was undoubtedly the only major reason why it did not join that scrap pile of so many (one-of-a-kind) military experimental types. A speed of 405 mph for a fighter in 1940 was as startling as seeing a Model T racing at Indianapolis. The Army Air Corps swallowed considerable pride when this large radial-engine fighter was shown capable of pulling away from any of the best liquid-cooled Air Corps fighters of the day.

When the Corsair design was first layed out the threat of war was dim, but with the rapid onset of hostilities in Europe, a complete redesign for

229

Belly view of a Corsair in a pullaway.

speedy production was instituted for the Navy's new hotrod.

The guns, normally in the fuselage of a pre-World War II fighter, were moved to the wings, and the fuel tank was moved from the center section of the wing to the center of the fuselage. This final tank movement meant sticking the cockpit aft of the wing and giving the pilot all the visibility of a train conductor in the caboose of a hundred-car freight train.

The construction of the Corsair, in spite of its impressive speed and unusual design, was a strange mixture of the antique and the modern. Few pilots realize that the wing of the Corsair was fabric-covered aft of the spar. Incidentally, this is a good way to win a free flagon of old Popskull

230

among the flying fraternity, for so far as I know, this is the only modern fighter ever designed and built with a fabric-covered wing.

The mighty 2000-hp Pratt & Whitney engine sat out on the end of the graceful oval fuselage like an eagle at rest, and the wheels on retraction rotated 90 degrees and tucked up flat in the wings in the same manner as for the Curtiss P-40.

All U. S. Navy fighters through the years have had the strength and stamina of water buffalos, and the Corsair was no exception. The massive box spar center section went through the fuselage forward of the pilot's cockpit and was joined on either side by the wing panels, which folded hydraulically.

Most civilians and non-Navy type aviators approach folding wings with all the enthusiasm and confidence of someone picking up a live cobra, but actually with any care the wing-fold system is as strong as the Brooklyn Bridge and about as reliable.

The forward fuselage, the center wing section area, and the tail cone area were the essential parts of the fuselage. These were all of aluminum-stressed skin construction and were flush-riveted. In direct contrast, the wing aft of the rear spar was fabric-covered, as were the elevators and rudders. The ailerons were plywood, covered with fabric, and the booster tabs were slabs of wood with two small wood screws holding the fitting!

It's perhaps time to mention that the use of booster tabs to increase control force is not new in aviation, but if they are shed at high speeds, you can lose your controls in somewhat less than the proverbial flicker of an eyelid. This particular feature of the Corsair was the only strength factor I ever had any grave doubts about. Wheels and brakes were ade-

quate, and the multiple-disc brakes were quite capable of dumping this 11,000-pound airplane on its nose, to the great consternation or embarrassment of the Navy or Marine pilot whose previous experience in stopping most Navy fighters of the period included standing on the always inadequate brakes and ending by throwing out an anchor in hopes that would help.

The 237-gallon rubber tank in front of the pilot was multiple-wall and self-sealing, and could be implemented for long range by either a 178-gallon Durahold drop tank or a 154-gallon standard Navy tank.

Not unlike the Twin Beech, the Corsair suffered a directional problem on landing as the tail settled down and was blanketed out by the flaps and wing. One had to have speed and dexterity on the brakes to stop ground loops.

Both hard rubber wheels and pneumatic tire tail wheels were fitted. The weight of the Corsair ate pneumatic tires like popcorn, but the hard rubber wheel made every rivet and nut and bolt in the structure of the U bird protest, and on landing you felt like you were being driven through a soup can factory that was falling apart. In war use the hard rubber wheel was most often used.

The armament of 6 .50s was carried in each outboard wing panel, and the convergence was boresighted for 300 yards. Armor was added to the basic Corsair design, and although it totaled 170 pounds of glass, steel plate and heavy aluminum, there were, I am sure, no pilot complaints as to its usefulness or desirability.

The Corsair's first combat experience came about flying as part of a cover for a squadron of B-24 Liberators. It was an unfortunate meeting of Marine squadron VMF 124 over

An intimate view of aerial power: the FG1D.

Bougainville with 50 Zeros. It was ruefully known as the St. Valentine's Day Massacre, because of the loss of 2 Corsairs, 2 Liberators, 2 P40s and 4 P38s. Japanese losses amounted to three or four Zeros.

Not unlike the baptism of fire suffered in World War I by the first-rate Bristol fighter, which suffered losses in initial combats, so also did the Corsair, but soon pilot skill, blinding speed, armor, and 6 .50s had enough wind up the Japanese that they preferred to be somewhere else when the U bird showed up.

The Corsair was a tough bird to land aboard a carrier, due primarily to the poor visibility and the rebounding the main gear struts made, and it was about as popular for carrier use as a lady of the evening in a Baptist prayer meeting. For many months all Corsairs were relegated to Pacific shore bases, and squadrons like Commander Blackburn's VF-17 were credited with 154 enemy planes in only 79 days of combat.

Before the awesome atomic blasts wrote the finish to Japan's rising sun, the Corsair was to proudly wear the claim of 2140 enemy aircraft destroyed, against a loss of only 185 Corsairs. And these fantastic victory ratios were in air-to-air combat!

Many modifications were to cross the Corsair's path, but one of the most successful was the conversion of a group of twelve to radar-

Profile from the chase plane.

equipped night fighters. Along with Japanese infiltration, heat, jungle rot, and pure terror, the Japanese had come up with a new discomfort for our fighting men. They sent over slow biplane aircraft at night and dropped small bombs and grenades in sufficient quantities to rob our Marines of rest. Like Rin Tin Tin to the heroine, the radar-equipped heavy Corsairs arrived on the scene, and in a few weeks the washing-machine Charlies, as they were known, had all gone to join their honorable ancestors.

The Corsair's wing brackets used for the drop tanks were also stressed to carry 500- and 1000-pound bombs, and on rare occasions, 2000-pounders. So, besides its superb fighter characteristics, the F4U served as dive bomber and skip bomber. Later on in the war, when the Japanese started holing up in caves that were enormously well protected and defended, it was the Corsairs that often skipped in a big pickle through the cave opening and effected a permanent sealing of the cave.

By May 1944 the Corsair had written a gallant page of honors, and the Navy evaluation board had stated that in comprehensive tests the F4U was a better fighter, a better bomber, and as good a carrier plane as an F6F. As soon as the Navy was able to get a captured Zero flying, it tested it against the Corsair. The Zero was obviously outgunned, out-armored, and was no match in speed, rate of climb, or ceiling. In further tests the Navy tried its aircraft against Army Air Corps birds. Up to 12,000 feet a P-51 and a Corsair were evenly matched; above 12,000, the Corsair was superior. The Corsair was considerably superior to the P-47, the P-38, and the P-39.

The author might be accused of some natural discrimination, having been a naval aviator, but for sheer loveliness of control feel and rate of roll, the Corsair is a graceful leopard compared to the P-51 Polar Bear. Through the years since World War II, I have had the distinct pleasure of owning and flying most of the Air Corps and Navy fighter planes, and while I am sure that most service pilots are partisan in their choice of fighter aircraft, I am also sure that the in-flight characteristics of the Corsair are so superb, as to have most of my Air Corps friends lucky enough to fly a Corsair ready to turn in their silver wings for Navy wings of gold.

The manufacturer of Poopy bags (the Navy's slightly scurrilous nickname for blimps) was of course Goodyear Tire and Rubber Company in Akron. Unknown to many was the fact that in World War II, Goodyear

also produced 4014 FG1Ds, their designation for the Corsair, while Chance Vought produced 4669, and Brewster Aircraft, 735 as F3A-1Dp.

Before my fortunate meeting with Paul Mantz and our ultimate joining hands as partners, I had been a competitor, and I operated from a small airport west of Riverside, California. One of my pilot visitors at Riverside spoke of having seen a group of Corsairs at Litchfield Park, Arizona—that sad repository of the United States Navy's gallant air armada in World War II. The Corsairs were being scrapped, along with such aircraft as the Douglas AD, later to be reproved in the heat and hell of Vietnam. Other aircraft going to the smelter were Grumman F9's, Lockheed Constellations, PB4Y's, Twin Beeches, and a smattering of SNJ's and F8F's. This news set me off on the case to bag my own U bird.

Following up the rumor, in a matter of two weeks. I located the firm smelting down the Corsairs. Agreeing on a price (a steak dinner more than scrap value), I picked out three Corsairs based on engine and aircraft time on the available lists. From these three candidates I'd be able to select the one in best condition.

To an aviator and a true lover of aircraft, the sight of these proud and great Navy airplanes waiting to be picked apart like buzzards over a dead burro never ceases to make me sad. My three Corsairs were at the end of a mile and a half drive between rows of Navy aircraft totaling in the thousands.

Getting out of our truck and surveying our find produced whistles from the assembled company like the last departing whisper from a deflated balloon. The Corsairs weren't pretty; they were weathered, sun-bleached and filthy, and when we made the steeplejacklike ascent to the cockpit and looked through the dusty canopy, we were appalled to look upon a floor of finely sifted Arizona desert just a few inches below canopy line!

With coolielike labor, in four days we had the desert cleaned out of the cockpits, but aside from using shovels, it was finally necessary to open all inspection plates on the bottom of the fuselage and give it a fire-hose washing. With typical Navy thoroughness, the carb scoops, radiator, and stacks had been covered, and except for flat struts and tires, the U birds weren't in too bad a shape.

We then examined each of the three candidates, with painstaking attention to details, before selecting as our very own the FG-1D (made by Goodyear). I hated to part with the two other Corsairs, but at that time purchasing and reconditioning one U bird was about all we could handle with all our other commitments.

After as thorough an overhaul as we could manage under the circumstances, we put in a new 3150 battery, filled up the tanks with clean fuel, and hooked up an APW (auxilliary power unit). As 3 mechanics watched yours truly improperly primed the huge R2800. With a barking cough that dropped the jaws of the mechanics like drawbridges, the R2800 engine enveloped itself in flames like an Indian funeral pyre.

With the fire out, a change of wardrobe, and a large CO_2 bottle replaced, I tried the start after a long visit with the *Pilot's Aircraft Handbook*. This time I got flame again but kept the engine turning, and with a strange dynamolike rapid increase of rpm the Pratt & Whitney started, settled down, and ran with almost watchmaker smoothness.

Eight o'clock the following morning saw a walk-around inspection of

the U bird by yours truly. The fabric looked sound but weathered—all gun hatches secured and controls free, with tires and struts as they should be. Climbing to the cockpit takes some agility because of the height, and it is very easy to slip.

Without too much trouble the Pratt & Whitney started with its characteristic dynamolike windup, and I taxied out following the Navy "Follow Me" Jeep. At the takeoff point I again checked my wing fold lever by my left elbow; the tail wheel was locked, the canopy was locked, the open engine was O.K., and all instrument readings were normal.

As I fed power I needed a lead foot, and before I could catch my breath, I was airborne at about 90 mph and climbing like a hungry hawk. With the gear up, prop and power back, and canopy closed, my heart decided it would beat again. With the opportunity to look around I realized what a powerhouse of an airplane this was.

Climbing on course to Blythe and settling down at 10,000 feet, I again consulted the *Pilot's Aircraft Handbook*. As long as I was paying for my own fuel, I began acting like Scrooge and dropped rpm to 1450 and began counting blades. I sailed along with 30 inches indicating, at over 200 knots.

On these earlier Corsairs you had 2 foot channels under the rudder pedals and then a free fall to the bottom of the fuselage. The hole consequently was quite large enough to lose a white-faced Hereford in, but it served another purpose. When you got tired and your legs got stiff, you could trim out the Corsair, loosen your chute, and just dangle your legs in the abyss.

Tucking my feet back on the pedals, still at cruise, I cleared myself ahead, pulled the nose above the horizon,

A fine view of the distinctive gull wing.

locked on a cloud, and rolled. Because of the long nose, you can put it on a point and lock on as beautifully in a roll as you would with the long-nosed liquid-cooled jobs like the P-51 and the P-40.

The ailerons are faultless and pure delight, above a third the stick load of a P-51 in any attitude. For all its light touch there is a pleasant feeling of size and strength in the F4U that I have never felt in any fighter, except possibly a P-38.

The R2800 Pratt & Whitney runs

with the liquid smoothness of a Merlin or Allison, and like all Pratt & Whitney products, pilots by and large have the same faith in these P & Ws that they do in their minister.

Going over again the *Pilot's Aircraft Handbook,* carefully removed from its resting place between my stern and the parachute, I reinforced my memory on the gear system and its emergency procedures. Slowing down to 130 knots, I moved the big knobbed gear lever into the down position, and I could happily feel the landing gears start down and rotate into lock. Chopping the throttle gave no blowing horn, so I settled into a descent for Flabob Airport in Riverside, where I then hangared my other aircraft.

Being up about as tight as an Oneeda bear trap, I went through my checkoff list, slid the canopy back, dropped flaps, and turned on base. Holding 100 knots with very little throttle produces a significant nose-down attitude.

As I turned on final, that lovely long nose blanked out the miniature runway of Flabob, and I made my final descent like a good seaplane pilot watching the trees on one side and the hangars on the other side gradually rise. With a little back pressure I put it down on the wheels at about 90 knots. It rolled nicely, with lots of rudder control. As the tail settled down it was necessary to apply the delicate brakes. You must be Joe Lightfoot, for the brakes are truly sensitive. Also, as the tail wheel came down, an unexpected stall buffet passed by the cockpit, much to my surprise. Taxiing back for shutoff required wide sweeps of the nose to clear the path ahead.

Some months later the Navy found I had an operational Corsair and asked me to do a show at Oakland Naval Air Station. On the flight up I enjoyed the unparalleled pleasure of the Corsair's lovely controls as the rocky coastline of California passed underneath the gray-blue wings.

On the high-speed pass and pullup during the show, the spectators and I were treated to a phenomenon that seems to be largely a Corsair trait. In pulling back at about five G's, I left magnificent contrails from both wing-tips that followed me up like a smoke writer's signature for more than a thousand feet.

Some time later, the fiftieth anniversary of naval aviation coincided with a flight of our Corsair and a Garland Lincoln Nieuport 28 to Pensacola over a course of thousands of miles, and it involved a tortoise-and-hare race between both of these aircraft, one of World War I vintage and one of World War II. Mike Hinn, a friend, flew the Corsair to Pensacola, and I raced behind him in the Nieuport. We covered some thirty states in seven days, and my tail (and I don't mean aircraft) was dragging when we finally reached Pensacola.

As it turned out, another Corsair was to do a stunt show very low over the ground, but for a variety of not so good reasons, the job was scrubbed and I was asked if I would take over. With twenty minutes to practice I went out in the Pensacola acrobatic area, cleared myself, dropped the nose, and looped. I estimated a rise of three thousand feet at the top and speed of just 100 knots. Cuban 8's required less altitude at the top because of faultless engine performance and lovely ailerons. Of course, snap maneuvers have no place in a high speed fighter, so these as well as altitude-devouring spins were not attempted.

Nostalgia and people were present the following morning in equal quantity, and to this naval aviator, who remembered Pensacola N.A.S. as his first duty station, as well as his father's in World War I, the festive crowds and air show were like a shot of adrenalin.

Following the Blue Angels, the Navy's crack stunt team, is like a vaudeville hoofer trying to follow Fred Astaire. I took off, tucked my gear up, and climbed with the rate indicating more than 3000 feet a minute. I reversed course, flattened out at better than 250 knots indicated, at about 50 feet over the runway. My pullup was smooth, and I hit just 3000 feet on my back, trailing beautiful contrails from both wingtips.

Starting down I had the same feeling that the lion tamer has when the cage door locks and he finds he has forgotten his whip, his gun, and his chair, and the lions are licking their chops. As I was coming vertical I realized I had only about 1400 feet to pull through. Having shown my own fair share of high-speed stalls to military students, I put the tips of my fingers on the stick so I wouldn't haul back unconsciously. With cold sweat pouring off my brow, I came level at about 20 feet above the field, going better than 300 knots.

It was a beautiful loop to the spectators so I pulled into another, and as I came over the top I made a roll and a half off my back for a Cuban 8 instead of the normal half roll. Each time it required the Corsair's full and very fast roll rate to complete the maneuver before I reached the deck.

Following this I did an inverted pass at about 100 feet, and everything fell into the canopy, including maps, a wrench, the *Pilot's Aircraft Handbook*, a half-eaten sandwich, and a dead mouse. Dodging the debris, I landed, and taxied up to the plaudits of my Navy friends, who thought my show great, but felt I was cutting things pretty fine. I didn't mention to them that a call for wardrobe was in order and/or tell them of the mental note I made that in the future I would give myself considerably more sky room in acrobatics when flying fast, clean military fighters for the first time.

Flying the Corsair back to California from Pensacola was delightful, and except for the U bird's propensity to catch fire because of its carburetor and the consequent necessity to always have a fire guard, the trip went well. The Corsair has many hours' range, when you cut your rpm to 1400 and your manifold press to 28 inches, your fuel costs will be below that of an SNJ on long trips. As for all interesting airplanes, each stop at any airport is like riding up on a rajah's show elephant, and the Corsair draws about as much attention.

Summing up the cranked-wing beauty, I can easily say it is my favorite Navy fighter; it is also the only one to serve in two wars and still be in limited service in some of the world's air forces today.

A B&B—Or a Look at Balloons and Blimps

THIS AUTHOR IS no great balloon pilot or blimp driver, but for the edification of my readers, let me pass along a few experiences and thoughts about the rubber and nylon cows.

A few years ago an opportunity to go ballooning came along to me as a sort of lark, and I don't mean the bird. Actually, flight by man was first accomplished, or at least properly recorded, on November 21, 1783, when Pilatre De Rozier and the Marquis D'Arlandes rose in an elegantly decorated Montgolfier hot-air balloon and flew five miles before alighting safely.

This flight was the culmination of more than five thousand years of man's dreams and aspirations. In myth and legend, flight was generally reserved for the gods and goddesses, and literature is replete with the stirring legends of Daedalus, Icarus, Pegasus the Winged Horse, and the aerial chariot of Aurora, Roman Goddess of the Dawn.

If we go back farther in time, the story of the shepherd who flew on the back of an eagle is preserved on a seal dated 3500 B.C. and Babylonian in origin.

In Persia, fifteen hundred years before Christ, King Kai Kaoos tried training eagles to carry him on a light throne. Accounts read that the king got airborne but that the eagles shortly ran out of hundred octane and dropped him. When he regained consciousness, his advisers were all for locking him up in the funny farm.

Because other religions, such as the Egyptian, worshiped the winged sun and deified birds, the legends grew

The great balloon race, with a busy Cliff Robertson and a dubious Frank Tallman in full dress.

apace, and the people dreamed of the day when man could fly.

Many men through the ages were to lose their lives in this quest to conquer space. As far back as A.D. 57, Nero watched Simon the Magician make a nasty mess in the Forum at Rome when unfortunately his magic failed him at the three hundred-foot drop. He was followed in another public exhibition in 1100, when Saragen of Constantinople strengthened his cloak with rods and jumped from the Hippodrome. In this attempt everything got broken except the paving. A contemporary account of this accident most succinctly stated that his body had more power to drag him down than his artificial wings had to sustain it.

With the onset of the Dark Ages, flight was to become a province of witches, demons, and familiars, and it wasn't until such geniuses as Da Vinci drew up designs for flying machines and parachutes that flying or the hope of it was acceptable again to both the clergy and the world at large. Until

the advent of Pitcher, Chanute, the Wright brothers, and other great pioneers of heavier-than-air craft, balloons were to dominate flight.

A surprise to many is the fact that hydrogen balloons were developed almost simultaneously with hot-air balloons, and would come in time to dominate nearly all ballooning. The very volatile hydrogen gas was extremely dangerous and was to claim the lives of many balloonists for nearly two centuries. A leaking gas cell and a spark statically induced, or lightning, could send the balloonist to a flaming end not unlike the Norsemen who sent their heroes to Valhalla by setting a longship adrift and lighting it as a funeral pyre.

Apart from the danger, ballooning with hydrogen or cooking gas is expensive, for even in Europe a single inflation costs between five hundred and eight hundred dollars, contrasted to the hot-air balloon's inflation cost of perhaps five dollars.

With the advent of spangled lights and state fairs in the middle and late

1800s, the daredevil parachute jump from a hot-air balloon became a major attraction.

From such historical beginnings have arisen the modern sport of hot-air ballooning today. In one area of the United States and a few other spots in the world, gas balloons are still used for sport racing, and recently I saw several gas balloons lazily drifting across northern Bavaria.

Off the coast of California lies an island that for sheer beauty and scenery rivals the loveliest in the world. Catalina, like many vacation spots, quiets to a whisper in winter, when the great white cruise ship is put away for the season.

To boost travel in the off-season, a hot-air balloon race was planned from Catalina in January some years ago. Being a slow motion-picture season, I enlisted Cliff Robertson to go as co-pilot, and we entered our names. Cliff Robertson is not only an actor's actor, but a rugged citizen who is pleasant to have around when the going gets tough.

To be sure of a vehicle, I bought an interest in a balloon without having ever seen one, a red-and-white nylon beauty. Then Cliff and I enlisted Don Piccard, a first-rate balloonist and a member of the famous scientific Piccard family, to brief us on the rudiments of ballooning.

An inflated balloon often acts like a rogue elephant and is every bit as difficult to control. Memories still come back of Cliff and I and Don racing across a stubble field trying to hold onto our partially inflated balloon and also trying to get aboard. We ultimately checked out in several ascensions shielded behind a high screen of eucalyptus trees and early enough in the morning to beat the wind that had previously caused us our gallop across the field.

The balloon can be inflated by the same type of blower unit that we used in the service for winter heating of engines, and this with the addition of asbestos gloves is the easy way, but most true balloonists scorn this, and consequently their hands, faces, etc., bear enough burns to look like they

With hand on gas value, Cliff is anxious for the starting signal. Our hefty handlers hang onto the frame to keep us down.

Spanning the years, a formation flight of the World
War II Corsair and a vintage Nieuport 28.

Rehearsing for a scene in an episode of the TV series
"F Troop."

were No. 1 target for a flame thrower. Once the neophyte has learned the rigging, the difficulties of balloon inflation disappear to some extent.

I for one never got over the wonder of looking up from a basket into the open throat of the balloon and seeing the top of the balloon a majestic fifty feet above like the vaulting roof of a red-and-white cathedral.

Cliff and I took our initial lumps and inflated and flew our balloon numerous times behind the eucalyptus screen for a careful FAA flight inspector, and we received our licenses the same day.

Having a trace of poland china ham in my makeup, I decided that in the upcoming big race we should look the part, so Cliff and I arrived on the scene dressed as in days of yore, wearing top hats and meticulous cutaways with red sashes. This created some consternation and a good deal of humor among the very much more experienced balloonists.

In case you haven't an atlas handy, Catalina Island is separated from the mainland of California by twenty-five miles of dull, green, white-capped Pacific rollers, and on this wet January day, in spite of being an ex-lifeguard, I didn't relish a swim *for distance* in my cutaway and top hat. With a background of naval aviation and its attention to survival equipment, Cliff and I carried Mae Wests in our basket as well as a single-man rubber boat quite capable of carrying several miserably wet humans.

The takeoff area was in a natural bowl, with the mountains rising on three sides. The sounds of hundreds of people milling about, the hiss of escaping propane and butane gases for inflation, plus curses because of burned hands and smashed fingers merged into a kaleidoscope of noise and color.

Then it was our time to take off.

With a strong wind from the south, I decided to overinflate the red-and-white parachute nylon envelope. With champagne toasts we bid the boat crew that was to follow us and our friends goodbye, and at signal, the four heavyweight handlers dropped off and we shot up into the dripping January skies like a stag pursued by the hunt.

The rate of climb must have been better than a thousand feet a minute. I released the honker or the gas valve that shoots a tongue of flame and hot air into the bag. But soon after leaving the island and its lovely boat-ringed harbor, the bag appeared to be descending. I began pulling full gas on the honker, but nothing appreciable

happened. Cliff looked at me and I looked down, and the dull green ocean was coming to meet us at an alarming rate. I believe I said, "We are going in the damn ocean," and at about that time we hit like a lead-lined safe. Cliff flew gracefully out when the basket hit, but my foot caught under a propane tank, and the next thing I knew I was looking up through ten feet of green winter ocean.

The bag, not having lost all its inflation, dragged the basket back to the surface. Cliff swam back, and a very wet movie star and a very cold pilot contemplated the whole balloon fiasco in a basket waist-deep in the winter sea. Through some fluke, the pilot light on the burner had not gone out, so with nothing else to do, we turned the gas full on, and in about five minutes the balloon was nearly fully inflated and the basket was skipping the whitecaps.

Our following boat had arrived by this time, and with more dash than good sense we bid them *adieu* and took off again from the ocean.

Going up in wet clothes and looking like a refugee from the local coin laundromat, makes a world of difference in ballooning, as we soon found out. The temperature at 3000 feet, where we stabilized, was a chilly 48 degrees, and my lack of comfort was considerably enhanced by a sweater that I had on underneath my formal clothes and that had some kind of cleaning fluid on it. I stood the itching and burning just so long before I stripped to my pants and suspenders, threw the offending sweater overboard, and put back my wet tailcoat and a slicker.

Misery followed misery as we drifted into clouds cold and damp, listening carefully, for we hoped no airplanes were flying blind this far out to sea. It required careful watching of

Earning my keep as I substitute for the actor. Actor Ken
Berry looks on.

balloon inflation, for the touch of a damp cloud rapidly changed the balloon's temperature, necessitating the use of more burner.

Being no lover of heights and suffering from acrophobia, I surely left my fingerprints in the aluminum basket frame, for in a barely waist-high basket 3000 feet is a long way down.

Going over our wet survival gear, we found a large bag of peanuts and a binocular case in which some kind soul had stuffed a bottle of first-rate brandy. To ward off incipient pneumonia, we ate the peanuts, watching the shells drift slowly down the thousands of feet to the ocean, and companionably nipped at the brandy.

Our compass was gone, and only once in a while did we see our following boat, but the general tenor of life had considerably improved, and the hours passed.

We had gone on our reserve tank

And off I go, hopefully for a successful film take.

of gas when Cliff and I decided to try to see where we were. As carefully as possible, we let down to about fifteen hundred feet, and wonder of wonders, the coastline of California at Oceanside appeared through the rain and soup about five miles ahead.

With available gas running out fast, we decided to ditch for the second time in the ocean. Our boat, which had been following our occasional appearances through the broken clouds, was now about a mile behind us, making very heavy weather in the huge seas.

Having got caught once in the basket, I decided to take French leave and jump this time before the balloon hit. Both of us got on the rear of the basket, and as the balloon slanted into the sea like the Tornado Roller Coaster at Coney Island, we both jumped. Cliff was first off, and followed with the rubber boat, and as I went over

I yanked the rip panel out of the top of the balloon.

While still in the air I saw Cliff hit a whitecap, and with swallow coat flying shoot over the top of the next two waves he looked for all the world like an eagle with his feathers afire. A second later I hit, and in spite of the freezing water and because of the nine hundred gallons of adrenalin we were pumping, the ocean felt like a hot bath at a German spa.

With the weight gone, the balloon rose to about five hundred feet before it gradually closed up like a shot mallard and dropped in the ocean about a half mile away.

Cliff and I swam about, and after a few minutes our rescue boat arrived and we got hoisted aboard. Their trip had been brutal in the rough seas and twenty-five-knot winds, and they had used fuel and liquid nourishment in about equal quantities. We couldn't

243

At the controls of the Goodyear blimp *Columbia.*

have cared less, and we were both as glad to see them as the British soldiers were to see Florence Nightingale at Balaklava.

The balloon resisted every attempt to get it in the boat, and we finally had to cut it like an animal in a slaughterhouse to let out the air.

We arrived at Oceanside at night, wet and worse for the weather to find one of the women contestants lost. Tragically, without adequate gear she died of exposure that night when due to some mixup her boat lost her and she landed in the water out of fuel.

Ballooning can be exciting to any-

You don't realize how big the bag really is until you approach to climb into the cab.

one, but also dangerous. Modern hot-air balloons have improved considerably, and the single burner has now been replaced by four, giving enormously greater response. The bags are multicolored gores of nontear waffle parachute and range in size from forty to sixty feet. But the beauty and apparent ease of their flight are sometimes belied by their shattering descents into trees, church steeples, and high-tension wires.

There are many fine balloonists about, and I have learned from them and from my own experiences that one must be at least twice as alert in a balloon as in an airplane. In the older balloons you cannot compensate fast enough for a drop in altitude if you are not on the ball, and strangely enough, it is hard at altitude to recognize anything but a graveyard fall.

I would never fly over land again without having a German variometer aboard, which can register a delicate rise or descent of two to three feet a minute.

Since the Catalina race episode I managed another balloon flight off Catalina. The motion-picture film unfortunately was never used, but it was beautiful. The balloon drifted away from Catalina with myself and lady stunt girl aboard. With better than usual skill, I managed to set down at sea next to a waiting boat, and we barely got our feet wet.

As we set down, the gas valve broke after I had pulled the ripcord on the balloon. I had to smother the gas with a towel but not before the settling bag had left smoldering nylon on my hand, and the scars still remain.

On another picture we set the balloon up for an "F Troop" episode supposed to take place in a frontier fort in the 1870s. With the limited space of a movie set, erecting and flying the balloon was a problem, and due to a mistake in signals I nearly flew off over Burbank. The roaring of the gas upset the animals on the show, and we nearly had a runaway when we placed the inflated balloon on top of the stagecoach.

Through the years our company has made many commercials using balloons and has used them in TV and motion pictures, but mindless monster aspects of a balloon have never left me, and consequently I have rarely ever flown them for fun.

Something in the same line but a little closer to a frustrated airplane driver is a blimp. After my nerves had calmed enough to face the prospect of powered ballooning, I was pleasantly surprised with the professional approach of the Goodyear people and their first-rate crews.

The blimp's history must start with the first successful flight of Henri Gifford, who piloted a steam-powered hydrogen-filled balloon of his own under controlled flight over Paris in 1852. The danger of a steam engine blowing sparks over the leaky bags of that day is akin to rolling in raw hamburger and going into a cage of starving lions.

Due to the pioneering of Santos Dumont and the rigid zeppelins of Count Von Zeppelin, powered ballooning came of age just prior to World War I. The blimps were used most successfully on antisub patrols. Following World War I, blimps were used intermittently for training and advertising purposes.

The rubberized fabric used in the envelope of the blimb is a natural product for Goodyear; consequently their background in the construction and operation of balloons and blimps goes back over half a century.

Perhaps one of the most spectacular incidents in the history of the blimp

The ground crew release the blimp from its mooring, pulls it down on its single wheel, and releases it as the pilot pours on the coal.

was its use as a flaming springboard for the first Caterpillar Club. Helium gas, which is nonflammable, is used in all blimps today, but throughout World War I and shortly thereafter all blimps, observation balloons, and zeppelins were filled with hydrogen.

The blimp *Wingfoot Express* (hydrogen-inflated) was circling Chicago in the early 1920s when a spark set the gas alight and it exploded. Only two of the crew got out in 'chutes, but the flaming wreckage and the rest of the crew fell in the heart of the Chicago Loop.

Unlike this peacetime disaster, the spectacular and horrifying sight of a zeppelin going down in flames over London or the Channel in World War

I makes one wonder how the Germans were able to recruit crews without handcuffing them to the dirigible's control car.

The United States possesses the only substantial stock of helium in the world, and all blimps in this country today must use the nonflammable gas. But in spite of the fact that all the dirigibles manufactured in the United States were helium-filled, our record for safe operations suffered due to a number of disasters, such as the loss in violent storms of the U. S. Navy's airships *Macon* and *Akron*. The U. S. lighter-than-air program came to a screeching halt and the Navy began phasing out their various remaining airships. The only surviving airships today of all the group of nonrigids or dirigibles are the Goodyear blimps.

The only U. S. dirigible to go into honorable retirement was the *Los Angeles*, made in Germany and delivered to the United States as a World War I reparation. The *Los Angeles* served long and faithfully until the middle 1930s and was finally retired and broken up at the Lakehurst Naval Air Station in New Jersey.

The *Shenandoah*, of American manufacture, but copied carefully after the German war zeppelins, broke up in a line squall. The nose section broke away, but with enormous skill the officers and men still surviving and hanging onto the framework free-ballooned the remnant to a safe landing.

History abounds with the incredible disasters that overtook lighter-than-air dirigibles in the 1920s and 1930s, and only men with an optimism and courage on the order of Jeanne d'Arc could have proceeded in developing and building new dirigibles in light of the enormous loss of lives and resources that these crashes caused.

Lloyd's bell in the famous old insurance exchange in London must have rung with the frequency of castanets:

In 1922, the Army's Italian-built semirigid *Roma* crashed in flames.

The French dirigible *Diximude* disappeared with complete loss of crew in the Mediterranean in 1923.

The British *R33* and *R34*, which crossed the Atlantic in 1919, were badly damaged in accidents.

The American *Shenandoah* was lost in 1925.

The British *R101* burned in 1930, taking forty-seven passengers to their deaths.

In 1933 the great Navy dirigible *Akron* went into the sea, taking one of the great proponents of dirigibles, Admiral William A. Moffett, and seventy-two others.

In 1935, the Navy dirigible *Macon* lost a tail fin; a survivor of the *Akron* crash, Lieutenant Commander Herbert V. Wiley made a skillful landing and only two crewmen lost their lives, but the *Macon* sank.

The death knell of dirigibles was sounded when the *Hindenburg*, coming in to land at Lakehurst, caught fire due to some unknown cause and burned, with considerable loss of life.

In spite of the history of rigid airship disasters, the Navy most successfully operated squadrons of nonrigid blimps in World War II from both coasts in this country and from Africa, and they very materially aided convoys and kept the German U-boat packs from surfacing. Early in the war their range and their ability to fly slowly were vastly better than aircraft, and blimps put more than five hundred thousand hours in the air during the war. By 1944 they were patrolling the tidy sum of nearly three million square miles of ocean.

For armament in the beginning of the war they started with lever-action Winchesters (shades of Custer's massacre), but by the end they had power turrets and depth bombs. And in spite of a lack of real firepower, one blimp captured the German U-boat *U258* by depth bombs and escorted her into port like a ship of the line in the days of our Revolution.

The working careers of nonrigid airships before and following World War II have been as varied and colorful as the life of a circus clown. People attached to airship operations have been married to blimps. They have

landed on Plymouth Rock to celebrate the Pilgrims' landing. They have hunted whales and towed water skiers, and an intrepid stuntman with an inordinate desire to be clean even took a bath in a tub slung underneath a blimp cruising over a surprised New York City.

Following the war, at one time in my Naval Reserve career, I almost put in for blimp training. Instead, I was assigned to helicopter training, which I certainly don't regret. However the silver whales didn't last very long in the Navy after that and I felt I had lost a golden opportunity.

The only airship training available in the world today is that sponsored by Goodyear and the only nonrigid or rigid airships still operating regularly all have the Goodyear winged foot boosting them along. The Goodyear airship I was lucky enough to fly was late in the series of more than 290 bags built by Goodyear and was captained by an ex-Navy pilot who had first been a pilot in *heavier*-than-aircraft and had later transferred to lighter-than-aircraft following the war.

All of Goodyear operations seem to have a "tight ship" naval flavor. They are immaculately clean and well run, and everyone from the handling crew to the pilots and PR men knows his job like an old pro, and like old pros the safety record of the Goodyear fleet, with literally hundreds of thousands of passengers, is unblemished.

Until one walks out to the line and gets into the car up short steps and a rail held by crew and sandbags, one really doesn't realize the immensity of the bag, for it overshadows everything like an enormous beach umbrella.

Seated in the copilot's position, you have a huge window area equal to the con position on a carrier, with the panel sloping sharply downward to give you very good visibility forward. Rudder pedals there are, but no stick or wheel, only an elevator wheel on the floor the size of a pony cart for the elevators. The throttles for the two continentals are in the center of the panel, plus prop controls, including reverse and mixture and carburetor heat. The gauges, apart from standard engine controls, are twin omnis, a transponder and a bewildering group of glass tubes that read *inches* of water and tell pressure inside the balloonets (the inner gas bag compartments), as well as gauges to tell the purity of the helium, which must remain above 96 percent to keep the lift of the airship from becoming affected.

After the six passengers are put in, the door is locked, and incidentally, there are no seat belts! The ship is weighted off by removing sandbags, and while slightly heavy, on a signal from the trained ground crew the dirigible is lowered down on its single wheel and thrown into the air, at which point our pilot poured the coal on the two continentals, and we took off in a breathtaking climb more than the equal of the Boeing F4B1. The speed in its climb was about 40 mph, and I must admit to a queasiness about stalls that had nothing to do with airships.

Forward of the pilot's and copilot's windows are the nose lines and an aluminum manhole, which kept winking like an affectionate teenager at a dance. This proved to be one of three air valves, which keep the air pressure constant in the blimp. This pressure is maintained automatically by air scoops behind the propeller, or by an auxiliary electrical pump if the blimp is drifting with engines dead. Without the constant valving of air or filling of air to compensate for temperature

249

In a really breathtaking climb.

and barometic conditions, the flying of a blimp would be nearly impossible. Toggles are used manually to valve air if the automatic relief valves don't function properly.

At two thousand feet the pilot moved over, and I sat down in the pilot's seat. Rudder pressure is great, and moving the enormous surfaces requires under certain conditions the strong calf muscles of a long-distance runner. At first, with the elevator wheel and the rudder controls, one has a tendency to be behind the movement of the blimp. Once the direction of movement has started to change, you have to compensate back in the opposite direction almost instantly to stop where you want.

The easy rolling movement of the blimp would seem to me to be a pretty good stimulation to seasickness, but I am told that less than one passenger in ten thousand has to "hang over the rail."

In a little while I felt comfortable flying the blimp, and cruised out over Long Beach Harbor following a Navy cruiser going to sea. I held altitude then and did both climbing and gliding turns for practice. Under way the airship has an aerodynamic lifting effect that it is easily recognizable, even to a neophyte like myself.

Cruising over Palos Verdes Peninsula with an air-up slope wind condition and minor turbulence, there was a need for control practice. Coming back over the crowded South Bay area, at a pleasant 40 mph, I looked back in the cabin and wondered if there were some additional locks on the cabin door, for it would be one hell of a first step.

Being in radio communication with the base, we found that the wind had picked up to 12 to 14 knots, so shifting seats again, the blimp commander carefully surveyed the area, circling once, then came in over a golf course where the players never even looked up. Our descent angle was not uncomfortable, and we were moving toward the waiting handling crews at about 6 or 8 mph ground speed. Just before the drag lines got to them, the blimp took a sudden puff of wind and drifted like a stubborn mule, and it took full rudder and many turns of the elevator to get us back to the crew. It was certainly not an emergency, but to a pilot it was a last-second, sweat-filled correction that the blimp skipper handled beautifully. Three men each grabbed one of the nose lines and eased us up to the spot.

Flying the blimp was a fascinating experience in an almost forgotten aircraft, and it's not hard to see why the requirements are high for blimp commanders who, even if they are experienced aircraft pilots, must go through a complicated flight and ground school of six months' duration.

After having looked at the *Pilot's Aircraft Handbook* (a volume the size of Webster's unabridged dictionary), and particularly its chapter on aerostatics, which should keep any graduate chemist happy with its formulas, I came away with a high regard for the knowledge required of a blimp commander.

Flying or even riding in a blimp is quite an eye-opener to a pilot of heavier-than-air craft.

In discussing the flight characteristics of the blimp and balloon, and of early flying machines, it occurred to me that the balloon and powered lighter-than-air vehicles also have their necessary places in our modern world of aviation, for they are really more in keeping with the legends and myths that brought the world ultimately to flight than are some of our planned future endeavors.

Index